Dual Language *Essentials*

for Teachers and Administrators

SECOND EDITION

Dual Language *Essentials*

for Teachers and Administrators

YVONNE S. FREEMAN

DAVID E. FREEMAN

SANDRA MERCURI

HEINEMANN
PORTSMOUTH, NH

Heinemann
361 Hanover Street
Portsmouth, NH 03801–3912
www.heinemann.com

Offices and agents throughout the world

The authors and publisher wish to thank those who have generously given permission to reprint borrowed material.

Cataloging-in-Publication Data is on file at the Library of Congress
ISBN: 978-0-325-09252-2

Editor: Holly Kim Price
Production Editor: Sonja S. Chapman
Typesetter: Eric Rosenbloom, Kirby Mountain Composition
Interior design: Suzanne Heiser and Seán Moreau
Cover design: Suzanne Heiser
Manufacturing: Steve Bernier

Printed in the United States of America on acid-free paper

22 21 20 19 18   PA   1 2 3 4 5

Dedication

Authors David and Yvonne Freeman

We dedicate this book to our children and grandchildren.

In the United States

To our daughter, Mary, who is bilingual in Spanish and English, and is teaching teachers how to support emergent bilingual students in mainstream, English as a second language, and dual language classrooms.

To our son-in-law, Francisco, who is a Spanish/English dual language teacher.

To our granddaughter, Maya, who is bilingual in Spanish and English, using English at home and Spanish with her Salvadoran relatives.

To our grandson, Romero, who is in first grade in a Spanish/English dual language school.

In Mexico

To our daughter, Ann, who negotiates her life in Mexico City equally well in Spanish and English.

To our son-in-law, Chris, who is Greek American and now has added Spanish to his linguistic repertoire as he negotiates at work in both English and Spanish.

To our grandchildren, Christiana and Alexander, who are fluent in English, understand and speak some Greek, and are emergent bilinguals in English and Spanish.

Author Sandra Mercuri

To my husband Freddy, who daily uses his multilingual abilities in English, Spanish, and German in his work and travels and is now adding Italian to his linguistic repertoire.

To my children and grandchildren.

In the United States

To my daughter, Stephanie, who is bilingual in Spanish and English and uses those skills in her work daily.

To my daughter, Jessica, who is a bilingual teacher who teaches emergent bilinguals in elementary school during the day and at the college level at night.

To my granddaughter, Olivia, who is fluent in English and is becoming trilingual by learning Spanish at home and in preschool and Tagalog with her paternal grandmother.

In Germany

To my daughter, Natascha, who is trilingual in Spanish, German, and English and uses all three languages in her teaching at an international school.

To my son, Aiko, who is also trilingual in Spanish, German, and English and uses those skills in his work daily. My granddaughters, Valentina and Catalina, who are bilingual in Spanish and German and are becoming trilingual by studying English at school.

To my grandson Tommy and granddaughter Elise, who are fluent in English and Spanish and are emergent trilinguals as they learn in German at their international school.

To my grandson, Tobías, who is fluent in Spanish and is an emergent trilingual in English and German.

From All Three Authors

In addition, we base many examples in the book on the work of dual language teachers and administrators in and around Houston, Texas. At the time of writing this book, these educators were suffering through Hurricane Harvey. We dedicate this book to all the schools in the greater Houston area and applaud the important work dual language teachers and administrators perform in these schools.

Contents

Video Clips

How to Access the Online Video

To access the online video for *Dual Language Essentials for Teachers and Administrators*, Second Edition, go to **http://hein.pub/DualLang-login** to **Log In.** If you do not already have an account with Heinemann, you will need to create an account.

Register your product by entering the code: **DUALLANG**

Once you have registered your product, it will appear in the list of **My Online Resources**.

Acknowledgments

This book would not have been written without the collaboration and cooperation of a great many people. We have attempted to list as many of them here as possible. However, there are undoubtedly others we have missed whose contributions have influenced our writing—presenters at conferences we have attended, teachers whose classrooms we have visited, colleagues at universities where we have worked, and graduate students in our classes. We owe all of these individuals a debt of gratitude as well.

We want to begin by acknowledging the support and guidance we have received from our editor, Holly Kim Price, at Heinemann. Holly always provides useful suggestions on ways to improve the drafts of chapters we send. For this book, she made an extra effort to travel to Houston to support the videotaping in dual language classrooms. Holly has edited several of our previous books, and we appreciate her long-term support of our work. We also want to give a special thanks to Lisa Fowler, the publisher of professional books at Heinemann. Lisa fully supported us in writing this second edition of *Dual Language Essentials.* Her encouragement was crucial in our decision to gather new information and update the first edition.

We certainly want to acknowledge each member of the team at Heinemann who helped produce, advertise, and market this book. Without their combined efforts what we write wouldn't reach the teacher educators, teachers, and administrators who read our books. Sonja Chapman served as the production editor. She oversaw the editing and all aspects of the book's production. Sherry Day, the video producer, oversaw the photo shoots her talented photographers, Michael Grover and David Stirling, carried out at the dual language schools featured in this book. She also traveled to Texas with her team to oversee the videotaping of teachers and administrators. Her video team included David Stirling, Dennis Doyle, and Scott Anderson. Kim Cahill, the product manager, coordinated all the marketing work for this book and Amanda Bondi was the editorial coordinator. Suzanne Heiser, the designer, helped create the cover and the graphic design of the book, a very important role. McKenna DeMelo is the event coordinator who ensures that our books are available at key conferences and at our speaking engagements. Sarah Fournier, the managing editor, is always available to answer questions and oversee the publication of our

books. The Heinemann team has been supportive throughout the process of writing and producing this new edition of *Dual Language Essentials*.

In researching and writing this book, we worked closely with schools in Spring Branch, Texas. Jeffrey Post, the principal at Cedar Brook Elementary School, and Vivian Pratts, the principal at Edgewood Elementary, provided specific examples of how they implemented the dual language essentials. In addition, their video interviews gave us many insights into the work of administrators in developing and supporting elementary dual language bilingual programs.

In this edition of *Dual Language Essentials*, we have included a number of examples of secondary dual language programs. The inclusion of secondary programs reflects the reality that more dual language bilingual programs have been extended into middle and high schools. Tom Koulentes, who was the principal at Highland Park High School in Township High School District 113, provided valuable insights into how he has worked with teachers in the dual language program. Tom and Jesse Villanueva, the EL/DL coordinator, presented their exceptional program with us at La Cosecha, a major dual language conference.

We thank the many teachers and administrators working in dual language programs who informed our writing. Omaly IsaacCura, an Assistant Principal at Ridgecrest Elementary School in Spring Branch ISD, appears in our videotapes doing a model lesson and has informed our understanding of how to support dual language teachers. Karina Avila, an Assistant Principal at Pine Shadows Elementary in Spring Branch and a former student, provided us with ways to support both teachers and parents. Efraín Tovar, an education technology expert in the Central Valley of California, provided an excellent example of the importance of bilingualism in our globalized world. We also want to thank the team at Edgewood Elementary who shared their curriculum revision for language allocation: Gladys Baez, Marietta Del Riego, and Yadira Roel.

The coauthor of this book, Sandra, has worked closely with Pascual Yacovodonato, the Director of Bilingual, English language learners, and migrant students, in New Caney, Texas. Sandra and Pascual have worked to develop an effective curriculum for the district's dual language schools.

The chapter on teacher essentials includes examples of a number of bilingual teachers, several of whom we referenced in the first edition of this book. They include Juan Carlos Veloso, Irma Villa, Kari Bejar, and Marcela Pinzon Richardson.

Their stories form an important element of this book. We also want to include three people who are especially close to us: our two daughters, Mary and Ann, and our son-in-law, Francisco. Ann Ebe worked with Ofelia García and her research team in New York. The team's research on translanguaging has informed our views of good practices in working with emergent bilinguals. Mary Soto is a teacher educator in California who prepares bilingual teachers and has worked with both elementary and secondary teachers in dual language classes. Francisco Soto is a dual language teacher in an elementary school in Hayward, California. All three of these individuals continue to inform our work.

This edition includes video excerpts that highlight effective practices in dual language programs. We wish to thank Jessica Tejada, principal of Edgewood Elementary, and Alejandra Perez, principal, and Michele Gabriel, assistant principal of Cedar Brook Elementary in Spring Branch ISD, for welcoming us into their schools and supporting the videotaping. We also want to thank the teachers whose classroom practices are featured in the videos. They include the following teachers at Cedar Brook: Dora Baxter, Prekindergarten; Sandra Cordúa, Kindergarten; Teresa Batres, Third Grade; and María Amaya, in Fifth Grade. At Edgewood Elementary we videotaped Francisco González' fifth-grade science class and interviewed Yadira Roel, the First-Grade Bilingual Grade Level Chair, who provided an insightful interview on planning with grade level teams.

Finally, although our work has been influenced by a number of researchers, we want to acknowledge the work of several who have especially influenced this book. They include Ofelia García and her colleagues, for their work on the New York Initiative on Emergent Bilinguals through the City University of New York; Julie Sugarman and her colleagues, who contributed to our understanding of equity in bilingual programs; Jim Cummins, whose theories have influenced so many teacher educators and teachers in bilingual education; James Crawford, for his work on the history of bilingual education in the United States; Sonia Soltero, for her insights into how to develop dual language programs; Else Hamayan, Fred Genesee, and Nancy Cloud, for their valuable books on implementing bilingual programs; and Kathy Escamilla and her colleagues, for their contributions to our understanding of biliteracy. These researchers and others helped us develop an understanding of bilinguals and bilingual education that serves as the theoretical basis for this book.

Dual Language Programs
Growth, Rationale, and Models

We live in a multinational, multicultural, multilingual world. With the ease of travel, interconnectivity in communications, economic globalization, and transnational mobility, it is critical to be able to communicate with others around the world. People need to be bilingual or multilingual.

Baker and Wright (2017) state:

> Bilinguals are present in every country in the world, in every social class, and in all age groups. Numerically, bilinguals and multilinguals are in the majority in the world: it is estimated that they constitute between half and two thirds of the world's population. (60)

The number is hard to determine, but probably many of these bilinguals are really multilingual, especially if we accept Grosjean's (2010) definition of bilinguals as "those who use two or more languages (or dialects) in their everyday lives" (4).

Education in the twenty-first century must change to reflect the realities of a rapidly changing world. Not only are science, math, and technology important, but so is the ability to read, write, and speak two or more languages. The P21 Framework for 21st Century Learning provides "A unified vision for learning to ensure student success in a world where change is constant and learning never stops" (www.p21.org). The Framework used by hundreds of schools in the US and abroad lists four skills for learning and innovation: creativity and innovation, critical thinking and problem solving, communication, and collaboration (Wagner and Dintersmith 2015). The Framework includes Global Awareness, and lists "Understanding other nations and cultures, including the use of non-English languages (www.p21.org).

The twentieth-century assumption that nations are comprised of people who all speak the same language can no longer be supported. People in France do not only speak French and people in the United States do not only speak English. Instead, in most countries, especially in urban areas, many different tongues are heard, and the environment is filled with print in a variety of languages. As Romaine observes:

> The concentration of the world's 6,900 languages into about 200 countries means that there are over 30 times as many languages as there are countries, or in other words, that bilingualism and multilingualism is present in practically every country in the world, whether officially recognized or not. (Baker and Wright 2017, 60)

People are aware that in this globalized society, it is important to be able to communicate in more than one language, and schools in the United States are implementing dual language programs to help all students become bilingual and biliterate.

Policy makers and educators have recognized the critical need for Americans to become multilingual in the growing global economy (Mansilla and Jackson 2011). In 2000, when Secretary of Education Riley highlighted the dual language approach as the most effective way to teach English and encourage biliteracy, he pointed out that the United States needed to invest in programs such as these because "in an international economy, knowledge—and knowledge of language—is power" (Riley 2000, 4).

Soltero (2016) explains clearly the importance of bilingualism and multilingualism in this country:

> Market analysts point to the increasing need for bilingual, biliterate, and cross-cultural professionals in the United States and abroad. Having multiliterate citizens enhances intercultural competences, intergroup relations, and global economic competitiveness. (7)

A good example of the importance of speaking more than one language comes from Efraín Tovar, a former bilingual education student of Yvonne's. Efraín is now a veteran teacher of English learners in the San Joaquín Valley of California. He is also an education technology expert and the Coordinator of Information and Technology Services for his district. In addition, he is a board member of the Central Valley Computer Using Educators and founded the Central Valley Coding Project.

Efraín recently attended a Google Mexico conference as part of Google's Innovator Program. There he joined the Global Certified family consisting of new colleagues from all over Central and South America. He reconnected with his own Mexican roots while in Mexico City, and as a result of his experiences there and at the conference, Efraín posted this conclusion on Facebook (2017), "One of my biggest takeaways from being at Google's Innovator Program: BEING MULTILINGUAL IS A MUST! When will our school districts promote biliteracy?"

Despite the benefits of bilingualism, for many people living in the United States, monolingualism is still the norm. Although 56 percent of those polled in the European countries reported that they were fluent in at least one other language, Grosjean (2016) estimates that only around 20 percent of people living in the United States are bilingual and those include people who pair "English with Native American languages, older colonial languages, recent immigrant languages, American Sign Language, and so on" (1).

Even though many Americans are monolingual, the number of bilingual and multilingual people in the United States has steadily increased. According to the Migration Policy Institute's 2016 SPOTLIGHT report (Bartalova and Zong 2016) on language diversity in the United States, 60 percent of those who do speak a language other than English at home reported that they are also fully English proficient, that is, they are bilingual. The numbers of immigrants and U.S. natives speaking a language other than English at home represents one in five U.S. residents, and the number of bilinguals has drastically increased from 23.1 million people in 1980 to 29.2 million in 2015.

Increasingly, the United States reflects the world in its multilingualism and multiculturalism. "Indeed the U.S. Census Bureau records the use of more than 350 languages" (Bartalova and Zong 2016, 1). The many signs advertising businesses and products in a variety of languages in cities, and even in rural areas, makes it clear that English is not the only language people use to buy, to sell, and to communicate messages. Schools have responded to the increase in multilingualism in their communities and have begun to offer more programs designed to help students become bilingual and multilingual.

Growth of Dual Language Programs
- -

Dual language programs are a type of bilingual program that have proliferated in all parts of this country. Dual language programs teach language through content by teaching in English and in another language. García (2009, 2010, 2014) is concerned that the term *dual language* by itself without the word *bilingual* attached to it has been used by educators to avoid the political controversy caused by English Only advocates. She refers to dual language programs as *bilingual dual language programs* to remind us that dual language is a type of bilingual program. Throughout this book we use both the terms *dual language* and *bilingual dual language* as we discuss these programs.

Bilingual dual language programs can be found in schools in both cities and rural areas. For example, Utah passed a bill in 2008 to develop dual language programs in Spanish, Mandarin, and French. Then, in 2010, the governor issued a challenge to open 100 new dual language schools in the state teaching in English and Mandarin, French, German, Portuguese, and Spanish. In New York City, the Chancellor launched an expansion of dual language schools in the city. These programs are in high demand. García (2015) reported that forty dual language schools were being added because of the demand for dual language, citing the example of one school that had 1,100 applicants for only twenty spots in the school. The number of dual language programs grew from 180 in 2015 to 239 in 2017 (Sonia Soltero, personal communication).

The Houston Independent School District's Multilingual Programs department lists 59 dual language campuses in 2017–2018 on their website (www.houstonisd .org).These include one dual language Mandarin program and one program in Arabic. Los Angeles Unified School District lists sixty-four dual language programs on their website including nine in Korean and programs in Mandarin, Arabic, and Armenian (www.lausd.net).

It is difficult to get an accurate count of the number of dual language programs in the United States, because new programs are constantly being implemented. A search of the Internet shows dual language programs in many states. The Dual Language Schools website (http://duallanguageschools.org) listed 1,442 schools as of November 7, 2017 and updates its numbers frequently.

A study on current state policies and practice of dual language programs carried out by the Office of English Language Acquisition (U.S. Department of Education 2015) reports that:

In their 2012–13 Consolidated State Performance Reports (CSPRs), 39 states and the District of Columbia indicated that districts receiving federal Title III funding implemented at least one dual language program that year. In total, these programs featured more than 30 different partner languages. States most frequently reported dual language programs with Spanish (35 states and the District of Columbia), Chinese (14 states), Native American languages (12 states), and French (seven states and the District of Columbia) as the partner languages. (x)

As this report shows, dual language programs are being implemented each year in many different states, and the number of partner languages is also increasing.

In our own experiences with dual language schools across the country, we find that many dual language programs are not included in any listing. Furthermore, many schools with dual language programs in the elementary grades are now extending the program into middle and high schools.

Bilingual dual language programs are growing in popularity across the country because of the academic success of students in these programs and because dual language students are becoming bilingual and biliterate. In 2008 California initiated the Seal of Biliteracy, an award given by a school, school district, or county office of education recognizing students who have studied and attained proficiency in two or more languages. By October 2017, twenty-eight states and the District of Columbia had laws approving the Seal of Biliteracy. The Seal of Biliteracy website is constantly updated. This website keeps bilingual educators aware of issues related to bilingual education (http://sealofbiliteracy.org).

Wilson (2011) reported on the rise of dual language programs across the United States and described the benefits for both English learners and fluent English speakers.

At a time when other types of bilingual education are on the decline . . . dual language programs are showing promise in their mission to promote biliteracy and positive cross-cultural attitudes in our increasingly multilingual world. (1)

Even in states that passed legislation requiring English-only instruction, dual language programs have become popular. And attitudes are changing. In 2016, California passed Proposition 58, which opened the doors for multilingual education in the state and nullified the 1998 Proposition 227, the English in Public Schools Statute that required that limited English proficient (LEP) students be taught mainly in English and effectively eliminated most bilingual instruction in the state.

The majority of dual language programs are offered in Spanish. This reflects the report from the National Center for Education Statistics (n.d.) that in the 2013–2014 school year, nearly 77 percent of English learners in U.S. schools identified Spanish as their home language.

In addition to Spanish, dual language programs have been established in a variety of other languages, including French, German, Mandarin, Cantonese, Khmer (Cambodian), Italian, Navajo, Japanese, Haitian Creole, Russian, Korean, Portuguese, Cape Verdean, Arabic, Hmong, and Hebrew. Most of these programs are offered regionally because of the numbers of native speakers of those languages. For example, Hebrew is offered as a dual program in a middle school in a New York Jewish neighborhood area, and Arabic is offered in Houston where a large Arabic-speaking population can be found. Cantonese dual language is offered in the San Francisco area where there are many Cantonese speakers, and Hmong dual language programs have been established in Sacramento, California, and St. Paul, Minnesota, where many Hmong language speakers live.

Although dual language programs are offered in many languages, most of the specific examples provided here are from Spanish/English dual language programs because the majority of the dual language programs in the United States are Spanish/English. It is our conviction, however, that the essentials laid out in this book are applicable to dual language programs offered in any languages.

Labels for Students in Dual Language Programs

Dual language programs are designed for students whose home language is English and for students who enter school speaking a language other than English (LOTE). A number of labels have been used to refer to these LOTE students. The label most frequently used in federal and state documents is *limited English proficient*. Students identified as LEP are placed in English as a second language (ESL) or bilingual programs, and their progress in learning English and academic content is reported by schools.

Many state documents use the term *English language learner* (ELL) or simply *English learner* (EL) to refer to students with low levels of English proficiency. Early childhood educators refer to "young children who speak a language other than English in the home and are not fully fluent in English" as *dual language learners* (DLLs) (Espinosa 2013, 3). Although this is a logical label, many DLLs are not in dual language programs, so the term may cause some confusion.

LEP, *ELL*, and *EL*, are labels that define students in terms of their English proficiency. These labels do not recognize any of the positive qualities these students bring to school. Many students whose home language is English are deficient in some area of education, but schools do not label them as limited math proficient or limited science learners. And even native English speakers are required to take a minimum of twelve years of English language arts and are, thus, English language learners.

García (2009) introduced a positive term, *emergent bilinguals*, to refer to students who are becoming bilingual during their schooling. In dual language programs both native English speakers and students who speak languages other than English become increasingly proficient in two or more languages. As García explains:

> According to our view of language as action, a speaker never "has" a language, never stops learning how to use it, especially as life experiences change. . . . A speaker only uses or performs a language according to the opportunities or affordances he or she is given. Thus, we're all emergent bilinguals in certain situations, at certain times. (Celic and Seltzer 2011, 5)

More recently, García, Ibarra Johnson, and Seltzer (2017) have used both *emergent bilinguals* and *experienced bilinguals* to refer to students. As they explain:

> Many, if not most, classrooms are multilingual, with students who speak languages in addition to English. Some of these students are highly bilingual and biliterate (experienced bilinguals), whereas others' bilingualism and biliteracy is emerging (emergent bilinguals). (x)

In dual language programs all students in the early grades are emergent bilinguals. Both LOTE students and English speakers are learning an additional language. As these students progress through the program, they become experienced bilinguals. We will refer to the students in dual language programs as *bilinguals* to refer to both emergent and experienced bilinguals.

Rationale for Dual Language

The goals of dual language programs are to promote academic development, language proficiency in two languages, and cross-cultural understanding. These goals are critical in a world where transnational mobility is the norm and economic globalization is rapidly increasing. The bilingualism students develop in dual language programs results in academic, cognitive, linguistic, and economic benefits as well as increased cross-cultural competency.

Academic Benefits of Becoming Bilingual

Research shows that students succeed academically in well-implemented dual language programs. Lindholm-Leary (2013) found that bilinguals who are biliterate score higher on standardized reading and math tests than monolingual students, and in a California study, she found the students in dual language programs scored higher on high school exit tests than students in monolingual classrooms.

In a longitudinal study of a large district, Valentino and Reardon (2014) analyzed standardized test scores of 13,750 bilinguals in English language arts each year from second through eighth grade and math from second to sixth grade. They compared results for students in the different programs that the district offered: English immersion, transitional bilingual, developmental bilingual, and dual language programs. The longitudinal data for tests of English language arts showed that "the effect through second grade in ELA is significantly higher for those in TB [transitional bilingual] than for EI [English immersion] . . . not significantly different for those in DB [developmental bilingual] and significantly lower for those in DI [dual instruction] than those in EI" (20). It is not surprising that bilinguals whose home language is Spanish in dual language programs score lower in tests of English language arts than bilinguals in the other three programs. Spanish speakers in a 90/10 dual language model would have received only limited instruction in English by second grade.

Test results in later grades are quite different. Although the scores of bilinguals in English immersion, transitional bilingual, and developmental bilingual programs all increase at about the same rate as the state average for all students, scores for students in dual language classes increase more rapidly than the state average. Valentino and Reardon (2014) comment that "this rate is so fast, that by fifth grade their test scores in ELA catch up to the state average, and on average by seventh grade ELs in DI are scoring above their EL counterparts in all of the other programs" (21). The study found similar results in math. The later gains offset the earlier low scores. As the authors note, "ELs in DI are the only ones whose test score trajectories are not slower than the state average, but rather mirror that of the average student in the state" (22).

In a large-scale longitudinal study, Umansky and Reardon (2014) found that Latino ELs in dual language programs had higher English proficiency and academic achievement than ELs in any other program. In another large-scale study, Steele and her colleagues (2017) concluded that ELs in dual language programs in Portland Oregon public schools, "outperform their counterparts in fifth-grade reading by 13 percent of a standard deviation, and in eighth-grade reading by more than a fifth of a standard deviation" (4).

In addition, several meta-analyses have shown that bilinguals in well-implemented, long-term bilingual education programs succeed academically at higher rates than students in transitional bilingual programs or ESL programs (Slavin and Cheung 2004; Greene 1998; Rolstad, Mahoney, and Glass 2005).

Linguistic, Economic, and Cognitive Benefits of Becoming Bilingual

In addition to the academic advantage, dual language programs provide economic, linguistic, and cognitive advantages for all students. The linguistic advantages are obvious. Bilinguals can communicate in more contexts with more people than monolinguals can. This proves beneficial when people travel to other countries as well as when they communicate with people living in the United States who do not speak English or do not speak it well. In addition, dual language programs enable students who enter school speaking a language other than English to develop high levels of proficiency in both their home language and English.

Dual language programs also provide economic advantages. Callahan and Gándara (2014) in their edited book, *The Bilingual Advantage: Language, Literacy, and the US Labor Market*, provide evidence of the economic benefits of bilingualism. The chapters present empirical studies from researchers in education, economics, sociology, anthropology, and linguistics showing the economic and employment benefits of bilingualism in the U.S. labor market. Unlike previous studies, this book focuses on individuals who have developed high levels of bilingualism and biliteracy. Such people have greater academic achievement, greater likelihood of attending a four-year college, and greater employment potential than monolinguals. Similarly, in a report on preparing a globally competent workforce, the authors point out:

> ...learning at least one additional language is a crucial element of global competence. Employers are increasingly identifying the ability to understand another language and culture as an important workplace skill. An analysis of 14.6 million job postings found bi- or multi-lingualism to be not only one of the top twenty skills required for high-growth/high-wage occupations, but also one of the top eight skills required for all occupations. In addition, 63 percent of employers rated knowledge of foreign languages as increasingly important for high school and college graduates. (Monthey et al. 2016)

A colleague of ours pointed out that her daughter, who is an accountant, was given a high-level position in her company because of her ability to read and write in Mandarin. She is the only person in the company with a knowledge of Mandarin, and the company does business with Chinese business people who need accounting assistance for documents written in Mandarin.

A second example is the Freemans' son-in-law, Chris, who works for Colgate Palmolive. Chris was given a promotion to live in Mexico City and oversee a team that develops innovations for certain products throughout Latin America. He reports that many of his team meetings are conducted in Spanish, and when he travels to other countries in Latin America, his knowledge of Spanish is essential. If Chris had not been able to speak, read, and write Spanish, he would not have received this promotion, and his growing competency in Spanish allowed him to succeed in his present position. More recently, he was given an additional promotion and is now Director of Marketing Communications for Latin America.

Sandra Mercuri's daughters provide us with final examples. Her oldest daughter, Natascha, lived some of her childhood in Germany and then moved with her parents to Argentina. She got married in Argentina and then moved back to Germany for work. After applying for a job in the United States and getting approved, she moved with her family to teach in a middle school in Texas where her parents were living. Natascha worked six years in the United States teaching Spanish-speaking children in a rural school district, and then she and her family emigrated back to Germany. She now teaches in English, Spanish, and German in a prestigious private school because of her trilingual abilities.

Sandra's second daughter, Jessica, came to the Central Valley of California from Argentina with her parents when she was in community college. She knew some English, but became more proficient as she attended junior college. She transferred to a nearby four-year college where she received her BA and bilingual teaching credential as well as an MA in TESOL (Teaching English to Speakers of Other Languages) and reading. She taught in dual language programs for two districts in the Central Valley. She is now teaching at the local community college as an adjunct and as an elementary third-grade teacher.

Stephanie is Sandra's youngest daughter. She came to this country from Argentina with her family in elementary school. Her schooling was all in English, but her parents helped her maintain her Spanish. In high school she took several AP Spanish courses that gave her college credit. When she graduated from college with a communications degree, she was able to get a job with Univisión, a major American Spanish language broadcast television network, because of her bilingual abilities.

Being bilingual has cognitive advantages as well as linguistic and economic advantages. Bialystok (2011) has conducted a series of studies showing that bilinguals have better problem-solving ability than monolinguals. In addition, the studies have shown that bilinguals have lower rates of dementia and Alzheimer's disease than monolinguals. As Bialystok reports, "The main empirical finding for the effect of bilingualism on cognition is in the evidence for enhanced executive control in bilingual speakers" (1).

Hamayan, Genesee, and Cloud (2013) explain the concept of executive control functions:

The advantages of bilingualism have been demonstrated in cognitive domains related to attention, inhibition, monitoring, and switching focus of attention. These processes are required during problem solving for example, when students must focus their attention if potentially conflicting information needs to be considered; in order to select relevant information and inhibit processing of irrelevant information; and when they must switch attention to consider alternative information when a solution is not forthcoming. Collectively, these cognitive skills comprise what are referred to as executive control functions. (8)

As Bialystok points out, considerable research has shown that both languages of a bilingual speaker are constantly active, even in contexts where only one language is being used. As a result, bilinguals must use the executive control functions during linguistic processing. As Bialystok comments, "A likely explanation for how this difficult selection is made in constant online linguistic processing by bilinguals is that the general-purpose executive control system is recruited into linguistic processing, a configuration not found in monolinguals" (2). She argues that the result of constantly using the executive control system in linguistic processing changes bilinguals' brains in ways that improve the ability to solve problems and resist diseases like dementia and Alzheimer's.

Hamayan, Genesee, and Cloud (2013) point out that "the bilingual advantage found by Bialystok is most evident in bilingual people who acquire relatively advanced levels of proficiency in two languages and use their two languages actively on a regular basis" (7). Well-implemented dual language programs are long term and help students develop the high levels of bilingualism and biliteracy needed for the academic, linguistic, economic, and cognitive benefits of bilingualism.

The Benefit of Cross-Cultural Understanding

Educators also support dual language education because they know that dual language schools promote increased cross-cultural understanding (Torres-Guzman 2002, Lindholm-Leary 2001). Cabezón, Nicoladis, and Lambert (1998) report in their study of the Amigos program in Massachusetts what has been the experience of schools implementing dual language across the country.

We notice . . . that both English- and Spanish-Amigos enjoy learning about a new and different cultural group through long-term daily contact with members of a second ethnolinguistic group, who become like brothers and sisters to them. (11)

The Amigos program results, as well as the findings from research on other early dual language programs such as the Oyster program (Freeman 1995), are a reflection of how important it is that children from different languages and cultures learn together in two languaes. Genesee and Gándara (1999) point out that bilingual dual language programs provide data that support the contact hypothesis. This hypothesis holds that improved relationships result when students work and study together — when there is increased contact.

> Dual-language programs present a particularly interesting case for examining the contact hypothesis because they provide sustained opportunities for direct intergroup contact and, in principle, they incorporate at least some of the situational characteristics that are considered critical for positive intergroup outcomes, namely, the potential for close and cooperative contact in a context that is anxiety reduced and equitable for all participating groups. (667)

Contact promotes cross-cultural understanding among the children participating in dual language programs. However, the discrepancies between the socioeconomic status of English speakers and Spanish speakers can work to hinder positive intergroup relationships. For that reason, it is especially important that administrators, teachers, and parents maintain high expectations for students from both groups. Students are more likely to develop positive attitudes toward their classmates in a school where all students are expected to succeed. A school in south Texas provides this kind of positive atmosphere. At a recent orientation, Yvonne and her student teachers were visibly moved as the principal passionately explained that:

> All our students are special. All of them have potential. It doesn't matter if they live in a "colonia" with no electricity or running water. It doesn't matter if their parents work in the fields. Everyone here is becoming bilingual and biliterate. Everyone can and will learn.

Dual Language Program Models

Not all programs for bilinguals confer the benefits of dual language programs. Some programs for bilinguals are compensatory programs designed to overcome what are seen as linguistic deficiencies. For example, transitional bilingual programs use students' home languages to teach academic content for two or three years as the students learn English. Then students are transitioned into all-English instruction. Other compensatory programs, such as structured English immersion (Clark 2009), make no use of students' home languages and teach English grammar and vocabulary directly for extended periods of time each day.

Bilingual dual language programs, in contrast, are enrichment programs that build on the language students bring to school and help all students expand their academic, linguistic, and cross cultural competence. In their publication, *Guiding Principles for Dual Language Education*, the authors state as their first principle, "All aspects of the program work together to achieve the three core goals of dual language education: grade-level academic achievement, bilingualism and biliteracy, and sociocultural competence." (Howard et al. 2018)

Hamayan, Genesee, and Cloud (2013) identify three types of enrichment programs: (1) foreign or second language immersion programs for native English speakers, (2) developmental bilingual programs for students who enter school with limited or no English proficiency, (3) two-way immersion programs for students whose home language is English and for students who enter school with limited or no English proficiency. The authors state, "These are enriched forms of DL education because they aim for full competence in two (or more) languages along with high levels of academic achievement and cross-cultural understanding and achievement" (8).

Lindholm-Leary (2001) writes, "In dual language programs, English dominant and target-language-dominant students are purposefully integrated with the goals of developing bilingual skills, academic excellence, and positive cross-cultural and personal competency attitudes for both groups of students" (30). These are the goals of an enrichment program.

Soltero (2016) also describes dual language as enrichment education. She states:

> Dual language education is a long-term additive bilingual and cross-cultural program model that consistently uses two languages for content instruction, learning, and communication, where students develop high levels of bilingual, biliterate, and cross-cultural competencies. (3)

In this book when we use the term *dual language* or *bilingual dual language* we refer to the enrichment program models that meet the criteria that Hamayan, Genesee, Cloud, Lindholm-Leary, and Soltero list. Figure 1.1 lists types and goals of compensatory and enrichment programs for bilinguals.

One-Way, Developmental, and Two-Way Dual Language Programs

Based on our experiences with schools in different parts of the country, in this book we focus on two commonly implemented models of enrichment dual language: one-way and two-way bilingual programs. We also describe developmental programs here. We view developmental programs as essentially the same as one-way programs. It may be that what are called *one-way programs* in one part of the country are labeled *developmental programs* in other areas.

One-Way and Two-Way Dual Language Programs

Principal Jeff Post explains the differences and similarities between the one-way and two-way dual language programs at this school.

Compensatory		Enrichment	
Type	Goal	Type	Goal
ESL or ELD	Use specialized instruction in English to build English proficiency	Developmental bilingual	Use home language and English to build bilingualism, biliteracy, and cross-cultural competence
Structured English immersion		One-way dual	
Transitional bilingual education	Use home language as a bridge to all English instruction	Two-way dual	

Figure 1.1 Compensatory and Enrichment Programs

One-Way Dual Language Programs

Most of the students in one-way programs come to school with a home language other than English. These programs have been developed in areas where there are large numbers of students who speak a language other than English. Because two-way dual language programs need to have a sufficient number of students whose home language is English, it may not be feasible to establish a two-way program in some areas.

One-way bilingual programs can include recently arrived immigrants with little or no knowledge of English. In addition, many of the students in one-way programs may have been born in the United States or may have lived here for several years. They often understand some English and may use both English and their home language every day. For example, all the students in a one-way dual language program may be Hispanics with varying levels of proficiency in both Spanish and English. The programs are considered one-way because English is not the home language of any of the students.

Jeff Post, the principal of Cedar Brook Elementary School in Spring Branch, Texas, near Houston, described the student populations of the one-way dual language (OWDL) strand at his school. He uses acronyms for fluent English speakers (FES) and for long-term English learners (LTELLs), those students in U.S. schools for several years and still struggling with English.

> The majority of our students in OWDL are those with little to no English. Some are recent immigrants and some are LTELL. Those in primary grades usually have limited to no English. Occasionally we will have one or two kinder students in OWDL that are FES but it's rare. In the intermediate grades (usually 4th and 5th) there are a good number of students (maybe 4–5 per class) that have become English dominant over the years. But many are still struggling in 5th grade to reach English fluency and meet exit criteria.

Developmental Bilingual Programs ◆ One-way bilingual programs are similar to developmental bilingual education (DBE) programs where students continue to develop their first languages while learning English. Crawford (2004) explains that the language maintenance approach then known as "bilingual-bicultural education" began in the 1970s as an alternative to transitional bilingual education. This model soon came under attack because there was a perception that English learners were being taught in their home language and were not learning English. As a result, bilingual-bicultural program models were declared ineligible for federal funding.

However, when the Bilingual Education Act was reauthorized in 1984, programs labeled as developmental bilingual education (DBE) were approved for funding. This model was similar to transitional bilingual education in the early years. As Crawford notes, the two programs had the same components: "ESL instruction, initial literacy in the native language, and subjects taught in sheltered as well as native language classrooms" (2004, 44–45). A major difference between DBE and transitional bilingual models is that transitional bilingual education has the goal of moving students into all-English instruction while developmental (or late-exit) programs have the goal of developing the native language as well as developing English.

Crawford explains that DBE programs typically begin with about 90 percent of the instruction in the students' home language. Instruction in core academic classes is given at first in the native language and later in sheltered classes. Classes like physical education, music, and art are taught in English, and emergent bilinguals are mixed with native English speakers in these classes. Even after students reach high levels of proficiency in English, in DBE programs they continue to take one or two classes in their home language.

Valentino and Reardon (2014) included a developmental bilingual program in their research on program effectiveness. They write:

> Developmental bilingual education programs are similar to transitional bilingual programs in that they incorporate EL students' home language into classrooms and exclusively enroll ELs, but these programs are longer term, and often lasting through the fifth grade or later, and have the goal of helping students develop competency in English while maintaining and continuing to develop competency in their native language. (6)

In many schools, what might once have been called developmental bilingual programs are now labeled as one-way dual language programs. The change in terminology emphasizes that both languages are valued and developed and avoids the suggestion that the program is designed solely to develop students' home language.

Two-Way Dual Language Programs ◆ Two-way dual language programs differ from one-way programs in that they include students whose home language is English as well as students who speak a language other than English. Ideally, half the students would be native English speakers and the other half would speak a home language other than English; however, this balance is seldom achieved. Generally, two-way bilingual programs require at least a one-third – to – two-thirds ratio of the two language groups.

At Jeff's school there is a two-way dual language strand as well as a one-way strand. Students in the two-way dual language (TWDL) strand are generally more diverse than the students in the one-way dual program at his school. Jeff explains how the school has to be flexible and must consider how the program's population will shift over time:

> In TWDL we have both Hispanic and Anglo native English speakers. We have a pretty diverse mix of Anglo, Hispanic, African American, and Asian English speaking students. The other half of TWDL, of course, is made up of native Spanish-speaking Latinos. Usually the mix of the TW class is even with half native English and half native Spanish speakers. However, we noticed this year that in pre-K, we are heavy on the native Spanish side by almost 1/3, which definitely makes a difference as Pre-K rolls up in the future. This occurred not by design, but it just so happened that last year as we were preparing class lists, and as people began to drop off for various reasons before the school year started, that our waiting list was predominantly Spanish speaking. We are seeing this year a more even applicant pool as we prepare lists for 2017–18.

Two-way programs include students from two or more different cultural backgrounds, so there is a greater likelihood of students' gaining increased cross-cultural understanding, one of the goals of enriched education. In both one-way and two-way programs, there may also be students whose home language is not either of the two languages of instruction. As shown in Jeff's two-way program, cultural and linguistic diversity is frequently found in dual language programs. For example, we observed a Hmong-speaking student in a Spanish/English two-way program in Fresno. Her parents thought that Spanish as well as English would be useful to her future. Because the teacher constantly sheltered instruction to make the input comprehensible in both Spanish and English, this was a good placement for her.

Language Allocation in Dual Language Programs

In both one-way and two-way dual language programs, instruction is delivered in two languages, but the time allocated for each language varies. The two most common models are referred to as 90/10 and 50/50. Both models have been widely used in the United States. In their summary of the research, Lindholm-Leary and Genesee (2010) conclude that "English learners in both 50/50 and 90/10 programs developed high levels of oral English proficiency" (350). They go on to add:

> Whereas English learners in 50/50 programs exhibited higher scores in English than English learners in 90/10 programs in the early grade levels, these differences disappeared by the upper elementary grade levels and the performance of both groups remained comparable throughout the secondary grade levels. (350)

90/10 Model ◆ The 90/10 model is sometimes referred to as a "full immersion model" because students are immersed in the LOTE for 90 percent of the day. This model is based on the French immersion programs implemented in Canada (Lambert and Tucker 1972) where English speakers were immersed in French for 90 percent of the day for initial instruction. Each year, the amount of English is increased until about fifth grade when students have equal instructional time in each language. Many schools have adopted this model with the early emphasis on the LOTE to help compensate for the dominant power of English outside the school context.

One variation within the 90/10 model involves literacy instruction. In many 90/10 program models, all students learn to read and write initially in the LOTE. However, in some schools, all students receive initial literacy instruction in both languages. In still another variation initial literacy instruction is given in the home language, and the rest of the day is divided, with 90 percent of the instructional time in the LOTE and 10 percent in English. With this variation, there would be both English language arts for English speakers and Spanish (or Mandarin or other) language arts for speakers of languages other than English. As more English is added at each grade level, the program adjusts which subjects are taught in each language.

There is also variation in the subject for instruction in English in a 90/10 model. Some schools teach science during the 10 percent English time in kindergarten and first grade because science offers many opportunities for hands-on collaborative activities. When the model moves to 80/20, an additional subject is added. In planning a 90/10 model, it is important to outline a schedule for the subjects to be taught in each language at each grade level.

Schools implement their programs in different ways, organizing the time in each language and the subjects taught according to what works for them. In Cedar Brook, Jeff's school, the 90/10 two-way model is implemented in the following way:

> In the TW program, we begin the Spanish immersion component in Kinder and 1st grades (90% Spanish—Pre-K is 50/50). This model is based on gradual release, and more English is introduced each year until 5th grade, where the language components are once again 50/50. Throughout the program grades, subjects are taught in different languages. For example, Kinder and 1st grades teach science in English, and then 2nd and 3rd teach it in Spanish. Math is taught primarily in Spanish, until 4th grade when it switches to English. Similarly, LA is taught in Spanish until 5th grade. Although we do teach English grammar pieces and guided reading beginning in 3rd grade (small group only).

50/50 Model ◆ In the 50/50 model, students are instructed in each language 50 percent of the time throughout the program. This model is sometimes referred to as a "partial immersion program" because all students are immersed in a second language for half of the day. Some schools choose this model because administrators feel pressure to show high test scores in English, and they worry that giving less time for English in early grades will result in low test scores on tests of reading and math in English on the high-stakes third-grade test. As the research summary by Lindholm-Leary and Genesee (2010) shows, students in both 50/50 and 90/10 programs score equally well on tests by the secondary levels, but English learners in 50/50 programs have higher English scores in early grades.

Time for the two languages in a 50/50 program model may be divided in various ways—half day and half day, alternate days, or even alternate weeks. For schools where teachers organize curriculum around units of study, the alternation may be by unit, and the each unit may last from two to four weeks.

A good example of a school that has worked carefully through the implementation of their dual language bilingual program is the Amistad Dual Language School in New York City. They have developed a complex language allocation policy. This model includes alternate-day, alternate half-day, two-week, and three- to four-week cycles for the elementary grades. Then in the middle school there is a two-week cycle. Allocating the language by units of study once all students have developed at least basic proficiency in the two languages works well because it would be difficult to alternate languages during a unit of study. The Amistad School has developed an approach that fits its students, faculty, and community context, and this plan will undoubtedly change over time as they monitor how well the current plan works..

For schools in areas where it is difficult to recruit bilingual teachers, teachers can team-teach, and the bilingual teacher can provide instruction in the language other than English to one group in the morning and the other group in the afternoon (or on alternate days or weeks). This maximizes faculty language resources.

In some 50/50 models, the division is by subject. For example, math may be taught in English and science and social studies in the LOTE. Generally, the time for math instruction equals the combined time for science and social studies, so the total time is still 50/50. Literacy instruction also varies in 50/50 programs. In some programs, all students receive initial language arts instruction in their home language, and then, by first or second grade, all students have language arts together in both languages. In other programs, all students receive language arts instruction in both languages from the beginning.

The Gómez and Gómez (2015) one-way 50/50 Dual Language Enrichment Model is one that has been widely implemented, especially in Texas. In this model literacy is taught in the native language prekindergarten through first grades and then in both languages second through fifth grade. Math is taught in English throughout the grades and social studies and science are taught in Spanish.

Students also receive instructional support in a computer/science lab. The instructional software in prekindergarten through second grade is in the language of instruction (math would be in English, social studies and science in Spanish). Starting in third grade, the software is in the opposite language (math in Spanish and social studies and science in English.)

The model has other important features including vocabulary enrichment and conceptual refinement in both languages. Gómez and Gómez suggest color-coding of environmental print with blue for English and red for Spanish. They also encourage a daily switch of "language of day" activities with Spanish for Monday, Wednesday, and Friday and English for Tuesdays and Thursdays. The "language of the day" activities suggested include the library, P.E., and specials like music and computers as well as daily activities such as journal writing and sustained silent reading. The language of the day is best implemented when the school implements dual language for all students rather than as a strand.

Some schools have modified and adapted the Gómez and Gómez model as their programs have developed. As in any dual language model, there should be flexibility in implementation to meet the needs of individual schools, teachers, and students. Jeff describes his 50/50 model as a slightly modified Gómez and Gómez (G&G) model:

For our OWDL program, we implement a variation of the G&G model. Math is taught and primarily tested in English, Kinder-5th (with exceptions made for recent immigrants). LA/SS is primarily taught in Spanish but we do add in 30 minutes of English beginning in 2nd grade. Science is also taught in English beginning in 2nd grade. We preview in Spanish for subjects that are to be taught in English, and we rely on sheltered strategies during the English components of the day. We ask that teachers label the environment (sticking with color-coding), and that they keep to the language of instruction concerning each content area. We also require them to adhere to Language of the Day for routines and transitions.

Both one-way and two-way programs can be either 50/50 or 90/10. At Jeff's school, the one-way program is 50/50 and the two-way program is 90/10.

Not only are there variations within the basic models (one-way or two-way, 90/10 or 50/50), there are also variations in the extent to which programs are implemented. Dual language programs may constitute a strand of one or two classes at each grade level within a school or the program may be implemented schoolwide or even districtwide. Many factors shape decisions regarding program design and implementation, including availability of bilingual faculty and materials, student population, and attitudes within the school and the community. Developing a successful program depends in part on choosing the model that best fits a particular context.

Utah 50/50 DLI programs: Foreign/Second Language Immersion

As mentioned earlier, in 2008 Utah passed the International Initiative, Senate Bill 41, to create funding for dual language instruction (DLI) programs in Utah. These programs now include instruction in Mandarin, French, German, Portuguese, and Spanish. In this model there is a strict separation of languages and teachers. Fifty percent of the instruction is in English, taught by one teacher, and 50 percent in the partner language, taught by another teacher. Students are taught language through content in the second language part of the day with the goal of helping them become bilingual and biliterate in two languages.

Utah schools offer both one-way and two way programs. However what makes the one-way programs more like foreign or second language immersion programs rather than DLI is that the student population of these one-way programs is made up of English speakers with no proficiency in the second language. The one-way DLI programs do not serve minority populations. The DLI programs are designed to prepare students with the global competence needed for the twenty-first century (Utah Dual Language Immersion 2017).

High School and Middle School Program Models

At the middle and high school levels, the division for instruction in each language is usually varied by subject. Generally, language arts is offered in the LOTE along with either social studies or science. Students take either two or three subjects in the LOTE. The subjects offered may vary from one year to the next. For example, science might be offered in Spanish in ninth grade and social studies in tenth grade. Decisions about the subjects taught in the LOTE are determined by the availability of resource materials and teachers who have both certification in the academic subject and academic language proficiency in the LOTE.

In many schools the LOTE teachers are first hired to teach science or social studies, and then, when the school extends dual language into the middle school level, they teach their subject in Spanish, Arabic, or another language. Language arts in the LOTE is usually taught by the foreign language teachers. Often, because students have been studying in Spanish or another language in the dual language program for several years, they take an AP language arts and/or literature course in that language, and they may do this as early as middle school.

In Illinois, the North Shore Elementary School District 112 and the Township High School District 113 on the outskirts of Chicago have been promoting dual language education since the first dual language program began in the elementary schools in 1996 with fifty-six students. In 2015, 700 students were in the dual language programs (K–8) in the district. The K–8 dual language programs have expanded into the Township High School District's Highland Park High School, which is now in its second year. Although the goal will be a 50/50 program eventually, it presently has a 75/25 model. Led by principal Tom Koulentes, this program is in the process of being fully implemented following a carefully planned timeline.

In 2014–15 the vision for the program was created and in 2015–16 the Spanish courses for dual language students were completely redesigned as a Spanish language arts curriculum. In 2016–17 core curriculum courses were introduced. In Highland Park's well-thought-out dual language program, students take Spanish language classes each of their four years including Spanish language arts, Spanish language, and Spanish literature classes. All of these Spanish classes are honors or AP classes. In ninth grade they also take world history and physical education in Spanish. In tenth grade, P.E. along with traffic safety are offered in Spanish. In the coming years the school plans to add geometry, art history, U.S. history, biology, graphic arts, and international business/international relations/civics in Spanish.

Many course decisions have depended on finding qualified Spanish-speaking faculty, securing grade-level texts, and addressing parent concerns about their child's college readiness and test scores. Highland Park High School students are meeting the requirements of the State of Illinois Seal of Biliteracy, and the school has set its own Seal of Dual Language guidelines to recognize students achieving high levels of bilingualism, biliteracy, and biculturalism. This school Seal of Dual Language is actually more prestigious than the state seal, which requires language proficiency only. As Tom, the principal, explains, "Students would earn the Seal of Biliteracy first, and dual language students would have the opportunity to earn this more prestigious Seal of Dual Language." Figure 1.2 explains Highland Park High School's Seal of Dual Language and the additional requirements students need to achieve this seal, including coursework and a portfolio. Many students work for both seals. Up to this point, Highland Park High School dual language students have outperformed the school's non–dual language students on ACT composite scores as well as ACT math and reading scores.

Effective Models and Effective Practices

Baker and Wright (2017) note that the notion of a program model is now being challenged and that the emphasis should be on effective practices rather than simply on effective models. Program models may be seen as reflecting what García (2009) refers to as a "monolingual" or "monoglossic perspective." This is the perspective that a bilingual is essentially two monolinguals in one person. In programs based on this view, bilinguals are instructed as though they were monolingual Spanish speakers during some parts of the day and as though they were monolingual English speakers at other times. This perspective keeps the two languages separate and discourages building cross-linguistic connections and metalinguistic awareness.

On the other hand, when educators take a bilingual or heteroglossic perspective, bilinguals are seen as individuals who have a complex linguistic system with features of two or more languages. Effective practices include helping students make cross-language connections and drawing on all students' language resources at all times rather than keeping languages strictly separate. As Baker and Wright (2017) comment, "Such a perspective opens up space to engage in optimal classroom translanguaging practices that maximize growth and gains for individual students, as well as positive outcomes for schools in an accountability era" (198).

In the following chapters we will further our discussion of translanguaging and translanguaging practices, and we will keep the focus on effective practices in bilingual dual language enrichment programs. The different enrichment models that we have described can provide optimal education for all students when the programs are based on effective practices.

The Dual Language Seal
in
Township High School District 113

The Dual Language Seal at Highland Park High School is a recognition that is designed to signal to universities and employers that students with this Seal are biliterate, bilingual, and bicultural, have completed content area coursework in both Spanish and English, and have met requirements that far exceed the Illinois State Seal of Biliteracy.
For the graduating class of 2017, students must meet the following requirements.

- Students have earned the Illinois State Seal of Biliteracy
- Students have taken four years of Spanish language courses which includes AP Spanish Language and Culture, AP Spanish Literature, and Spanish Seminar Honors.
- Students have taken four years of English language courses.
- Students will complete a portfolio that demonstrates cultural proficiency in both Spanish and English.
- Students will participate in one of several approved cultural experiences in the community.

Highland Park High School
Dual Language Program

Grade Level	Spanish Language Arts	Spanish Content Courses
9th grade	Spanish Language Arts II Honors	Patterns of World History Physical Education
10th grade	AP Spanish Language	Physical Education Traffic Safety
11th Grade	AP Spanish Literature	
12th Grade	Spanish Seminar Honors	

State of Illinois Seal of Biliteracy Requirements	HPHS Seal of Dual Language Requirements:
• Proficiency in English equivalent to an Intermediate High level of proficiency. • Proficiency in a second language equivalent to an Intermediate High level of proficiency.	• 4 years of Spanish • 4 years of English • Dual Language Portfolio Presentation

Figure 1.2 The Dual Language Seal

Overview of Chapters

We began this first chapter by reviewing the importance of bilingualism and biliteracy in the twenty-first century as transnationalism and economic globalization have transformed twentieth-century notions of a nation state with a single language into the reality of a multilingual and multicultural world. We reviewed the growth of bilingual students in schools and then described compensatory and enrichment programs for English learners. We also discussed the labels for students in dual language programs and the benefits of becoming bilingual and biliterate through bilingual dual language education.

In Chapter 2 we review the historical content of dual language programs and the history of dual language programs in the United States, connecting that history to different orientations toward the language of English learners. We look at the growth of dual language programs in the United States and consider changing views of bilinguals and the shifts in the goal of dual language programs. We conclude Chapter 2 by examining misconceptions about language use in bilingual programs. We suggest ways to draw on the full linguistic repertoires of emergent bilinguals by using translanguaging strategies.

We organized this book around a set of essentials for dual language. Chapter 3 begins the discussion of the essentials by considering essentials for the whole school. In Chapter 4 we explain essentials for administrators and for administrators and teachers working together. Chapter 5 focuses on teacher essentials, and we also discuss the different kinds of teachers in dual language classes. Chapter 6 focuses on curriculum essentials, including goals, planning, and implementation, and Chapter 7 describes biliteracy essentials. In each chapter we outline the essentials for the chapter in detail providing examples of how schools have implemented these essentials. Below we list the dual language essentials:

- **Whole School Essentials**
- **Administrator Essentials**
- **Administrator/Teacher Collaboration Essentials**
- **Teacher Essentials**
- **Curriculum Goals, Planning, and Implementation Essentials**
- **Biliteracy Essentials**

Throughout the book we showcase wonderful schools and educators we have come to know as we have researched this book. We hope that these examples, along with the essentials, will assist teachers and administrators as they plan for or review dual language programs. We share a common goal: We all want to provide the best possible education for all students.

Reflect and Apply

1. Some programs for bilinguals are compensatory and others are enrichment. Consider the program for bilinguals in the school where you teach or in a school you have observed. Describe the program and explain what makes it compensatory or enrichment.

2. We discussed different labels for students whose home language is other than English. Which term is most commonly used in your area? Which term do you think is best? Take down some notes and prepare to discuss this.

3. We explained some of the benefits of becoming bilingual and biliterate. Rank the benefits from most to least important and be prepared to explain your decisions.

4. Reflect on a dual language program where you teach or that you are familiar with. Describe the model it follows and the time allotment for different subjects. Does this model fit the school context well? Be prepared to share.

History and Language Use in Dual Language Programs

Bilingualism and encouragement of linguistic diversity have been common since ancient times. The Greeks, for example, conquered large areas of the Mediterranean and schooled those whom they conquered in the Greek language and culture. However, they did not try to replace local languages. When education was available, it was common to provide formal schooling in more than one language. In fact, because there was so little written material available, a literate person had to be able to read in more than one language. When the Romans conquered Europe, formal schooling included Latin for all students, and only in recent times has Latin been replaced with modern languages. However, the precedent for learning in more than one language in Europe was well established by the early occupations (Lessow-Hurley 1996).

Multilingualism was common when this country was founded. Crawford (1999) reports that "In 1664, when the settlement of New Netherlands was ceded to the

British crown, at least eighteen tongues were spoken on Manhattan Island, not counting the Indian languages" (21). In addition, teaching in languages other than English is not new to the United States. In areas where a great many people spoke a language other than English, instruction in the non-English language was often offered. In the 1800s, with the influx of large numbers of immigrants, schools in more than a dozen states provided instruction in a variety of languages, including German, Swedish, Norwegian, Danish, Dutch, Polish, Italian, Czech, French, and Spanish (Lessow-Hurley 1996; Ovando and Collier 1998).

There were German-English schools in Baltimore, Cincinnati, Cleveland, Indianapolis, Milwaukee, and St. Louis. Louisiana authorized instruction in English, French, or both languages, and in 1912, the Territory of New Mexico included in the writing of their state constitution the following provision:

> The legislature shall provide for the training of teachers in the normal schools or otherwise so that they may become proficient in both the English and Spanish languages, to qualify them to teach Spanish-speaking pupils and students in the public schools and educational institutions of the State. (U.S. Commission on Civil Rights 1972)

Native Americans also provided instruction in their indigenous languages and English. In fact, Crawford (2004) reports that by 1850 the Cherokees had achieved a 90 percent literacy rate and used bilingual materials "to such an extent that Oklahoma Cherokees had a higher English literacy level than the white populations of either Texas or Arkansas" (92).

Even though the history of America at times has shown an acceptance of instruction in languages other than English, negative attitudes toward bilingualism have been evident as well. For example, the accomplishments of the Cherokees were resented, and by 1879 the government began to force Native American children to attend off-reservation boarding schools in an attempt to eradicate native languages and replace them with English. About the same time, Italian, Jewish, and Slavic immigrants began to outnumber the already established Irish, German, and Scandinavian immigrant populations. Public sentiment toward these newcomers was negative, and those who did not speak English were criticized.

In 1906 Congress passed the first federal language law requiring knowledge of English for naturalization. Proficiency in English began to be equated with political loyalty. Around the time that the United States entered World War I, it was clearly un-American to speak a language other than English in public. By the 1930s bilingual instruction was virtually eradicated throughout the United States (Crawford 1999), and there was little interest in learning in two languages in public schools for the next thirty years.

Orientations Toward Language

The shifting attitudes toward speakers of non-English languages are reflected in the kinds of programs for English language learners that have been offered in U.S. schools during the last half of the twentieth century and now in the twenty-first century. Ruíz (1984) has described the historical development of three different orientations toward students' home languages: language as a handicap, language as a right, and language as a resource. He defines an orientation as a "complex of dispositions toward language and its role, and toward languages and their role in society" (16).

During the fifties and sixties, language as a handicap was the prevalent orientation. Ruíz points out that at this time, educators saw English language learners as having a problem, so that "teaching English, even at the expense of the first language, became the objective of school programs" (1984, 19). In other words, educators with this orientation believed that to overcome the handicap they had, English learners had to transition to English as quickly as possible. This orientation resulted in the establishment of ESL and transitional bilingual programs. These programs were designed to compensate for the language handicap these students were thought to have.

Ruíz explains that in the seventies, the language-as-a-right orientation emerged. As a part of the Civil Rights movement, bilingual educators called for the rights of nonnative English speakers to bilingual education. In many districts instruction given in English excluded some students from access to a meaningful education. This began to change in 1974 when Chinese parents in San Francisco sued the school district for violation of the civil rights of their children.

The school district claimed that the Chinese students were given an equal education because they were provided the same materials and taught the same content as native English speakers. The Chinese parents argued that by teaching non-English speakers in English, a language they did not understand, the district was denying them an equal opportunity to learn and discriminating against them under Title VI of the Civil Rights Act of 1964.

The Supreme Court sided with the parents in the Lau v. Nichols case. Although it did not require a specific program for English learners, the Supreme Court did issue guidelines for districts to follow. These guidelines called for schools to identify students with limited English proficiency and to provide special services that would give them access to the core curriculum. According to the Lau decision, schools could meet these requirements in different ways, including providing bilingual instruction or ESL. Students could be given some instruction in their home language or be placed in ESL classes. ESL teachers could pull out groups of students or work with mainstream teachers by providing extra support in the classes.

In 1981 a second civil rights case provided clearer guidelines for the kinds of programs that schools are required to implement in educating emergent bilinguals. In the case of Castañeda v. Pickard, the Fifth Circuit court ruled that a school district in Texas had not provided an appropriate program for English learners. Because of their low proficiency in English, the students could not participate equally in the school's instructional program.

This case was important because the court established three criteria for any program serving English learners: (1) The program must be based on a sound educational theory; (2) it must be implemented effectively with adequate resources and personnel; and (3) after a trial period, it must be evaluated as effective in overcoming "language handicaps." Although the ruling still used the negative terminology of a language-as-a-handicap orientation, it established guidelines for programs for which English learners have a legal right. These three criteria have often been used by states and districts in evaluating programs for English learners.

Ruíz also identifies a third orientation, language as a resource. He sees this orientation as a better approach to language planning for several reasons:

> It can have a direct impact on enhancing the language status of subordinate languages; it can help to ease tensions between majority and minority communities; it can serve as a more consistent way of viewing the role of non-English languages in U.S. society; and it highlights the importance of cooperative language planning. (25–26)

Bilingual dual language programs are all based on the language-as-a-resource orientation. These programs have raised the status and importance of languages other than English in many communities across the United States. They raise the status of non-English languages, in part, because as native English-speaking children become bilingual, parents and students alike see the value of knowing more than one language. In some communities dual language programs have eased tensions between groups who speak different languages. The programs have helped build cross-cultural school communities and cross-cultural friendships among students and parents, relationships that probably would not have developed without the programs.

Dual language programs benefit both native speakers of English and native speakers of languages other than English. These programs serve English language learners in a unique way because the learners become proficient in English and, at the same time, develop and preserve their home language. Because their peers are also learning their language, they maintain pride in their home language and culture. Native English speakers add proficiency in an additional language and increase their cross-cultural understanding. These benefits are the direct result of viewing all languages as valuable community resources.

Early Dual Language Programs — New Mexico

The first dual language programs in the United States were developed in New Mexico and Florida. New Mexico, a state whose people have been multilingual since before it became a territory, stands out as an exception in its openness to bilingual education. From the early 1500s up to the mid 1800s, Spain and then Mexico ruled the area, and the governance was known for encouraging bilingualism and cultural pluralism. Under Mexican rule native New Mexicans were even appointed to government posts, giving New Mexicans both the responsibility for and voice in self-governance.

When New Mexico became a U.S. territory in 1850, New Mexicans could run for the legislature. New Mexico not only allowed bilingual citizenry but also passed constitutional provisions to maintain dual citizenship rights. During this period, the territory officially authorized bilingual education in Spanish and English. In the early 1900s. when some in the United States were mandating English-only instruction, New Mexico still acknowledged the importance of Spanish and bilingualism, even passing provisions for bilingual teachers. In 1935 a state house bill called for rural teachers to teach Spanish reading to Spanish-speaking pupils and to English speakers who wanted to learn Spanish (López 2003), a kind of precursor to dual language education.

One of the earliest dual language programs in the United States was initiated through the National Defense Education Act funding in 1967. Las Cruces Public Schools began an innovative 50/50 K–3 sustained bilingual program with mainly Spanish speakers but including around 10 to 15 percent English-speaking participants. Children developed high levels of proficiency in English and Spanish, and a study of the students through twelfth grade showed there were no dropouts from this program (López 2003).

Between 1967 and the present, New Mexico is one state that has continued to support bilingualism by passing a bilingual education act, providing state guidelines for bilingual certification, forming an educational partnership with Spain, increasing state funding for bilingual programs, and calling for proficiency in English and another language (López 2003). In view of the state's history, it is not surprising that New Mexico hosts the La Cosecha Conference, one of the country's most important dual language conferences.

Early Dual Language Programs — Florida

The 1959 revolution in Cuba brought bilingual education to Florida when professional Cuban refugees arrived on the coast with education, job skills, and a pride in their language and culture. By the early 1960s the huge influx of Cuban refugees into the area brought over 18,000 Cuban students into the Miami Dade County public schools. The school district, overwhelmed by the enrollment of over 3,000 non-English-speaking students per year, began recruiting experienced Cuban teachers and, through the Miami Cuban Teacher Retraining project, gave them special certification. With the help of these educators and grants, Coral Way Elementary School, a bi-ethnic, bilingual school, was opened in 1963. By 1975, eight bi-ethnic, bilingual schools were established with bilingual curriculum available in eighteen secondary schools (Feinberg 1999).

However, as the Hispanic community expanded, antagonism toward Hispanics and the Spanish language grew; so, for the next ten years, between 1978 and 1988, there was a yearly battle to maintain any of the bilingual support that had been provided. Most of the bilingual programs disappeared. However, with the formation of advocacy groups including the Spanish American League Against Discrimination (SALAD) and the American Hispanic Educators Association of Dade (AHEAD), and the realization that bilingualism was an asset in a globalized economy and multicultural society, the Dade county school board responded to this need for bilingualism and biliteracy. By June 1999, five dual language schools were established, and seventeen other schools offered support for the development of bilingualism and biliteracy.

> The combination of increased Hispanic representation on the board, the influence of prestigious community and chamber organizations, academic support in the form of well publicized research studies, and the active involvement of politically savvy members of the bilingual education community was successful in repelling if not eliminating resistance to bilingual schools and programs. (Feinberg 1999, 60)

Growth of Dual Language Programs and Some Setbacks

The factors that led to the resurgence of dual language in Florida were similar to the factors that resulted in the growth of these programs across the country. Howard and Christian (2002) explain that between 1963, when Coral Way opened, and the mid-1980s, the growth of dual language programs was relatively slow. Nevertheless, several successful programs were implemented during this period. Some particularly well-known sites that have been the basis of much research and study include the Oyster School in Washington, D.C., begun in 1971, the Amigos Two-Way program that was started in Cambridge, Massachusetts, in 1985–1986; the Francis Scott Key Elementary School program implemented in Arlington, Virginia, in 1986; and the River Glen Elementary school dual language program in San José, California, that began in 1987.

Despite the success of dual language programs and the recognition of the need to prepare students to compete in a global economy, the anti-immigrant attitudes that had led to the elimination of most dual language programs in Florida surfaced again.

In 1998, California, the state with the highest number of English learners, passed Proposition 227, the English for the Children bill, which severely limited the use of students' home languages in school programs and made it difficult for schools to offer bilingual programs. Ron Unz, who had promoted Proposition 227 in California, campaigned successfully for similar measures that eliminated or severely restricted bilingual education in Arizona and Massachusetts as well. Although these states passed specific laws about English-only instruction, it should be pointed out that in several other states where we have worked we have been told that either the state or the district or the individual school has a policy of English-only instruction.

However, studies of English learners in structured English immersion programs in California by Olsen (2010, 2014) and others (Krashen 2004) showed that students who had been placed in structured English immersion programs were not becoming proficient in English and were not succeeding academically. Many of these students were becoming long-term English learners, students who continued to struggle with learning English and learning academic content in English well into middle and high school. Olsen's research and the advocacy of Californians together led to legislation that overturned Proposition 227. Proposition 58 provides more flexibility to schools and parents to choose how to teach emergent bilinguals. Schools no longer are required to place English learners in English-only programs. Now California schools can offer bilingual programs, and parents do not have to sign waivers to have their students placed in bilingual education.

Changes in state laws and the academic success of students in dual language schools has led to a steady increase in the number of dual language programs in recent years. As we reported in Chapter 1, the number of dual language programs has been growing each year, and more dual language programs are being offered for students in middle and high schools. Research has shown that English learners in well-implemented bilingual programs achieve higher scores on tests of reading and math given in English than English learners in other programs. At the same time, both native English speakers and English learners develop high levels of bilingualism and biliteracy in dual language bilingual programs (Thomas and Collier 2012).

Changing Views of Bilinguals

As more dual language programs are implemented, there is an increased need for effective pedagogy for bilingual classrooms. Research in both cognitive science and sociolinguistics has provided a better understanding of bilingualism (Bialystok 2011; Grosjean 2010; García 2009). This research has implications for language use in bilingual programs. However, some misconceptions about bilingualism have resulted in pedagogical practices that make learning more difficult for bilinguals.

One commonly held assumption of bilingual educators has been that the goal of bilingual education should be to produce balanced bilinguals (Baker 2011; Grosjean 2010). A balanced bilingual is someone who is equally competent in two languages. This would mean that students in a bilingual Spanish-English program should develop the ability to speak, read, and write both English and Spanish equally well in all settings. An image used to represent the two languages of a balanced bilingual is a bicycle with two wheels that are the same size and do the same work. In contrast, a monolingual is represented by a unicycle with just one wheel (Cummins 1989).

The concept of a balanced bilingual comes from a monolingual perspective. From this view, a student in a dual language program would start as a monolingual in one language and then add a second language to become two monolinguals in one person. Both the idea of a bilingual being like two monolinguals and the idea that balanced bilingualism should be the goal of a dual language program are called into question by empirical research.

Studies in cognition have found that bilinguals are not simply two monolinguals (García 2009; Grosjean 2010). As we discussed in Chapter 1, both languages of a bilingual are always active, even when only one of the languages is being used. Over time, the neural structures in the brain of a bilingual change as the result of using two languages, As Bialystok (2011) states:

> The effect of bilingualism on cognitive performance is a striking example of how ordinary experience accumulates to modify cognitive networks and cognitive abilities. The bilinguals included in these studies did not typically learn a second language because of a preexisting talent or interest but because life required it. Their lives included two languages, and their cognitive systems therefore evolved differently than did those of monolingual counterparts. The research with bilinguals, therefore, provides clear evidence for the plasticity of cognitive systems in response to experience. (8)

As cognitive scientists have found, the neural networks of bilinguals are modified to accommodate their development and use of two languages. In very fundamental ways, bilinguals are different from monolinguals because of their experience of living with two languages.

Rather than picturing a bilingual as two monolinguals, Grosjean (2010), a sociolinguist, takes a holistic view. He argues that from a bilingual perspective, "the bilingual is an integrated whole who cannot easily be decomposed into two separate parts . . . he has a unique and specific linguistic configuration" (75). This is the same conclusion that Bialystok and other cognitive scientists have reached.

Grosjean compares a bilingual to a high hurdler in track and field. The hurdler has to have the skills of a high jumper and the skills of a sprinter and combines both jumping high and running fast into a new and different skill. That is, the hurdler does not have to be the highest jumper or the fastest sprinter to be a very proficient hurdler. Not only are bilinguals not two monolinguals, they don't develop their two languages equally. Research by sociolinguists into how bilingual people use their languages during communicative interactions has shown that they do not use their two languages in a balanced way. Instead, as Grosjean (2010) states:

> Bilinguals usually acquire and use their languages for different purposes, in different domains of life, with different people. Different aspects of life often require different languages. (29)

Grosjean refers to this phenomenon as the *complementarity principle*. Rather than developing equal abilities in each language, bilinguals develop the language they need to communicate with different people in different settings when discussing different subjects. Each language complements the other.

A good example to show that most bilinguals are not balanced comes from a friend of ours who is a bilingual educator. He is a Hispanic whose home language is Spanish. He speaks Spanish well. However, when he teaches bilingual education classes at the university, he teaches in English. He can explain Cummins' quadrants or the threshold hypothesis very well in English. Nevertheless, when he was asked to give a lecture on bilingual theory in Spanish, he had a very difficult time. All his reading, writing, and speaking about bilingual theory had been in English. He had not previously needed to discuss this subject in Spanish and had not developed the language he needed to communicate bilingual theory in Spanish. Like other bilinguals, his two languages are not balanced. Instead, he uses each language for different purposes with different people to communicate about different subjects.

Grosjean points out three consequences of the complementarity principle. First, most bilinguals are more fluent in one language than the other. As Grosjean (2010) explains, "In general, if a language is spoken in a reduced number of domains and with a limited number of people, then it will not be developed as much as a language used in more domains with more people" (31).

Fluency develops through use. Someone teaching English as a foreign language in China, for example, may not acquire full fluency in Chinese simply because he spends most of the day speaking English to his students and at home with his family. This teacher may only develop the language of the country in limited domains, such as speaking to clerks in stores about purchases. He may live in China for several years without becoming equally fluent in Chinese and English.

This leads to a second consequence. The language that bilinguals are more fluent in is their dominant language. Because bilinguals tend to use one language more often with more people in more situations than the other language, they don't use the two languages equally. For that reason, very few bilinguals are "balanced." Instead, they are more dominant in one of the languages.

For example, in the South Texas university where we taught, many of the students used Spanish with their peers, at home, at church, and in social functions. Even though they studied almost exclusively in English, these students were more dominant in Spanish. At the same time, they often struggled in Spanish classes. Although they had good levels of conversational Spanish, they had difficulty reading and writing Spanish. All of their schooling had been in English, and they had learned to read and write in English, but their reading and writing proficiency in Spanish was much less developed. As this example shows, the students were not balanced in either their use of oral language or their use of written language.

The lack of balance shows up in a third consequence of the complementarity principle: the difficulty bilinguals have in translation. Because bilinguals develop fluency in different domains rather than an equal ability in each domain, they often find it difficult to translate. Often, bilingual teachers are asked to translate a letter to be sent out to parents with the expectation that this will be an easy task. In fact, translation is difficult and takes a great deal of time.

As Grosjean explains, to translate, a person must be equally proficient in both languages in the topic being translated. Because teachers usually write about school topics in English to parents, they may not have developed the language needed to write about these topics in Spanish, and even if they can provide a basic translation, they may not use the right style or wording for a letter in Spanish that communicates effectively. For this reason, parents with academic Spanish ability may complain that a letter the school sent out in Spanish was poorly written.

Grosjean (2010) concludes his discussion of the complementarity principle by stating that most bilinguals "simply do not need to be equally competent in all their languages. The level of fluency they attain in a language . . . will depend on their need for that language and will be domain specific" (21). Because bilinguals develop their two languages for use in different domains, very few are completely balanced.

Views of Bilingual Education Programs
- -

The ideas that bilinguals are two monolinguals in one person and that the goal of bilingual education programs is to produce balanced bilinguals have shaped the way bilingual programs have been conceptualized and implemented. Traditionally, programs for bilingual students have been categorized in one of two ways: as subtractive when children go to school speaking a home language other than English and lose their home language in the process of learning English, or as additive when children go to school speaking a home language other than English, maintain and develop their home language, and learn English.

Lambert (1974) used the terms *additive bilingualism* and *subtractive bilingualism* in discussing his work on the Canadian immersion bilingual model. In this program, English speakers were immersed in French. This was a program for majority English speakers. He described their acquisition of French as adding a second language. Subtractive programs, on the other hand, are programs such as transitional bilingual programs, designed for language-minority students. A French speaker in an area of Canada where English is the dominant language might begin learning in French and English and then be transitioned into all English classes, and the result could be that this student would lose or would fail to develop proficiency in French.

Rather than viewing programs for emergent bilinguals as additive or subtractive, García (2009, 2010) looks at bilingualism through a different lens. She discusses two models of bilingualism that are based on a holistic view of bilinguals: *recursive bilingualism* and *dynamic bilingualism*.

Recursive bilingualism occurs when a community whose language is being lost makes an effort to revitalize that language. García uses the example of the Maori of New Zealand. The Maori language had been marginalized and was dying out, but now it is being taught in the schools. García explains that as they regain their language the Maori people are drawing on past knowledge. They move back and forth between Maori and English as they reconstitute the heritage language, using it for new functions as well as old. This reconstitution is not simply a new language being added; rather, it draws on the language knowledge already known, though not complete, to develop the language more fully to meet the present needs of the speakers.

The term *dynamic bilingualism* reflects the fact that the languages of an emergent bilingual are always active in the brain, and bilinguals draw on all their language resources, what García refers to as their full *linguistic repertoire*, as they communicate. García and Kleyn (2016) explain:

> Dynamic bilingualism goes beyond the notion of additive bilingualism because it does not simply refer to the addition of a separate set of language features, but acknowledges that the linguistic features and practices of bilinguals form a unitary linguistic system that interacts in dynamic ways. (16)

Dynamic bilingualism is the appropriate term for bilingualism in a globalized society. From a dynamic perspective, bilinguals and multilinguals use their languages for a variety of purposes and in a variety of settings. They are more or less proficient in the various contexts where they use the languages and are more or less proficient in different modalities (visual, print, and sound). Their languages continually develop as they use each language in a variety of settings. García (2009) draws on the Language Policy Division of the Council of Europe's definition of bilingualism to set a goal for students in U.S. schools: "the ability to use several languages to varying degrees and for distinct purposes" (54).

García argues that instead of picturing the languages of a bilingual as a unicycle (for subtractive programs) or a bicycle (for additive programs), a better image for dual language programs that promote dynamic bilingualism is an all-terrain vehicle. The wheels may be of different sizes, they can move up and down independently, and they can move in different directions as the vehicle negotiates an uneven landscape.

Consequences of Basing Dual Language Programs on Traditional Views

The twentieth-century views that bilinguals are two monolinguals in one person and that the goal of bilingual education is to produce balanced bilinguals have led to practices that Cummins (2007) argues are based on misconceptions. One of these misconceptions applies specifically to dual language programs. Cummins refers to this as the "Two Solitudes assumption." The misconception is that in bilingual programs the two languages should be kept rigidly separated. Cummins points out:

> This assumption was initially articulated by Lambert and Tucker (1972) in the context of the St. Lambert French immersion program evaluation and since that time has become axiomatic in the implementation of second language immersion and most dual language programs. (233)

The practice of keeping the two languages strictly separated is based on common sense rather than on empirical research. In dual language programs where the two languages are strictly separated, students are treated like two monolinguals. For example, in a Spanish-English dual language program during English time, all students are taught like monolingual English speakers and during Spanish time they are treated like monolingual Spanish speakers. Although the teachers make the input in English or Spanish comprehensible, they do not draw on students' home languages as a resource.

In many dual language programs there is one teacher for each language; in others, different subjects are taught in each of the languages. For example, math might be in English and science in Spanish. In other programs the languages are distributed by time—mornings in English and afternoons in Spanish. Still other programs alternate languages on a daily or weekly basis. In all cases, there are specific times, subjects, or teachers for each language with no overlap.

Many effective practices are excluded when instruction is limited to one language at a time. For example, having students access cognates depends on using both languages simultaneously. When the languages are not separated, students can carry out linguistic investigations and build metalinguistic awareness by comparing and contrasting languages. For example, students could compare and contrast the placement of adjectives in English and Spanish sentences.

Cummins (2007) writes:

> It does seem reasonable to create largely separate spaces for each language within a bilingual or immersion program. However, there are also compelling arguments to be made for creating a shared or interdependent space for the promotion of language awareness and cross-language cognitive processing. The reality is that students are making cross-linguistic connections throughout the course of their learning in a bilingual or immersion program, so why not nurture this learning strategy and help students to apply it more efficiently? (229)

Cummins points out that there is theoretical support for using both languages for instruction. Research has shown that new knowledge is built on existing knowledge, and if that knowledge was developed in the home language, it can best be accessed through the home language (Bransford, Brown, and Cocking 2000). In addition, literacy skills are interdependent, so teaching should facilitate cross-language transfer. He concludes his discussion of the Two Solitudes misconception by stating that "the empirical evidence is consistent both with an emphasis on extensive communicative interaction in the TL [target language] (ideally in both oral and written modes) and the utility of students' home language as a cognitive tool in learning the TL" (226–27).

Cummins' Hypotheses

Two hypotheses based on research Cummins (1979) conducted provide support for viewing bilingual students holistically and drawing on their full language repertoire: the interdependence hypothesis and the common underlying proficiency (CUP) hypothesis.

A commonsense assumption that is made in teaching emergent bilinguals in many places is that "more English equals more English." This idea seems logical. It is a variation of the time-on-task assumption that the more time spent on a task, the greater the proficiency a student develops. In this case, the assumption is that the more time students spend studying English, the more proficient they will become in English. However, Cummins explains that this seemingly logical assumption fails to recognize that languages are interdependent, and the development of the first language has a positive effect on the development of a second language.

As Cummins (1979) states:

> To the extent that instruction in L^X is effective in promoting proficiency in L^X, transfer of this proficiency to L^Y will occur provided there is adequate exposure to L^Y (either in school or the environment) and adequate motivation to learn L^Y. (29)

In other words, when students are taught in and develop proficiency in their home language, L^X, that proficiency will transfer to the second language, L^Y, assuming they are given enough exposure to the second language and are motivated to learn it.

Cummins (2000) explains that the reason proficiency transfers from one language to another is that a common proficiency underlies an emergent bilingual's languages. Because of this common underlying proficiency (CUP), there is an "interdependence of concepts, skills, and linguistic knowledge that makes transfer possible"(191).

According to Cummins the common underlying proficiency can be thought of as "a central processing system comprising (1) attributes of the individuals such as cognitive and linguistic abilities (memory, auditory discrimination, abstract reasoning, etc.) and (2) specific conceptual and linguistic knowledge derived from experience and learning (vocabulary knowledge)" (191). As a result of this interdependence, an emergent bilingual can draw on cognitive and linguistic abilities and skills in the home language to develop literacy and content knowledge in a second language. For example, if the home language shares features, such as cognates or syntactic structures, with English, those components of the home language can transfer to English if teachers use strategies to bridge between the two languages.

To take a simple example of how CUP operates, young children learn how to distinguish different animals quite early. At first a young child might call a cat or a cow a dog, but soon the child begins to understand the different features of those three animals. When they begin to learn the names of these animals in another language, they simply learn the label. So, for example, a Spanish speaker learns that *gato* is cat, *vaca* is cow, and *perro* is dog. However, she does not have to learn the distinguishing features of these animals all over again in English. She already understands the concepts of cat, cow, and dog. That is part of her background knowledge, and this knowledge is part of her common underlying proficiency. What she does need to learn is that the animal she calls *gato* in Spanish is called *cat* in English. This is an easier task than learning the distinguishing features of different animals.

Cummins' CUP hypothesis can help account for the difference in academic performance of students with similar levels of English proficiency. Because content knowledge and literacy skills transfer, a fourth-grade bilingual who can read and write in his home language and who has developed grade-level content knowledge in that language will succeed academically in English much more quickly than another fourth grader with limited or no prior schooling in the home language even if they are both classified as low intermediates in English proficiency.

Cummins uses the image of an iceberg with two peaks to illustrate his CUP hypothesis. The two peaks of the iceberg that are above the waterline represent the surface features (the sounds or writing) of the two languages. The part of the iceberg below the surface of the water represents the knowledge and skills that are common to the two languages and can transfer from one language to the other. Figure 2.1 is a representation of the iceberg with two peaks.

Students who have more schooling in their home language can draw upon that knowledge as they are learning the features of an additional language. Over time students with greater total underlying proficiency can do well academically in the second language. Students without the underlying academic proficiency in their home language, however, struggle because they have less to draw upon as they are learning academic content and literacy in a second language.

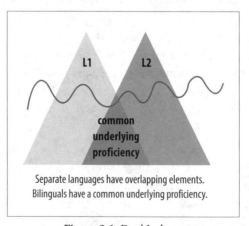

Figure 2.1 Dual Iceberg

Translanguaging

García, Ibarra Johnson, and Seltzer (2017) take Cummins' concept of a common underlying proficiency a step further. Instead of viewing the bilingual as having two separate languages with a common underlying proficiency, they argue that bilinguals have one complex linguistic system that has features of two or more languages. As they explain, from the perspective of dynamic bilingualism, "The linguistic features of what are considered two languages function in interrelationship and adapt to the communicative circumstances at hand" (19). Figure 2.2 represents this holistic view of dynamic bilingualism.

In the process of making meaning, bilinguals draw on their full linguistic repertoire in a process García and Wei (2014) refer to as translanguaging. They explain, "Translanguaging is the discursive norm in bilingual families and communities" (23). In bilingual dual language programs based on a model of dynamic bilingualism, teachers can implement translanguaging strategies that use "the entire linguistic repertoire of bilingual students flexibly in order to teach both rigorous content and language for academic use" (2). They do this by tapping into what García, Ibarra Johnson, and Seltzer (2017) term a translanguaging *corriente*. They explain:

> We use the metaphor of the translanguaging corriente to refer to the current or flow of students' dynamic bilingualism that runs through our classrooms and schools. Bilingual students make use of the translanguaging corriente either covertly or overtly to learn content and language in school and to make sense of their complex worlds and identities. (21)

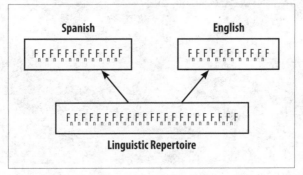

Figure 2.2 Linguistic Repertoire, adapted from García, Ibarra Johnson, and Seltzer (2017). Used with permission from García, O., S. Ibarra Johnson, and K. Seltzer (2017). *The Translanguaging Classroom: Leveraging Student Bilingualism for Learning.* Philadelphia: Caslon. © Caslon, Inc. All rights reserved.

Figure 2.3 illustrates the translanguaging *corriente.*

García, Ibarra Johnson, and Seltzer (2017) state that teachers can use the translanguaging *corriente* to:

1. Support students as they engage with and comprehend complex content and texts.
2. Provide opportunities for students to develop linguistic practices for academic contexts.
3. Make space for students' bilingualism and ways of knowing.
4. Support students' socioemotional development and bilingual identities. (ix)*

In her foreword to *The Translanguaging Classroom: Leveraging Student Bilingualism for Learning*, Valdés (2017) comments that the authors have provided by far the most compelling example proposed to date of a *culturally sustaining pedagogy* as defined by Paris (2012, 95):

Figure 2.3 Translanguaging *Corriente*

---

*Used with permission from García, O., S. Ibarra Johnson, and K. Seltzer (2017). *The Translanguaging Classroom: Leveraging Student Bilingualism for Learning*. Philadelphia: Caslon. © Caslon, Inc. All rights reserved.

The term *culturally sustaining* requires that our pedagogies be more than responsive of or relevant to the cultural experiences and practices of young people—it requires that they support young people in sustaining the cultural and linguistic competence of their communities while simultaneously offering access to dominant cultural competence. Culturally sustaining pedagogy, then, has as its explicit goal supporting multiculturalism and multilingualism in practice and perspective for students and teachers. (vii)

In dual language classrooms where teachers take what García and her colleagues call a translanguaging stance, they promote a culturally sustaining pedagogy for all their students.

Isn't Translanguaging Just Code-Switching?

When we discuss translanguaging with teachers, they often ask about the difference between translanguaging and code-switching. *Code-switching* is a term that has been used by linguists to describe the process of switching from one language to another, sometimes in the same sentence. For example, a Spanish/English bilingual might say, "I'll bring an umbrella *porque va a llover hoy*" (because it's going to rain today). From an external perspective an observer might interpret this sentence as an example of code-switching from an English linguistic code to a Spanish code. This interpretation reflects the belief that a bilingual is really two monolinguals in one person who has two separate language codes that operate independently. Code-switching is often viewed negatively. People may think that bilinguals code-switch because they have only low proficiency in one or more of their languages.

From a holistic view of a bilingual as a person with one complex linguistic system, however, there is no switching between codes of separate languages. Instead, the bilingual is drawing on features of one complex linguistic system to communicate effectively. As García and Wei (2014) state:

Translanguaging differs from the notion of code-switching in that it refers not simply to a shift or shuttle between two languages, but to the speakers' construction and use of original and complex interrelated discursive practices that cannot be easily assigned to one or another traditional definition of a language, but that make up the speakers' complete language repertoire. (22)

From this perspective, bringing in words and phrases from both languages allows a bilingual to communicate more effectively in the same way that having a large vocabulary in one language allows a person to express herself more fully.

Bilinguals translanguage in certain contexts. In the previous example, the speaker would only draw on features from two languages when communicating with another bilingual. In the same way that speakers shift from formal to informal registers depending on who they are talking with and the context, bilinguals shift languages to communicate effectively in different situations with different people. In dual language classrooms, translanguaging would not be informal as in the example above, but instead would be a planned strategic opportunity for the use of students' full linguistic repertoires designed to build students' content knowledge and linguistic abilities.

Translanguaging in the Bilingual Dual Language Classroom

Teachers in dual language classes who view their students positively as bilinguals employ translanguaging strategies to affirm their students' cultures, identities, and bilingualism. In traditional dual language classes where the two languages are kept separate, students are not given good models of bilinguals. Even when the teacher is bilingual, she is expected to model the practices of a monolingual teacher during certain times of the day or when teaching certain subjects. Furthermore, by separating the languages, teachers treat students as monolinguals. They do not affirm their students' emerging bilingualism, an important component of their identity. In contrast, in classes where teachers use translanguaging strategies, they affirm their students' bilingualism.

Both monolingual and bilingual teachers can use translanguaging strategies to promote metalinguistic knowledge by comparing and contrasting the two languages. For example, teachers and students can create cognate walls of key words in the content areas they are studying. During a review lesson on math measurement vocabulary one teacher gave her students a short reading on measurement in English and included a translation of the reading next to it in Spanish. Students first read the English version and then read the Spanish translation. They highlighted the words that looked similar in both languages and found cognates for measurement words, such as *centimeter* in English and *centímetro* in Spanish. They added these words to their list of math-related cognates. The teacher compiled these cognates into a whole-class math cognate chart. Figure 2.4 shows another teacher's social studies cognate chart listing key concepts around European expansion and colonization.

Teachers can also ask students to compare and contrast texts in bilingual books looking at the differences between how the same idea is expressed in each language. Teachers can have students compare the morphology or spelling patterns in the two languages. For example, if students speak both Spanish and English, teachers could point out that *-ción* in Spanish is usually written *-tion* in English in words like *acción* and *action*. Words that begin with *sp*, *st*, or *sc* in English start with an *e* in Spanish as in *Spanish* and *español*, *station* and *estación*, and *school* and *escuela*. To show differences in syntactic patterns, a teacher might contrast possessives in Spanish and English to show that *El libro de Juan* in Spanish becomes *John's book* in English.

Translanguaging Using Cognates

Francisco González draws on cognates to reinforce academic vocabulary.

In their book, *Teaching for Biliteracy: Strengthening Bridges Between Languages*, Beeman and Urow (2013) discuss a number of ways that teachers in dual language classes can bridge from one language to another. They provide specific comparisons of Spanish and English capitalization, punctuation, prefixes, suffixes, and orthography. These bridging lessons help students build metalinguistic awareness.

Escamilla and her colleagues (2014) include a chapter on the development of metalanguage (linguistic terms like *verb* used to describe language) in their book on biliteracy development. They describe cross-language strategies, such as using bilingual books and teaching about cognates. These translanguaging strategies help

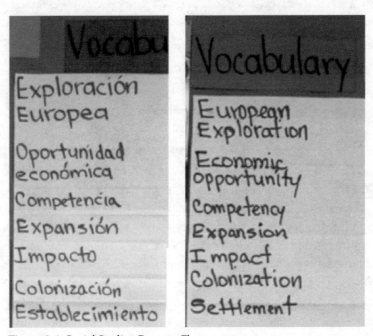

Figure 2.4 Social Studies Cognate Chart

students in dual language classes build metalinguistic awareness through a process of comparing and contrasting the languages and increase their bilingual proficiency.

Translanguaging also serves as a cognitive scaffold that helps students learn academic content. For example, during science a teacher might explain the water cycle stages using English and support the presentation with a clearly labeled visual. Then the teacher could have the students work in home language groups or pairs and encourage them to discuss their understanding of each stage of the water cycle using their home language or English. The students could then draw and label the stages using English, and each group could explain one of the stages to the whole class using English.

There are a number of other ways that both monolingual and bilingual teachers can use access the translanguaging *corriente* that runs through a bilingual classroom. For example, students can turn and talk with a bilingual partner using the home language to clarify procedures during a science lesson. Students can write drafts of papers in their home language and the final draft in the target language. *Translanguaging: A CUNY-NYSIEB Guide for Educators* (Celic and Seltzer 2013) and *Translanguaging in Curriculum and Instruction* (Hesson, Seltzer, and Woodley 2014) are two useful free resources that list a great number of translanguaging strategies. There is also an abbreviated guide available in Spanish, *El translenguar: Una guía de CUNY-NYSIEB para educadores* (Celic and Seltzer 2011). These documents can be downloaded from the CUNY-NYSIEB website (www.cuny-nysieb.org). In the following chapters we provide additional examples of effective translanguaging pedagogy.

Chapter Overview

From its earliest years, the United States has been a multilingual nation. When large numbers of immigrants settled in an area, education was often provided in their home languages. By the early twentieth century, however, attitudes toward teaching in languages other than English became increasingly negative. A case in point is education for Native Americans, such as the Cherokees, who had developed high levels of literacy in their home language. The establishment of boarding schools to teach Native Americans English provides an extreme example of English Only attitudes. These attitudes were fueled by World War I and II. During this time, foreigners and their languages were looked at with suspicion, and bilingual education programs were seldom implemented.

Changes in the kinds of programs offered for bilinguals since the 1950s can best be understood by considering different orientations toward the languages of speakers of non-English languages. Ruíz (1984) describes three orientations. During the 1950s and 1960s the language of students who spoke a language other than English was seen as a handicap, a deficit to be overcome. Students were provided instruction in English through English as a second language classes, or they were taught in English with no support. The idea was that students could learn English through immersion.

As a result of the Civil Rights movement in the 1960s the orientation toward students' languages shifted to language as a right. Court cases, such as Lau v. Nichols and Castañeda v. Pickard established that English learners had a right to receive education in a language they could understand. This led to transitional bilingual programs being established in many schools.

A third orientation sees language as a resource. This orientation supports programs, such as developmental bilingual and dual language programs, in which emergent bilinguals' languages are viewed as a resource that should be developed and maintained. Early dual language programs were established in New Mexico and Florida, two areas with large numbers of Spanish speakers. Other early programs included the Amigos program in Boston, the Oyster School in Washington, D.C., Francis Scott Key in Arlington, Virginia, and River Glenn in San Jose.

Despite the success of these programs, anti-immigrant sentiments led to laws in several states banning or severely limiting instruction in languages other than English. However, as research has shown, bilinguals in English-only programs, such as structured English immersion, do not learn English well and do not succeed academically. Research on bilingual dual language programs, meanwhile, has shown consistently positive results, and there has been a rapid growth in bilingual dual language programs.

In the same way that orientations toward language have changed over time, views of bilingualism have also changed. Earlier, bilinguals were seen as two monolinguals in one person and bilingual programs were considered additive or subtractive. The goal of additive programs was to produce balanced bilinguals. In dual language programs based on this view, the two languages were strictly separated.

However, research in cognitive science and sociolinguistics has shown that bilinguals are not two monolinguals and that bilinguals are not balanced. García (2009) argues that bilingualism is a dynamic process, and bilinguals constantly draw on features of both languages as they communicate. She labels this process "translanguaging." By employing translanguaging pedagogical strategies, teachers affirm the identities and bilingualism of emergent bilinguals. These strategies help students build metalinguistic awareness, and they serve as linguistic scaffolds that increase students' academic proficiency. These new understandings of bilinguals and bilingual education can guide educators as they plan curriculum and literacy instruction in dual language programs.

Reflect and Apply

1. Consider early bilingual programs in this country. Discuss why these programs might have been accepted. Compare those reasons to why dual language programs are popular now.

2. Consider Ruiz's (1984) three orientations toward language in schools: language as a handicap, language as a right, and language as a resource. Discuss why dual language programs fall under the language-as-a-resource orientation.

3. Do you believe that bilingual people can be linguistically balanced? Is that the ideal? What does the chapter say about a balanced bilingual?

4. Grosjean (2010) developed the *complementarity principle* to explain how bilinguals interact with one another. Discuss this with your classmates. Give some examples from your own experiences.

5. We discussed Cummins' (2007) Two Solitudes misconception. What is it? How is it played out in some dual language schools?

6. What is your view of translanguaging? Do you think it has a place in dual language classrooms? Why or why not?

Whole-School Essentials

As we have visited schools, interviewed educators, and worked with teachers planning for and teaching in dual language programs, we have seen a great deal of variation among the programs and those working and learning in those programs. However, even within that variation, it is clear that programs must have certain essential elements to fully meet the academic needs of the students they are intended to serve. In this and the following chapters, we offer what we consider to be the essential elements of effective one-way and two-way dual language programs.

We have developed these essentials based on the information that we have read, our own backgrounds of working in schools, and the ideas we have gained from interviews with teachers and administrators and visits to bilingual dual language schools. It is important to stay current in this field as our understandings about bilingualism and how to support it deepen and change. As more and more programs are being implemented, educators are discovering innovative ways to make dual language programs work well in a variety of settings. In this chapter we address whole-school essentials for dual language programs.

Whole-School Essentials

Whether a dual language program is a strand within a school or encompasses the entire school, there are several whole-school essentials that should be present for the program to succeed. The list below outlines whole-school essentials.

- **Understanding and supporting the goals and benefits of the program**
- **A vision and mission statement**
- **Flexibility and openness to change**
- **A multilingual ecology**
- **Academic and social equity and equal status for both languages**
- **Parent education and support**

If any of these six essentials is missing, the program will not be as effective as it could be. In the following sections we discuss each of these essentials and offer specific examples to help readers understand how to provide the essentials and what to avoid.

Understanding and Supporting the Goals and Benefits of the Program

Howard, Sugarman, and Christian (2003) review the research on two-way immersion education and summarize the common features of successful programs. The first item on their list supports our first whole-school essential:

> 1. It is important to have all stakeholders involved in program planning from the earliest stages in order to ensure that everyone understands the model, has a shared vision for implementation, and is clear about others' motivations for starting the program. (9)

When we refer to all the stakeholders, we include administrators, all teachers in the school even if they are not involved in the dual language program, parents, community members, school support staff, and, of course, the students themselves. The following experiences we have had provide examples of what can happen when any of these stakeholders does not understand or support the goals and benefits of a dual language program. We follow these examples with success stories to show what can be accomplished with positive supports in place.

Elementary School in a Large Urban District ◆ An elementary school in a large district in Texas was designated by the district as a new one-way dual language school because of the large numbers of Latino students in the school and because other dual language programs in the district had been successful. An administrator, who was known for her no-nonsense approach and her success in another school with raising test scores, was assigned as principal. She had no background in bilingual education or dual language programs and was a strong English Only proponent.

She was convinced that students needed to study in English to do well on standardized tests given in English. Soon newly assigned dual language teachers who were teaching content in Spanish complained to district bilingual staff that they were told by their principal to use English for most of their instruction. When the district sent consultants to work with teachers, the teachers were receptive but fearful they could not implement the kind of instruction in Spanish that the consultants promoted. As the school year progressed, the principal took a hard-line approach and mandated almost all-English instruction. Soon both central office bilingual staff and the dual language consultant assigned to the school stopped going there to offer support because their work was being undermined. The principal's lack of support for the dual language program may lead to phasing out the program in the future.

A Secondary School in a Rural District ◆ In a rural district the superintendent and bilingual director decided to implement Spanish/English dual language strands in the middle and high schools because of the success of dual language in elementary schools. Several secondary teachers who were not bilingual felt threatened by this change, fearing their jobs might be affected because they were not bilingual. Soltero (2016) found this concern among monolingual teachers in her work in New York City and explains "Dual language programs should never be implemented on the condition that any teacher in the school would lose his or her job" (124).

In addition to the concern of monolingual English-speaking teachers, some bilingual teachers teaching in English did not understand bilingual education theory and research and did not want to be forced to teach in Spanish. They were convinced that students needed English and that providing Spanish instruction was simply a kind of crutch.

These teachers took their complaints to the school board, and the community called for a halt in the implementation of dual language at the secondary level. It was only after several confrontational meetings with assurances from the superintendent that no teachers would lose their jobs and that no teacher would be forced to teach in Spanish that the secondary faculty accepted the change. They, then, agreed to listen to explanations of bilingual education theory and dual language goals and testimonies to the success of the program by elementary principals and teachers.

A Rural One-Way School ◆ In a successful rural-one way dual language school, the principal was often approached by immigrant parents who were concerned that teaching their children in Spanish would keep them from learning English, and important community members expressed the same concerns. The principal found herself under constant pressure to defend the program, especially because some teachers didn't understand the program well enough to support it when parents approached them. Without support from teachers, parents, and community members, it is extremely difficult to maintain a dual language program.

A Middle School ◆ Counselors in a middle school that offered a dual language strand complained that planning student schedules was very difficult. Because students in the dual program needed to take additional Spanish classes, their schedules were full. If they wanted to take electives, such as band or choir, the electives conflicted with the dual language courses.

The dual language coordinator was concerned that the counselors did not understand the importance of the continued development of the bilingualism of the students in the dual language program. The counselors could not explain to the students why they needed to continue their work in two languages. The coordinator wanted the counselors to understand about the Seal of Biliteracy students could earn with their high school diplomas if they took the Spanish courses, but the counselors were not open to an extra meeting with her so that she could help them understand. Many students dropped out of the dual language strand so they could take electives. If all stakeholders, including the counselors, had been involved in program planning, this conflict could have been foreseen, and the schedule could have been arranged to avoid setting up the choice between taking electives or taking dual language courses.

An Elementary School Success Story ◆ After attending a workshop on dual language at a state conference, administrators in a small town in Iowa decided that dual language would be a good option to help the many Spanish-speaking children in their school district. They read several books and articles about dual language theory and research. They were aware that there was little known about dual language and its benefits among the teachers and community, so they brought in consultants to speak to parents, teachers, and all school support staff including custodians, yard monitors, and cafeteria staff.

The administrators conducted book studies with the teachers and provided short readings for everyone. At community and schoolwide meetings, they set aside time for questions and answers. Together the school community planned for a dual language strand at the school and formed mission and vision statements. The administrators also addressed practical issues, including finding appropriate materials to teach content in Spanish and looking for bilingually credentialed teachers or potential bilingual teachers living in the community whom they could support. This early planning was crucial as they moved to implement the program.

A Secondary School Success Story ◈ At Highland Park High School, the Illinois high school we discussed in Chapter 1, the principal, Tom, is well aware of the need to involve all faculty, even those not teaching in the program, as they implement their dual language high school strand. He explained:

> As principal, you have to build the case for dual language so that your community embraces the changes required to bring the program to the school. Our strategy was to combine student demographic data, with dual language research and with a vision of what twenty-first-century students need to be successful in an increasingly globalized, interconnected world.

He pointed out to faculty that the demographic data demonstrated the growth of Latino Spanish-speaking families in their community, and he shared research that shows that dual language is the only program that effectively eliminates the achievement gap for those students. He also organized book studies with faculty, choosing books that show how bilingualism, biliteracy, and biculturalism are assets for students in U.S. society.

In addition, Tom believes that "a high school dual language program that fails to get counselors fully on board is missing a key ally." His team provided presentations for counselors to help them understand the program, including course sequences for bilinguals. He wanted them to understand the research on the positive impact of bilingualism on students' lives. He noted, "Our counselors spend a lot of time helping sell the program with parents or with students who come to them and want to drop a course. The counselors work to help the students remain committed to the program." The counselors in Tom's program are in sharp contrast to our fourth example. This shows how powerful the role of a counselor is, especially at the secondary level.

One final example Tom provides shows how K–12 schools that are implementing dual language programs can ensure there is an understanding of and support for the goals and benefits of the program:

> Our K–8 district has a dual language night for parents whose child will be enrolling in kindergarten and a dual language night for parents whose children will be moving to the middle school from the elementary schools. We send our high school staff and a

few high school dual language students to these meetings. It's amazing, but the parents need to hear that the high school faculty and staff love dual language and that we will view all the dual language kids who come to us as gifted. We share data about how the dual language kids do academically at the high school, and we show what colleges they are getting into. This is so important because at the kindergarten level, we need parents to enroll their children in the program. At the middle school level, we need parents (whose children are essentially fluent in oral Spanish) to leave their children in the dual language program when they go to middle school. If we don't provide reassurance to the parents at these two critical junctures, we believe our enrollments would drop as parents get nervous that they are doing something that will harm their child. By high school people showing up to these meetings, we have reinforced the message of the elementary district, and now we have a wait list to get into the dual language program.

Tom's program is a success because he works strategically to ensure that everyone associated with the program understands and supports the goals and the benefits of the dual language program.

Vision and Mission Statement for Dual Language Programs

Whether the dual language program is a strand within a school, like the Iowa school, or is a whole-school one-way or two-way program, it is important for all the stakeholders to participate in the process of creating a mission/vision statement, preferably with goals included. Too often vision and mission statements can be overlooked as dual language programs are being created. Those promoting the program and teaching in it have so much to do as they begin to develop their programs that the creation of a mission/vision statement can seem to be an added burden, and the importance of developing it and including all those affected by it is misunderstood. However, a vision/mission statement helps to guide a dual language program as it is being conceptualized, and it serves as a resource as the program matures. Revisiting these statements often helps guide difficult decisions that need to be made as programs grow.

In their *Guiding Principles for Dual Language Education*, Howard and her colleagues (2018) state:

Studies of effective schools consistently and conclusively demonstrate that high-quality programs have a cohesive school-wide shared vision; a set of goals that define their expectations for achievement; and an instructional focus and commitment to achievement and high expectations that are shared by students, parents, teachers, and administrators (10).

One of the most difficult parts of creating a vision/mission statement and coming up with goals is to involve all the stakeholders affected by the program. This becomes quite difficult, because not everyone is usually equally invested in the dual language program, and some who are involved may be reluctant participants. Soltero (2016) explains, "This can be a sensitive process because not all the staff may share the same beliefs and attitudes toward bilingual education or linguistic and cultural diversity" (35). Developing the mission/vision together may prevent resentments from those less involved in the program or less committed to the program as the program gains attention and resources are allotted to it.

Mission/vision statements may be quite long, or they may be short and simple. Often they are written in both languages being taught in the program. We have provided a variety of statements we found through program leaders or on the Internet that might help guide schools or districts as they consider implementing dual language.

Jacksonville, Florida ◆ Duval County Public Schools in Jacksonville, Florida, has four dual language schools including San José Elementary, whose website provides a short mission/vision statement in English and Spanish for all dual language schools in the county. School officials can go back to it often to see if their programs are accomplishing these goals.

> The Dual Language Program is designed to prepare children to succeed in a culturally diverse world and a global economy through academic achievement and proficiency in a second language.
>
> *El programa Dual de Lenguaje esta diseñado para preparar a los niños a tener éxito en una economía global y un mundo de diversas culturas a través de logros académicos y la habilidad de hablar un segundo idioma.* (San Jose Elementary School 2017)

Hayward, California ◆ Stonebrae Elementary School has had an English and Mandarin 50/50 program since the 2007–2008 school year. Their program has grown to offer dual language instruction from kindergarten through sixth grade. Students spend half their day learning in English and the other half learning in Mandarin. Below is the vision/goals statement:

> **Vision**
>
> We are preparing our students to be linguistically competent and culturally sophisticated in making business or government transactions internationally in the global economy of the twenty-first century.

Program Goals

The goal is acquisition of academic proficiency in two languages: English and Mandarin, together with mastery of academic core content and multicultural proficiency. Instruction is in Mandarin and English. The program will give students an opportunity to become bi-literate and bi-cultural. Using Mandarin and English as the vehicle of instruction, students will be able to communicate effectively in both languages and to achieve academic proficiency that meets or exceeds the State Standards in all academic areas. (Hayward Unified School District 2017–2018)

Austin, Texas ◆ Austin Independent School District is a large district in Texas that offers both one-way and two-way dual language programs depending on the student populations in the schools. In 2016–2017, they offered one-way programs in thirty-six of their district's schools, two-way dual language programs in twelve schools, and both one-way and two-way programs in three schools. One of the two-way schools is an English/Vietnamese dual language school. The following lists the Vision/Program Goals and the Mission for dual language programs in Austin ISD.

Vision/Program Goals

1. Students will participate in a rigorous academic program that accelerates their learning.
2. Students will develop a high linguistic proficiency in two languages.
3. Students will develop a high academic proficiency in two languages.
4. Students will develop positive cross-cultural attitudes.

Mission

Austin ISD [Independent School District] Dual Language students will develop a high academic and linguistic proficiency in two languages by participating in a rigorous academic program that enhances the development of bilingualism, biculturalism, and biliteracy so that students will graduate ready for college, career, and life in a globally competitive economy. (Austin Independent School District n.d.)

Highland Park High School, Highland Park, Illinois ◆ A final example comes from Highland Park High School, the secondary school discussed in Chapter 1. At the Illinois State Conference for Teachers Serving Linguistically & Culturally Diverse Students, the principal, Tom, and two colleagues made a presentation entitled "How to Create a High School Dual Language Program" (Koulentes, Villanueva, and Russell 2016). In this presentation, Tom and his colleagues showed the vision statement that the key players in developing the program created as one of the first steps in their preparation for creating a dual language program in their high school.

District 113 and Highland Park High School's Dual Language Vision Statement

We aim to become a dual language school that provides a world-class education where children become bilingual and biliterate while developing an ability to navigate many cultures.

As these examples show, mission/vision statements can vary widely. They may also include specific program goals. What is important is that everyone involved in creating and participating in the program should have a voice in developing the statements. In addition, these mission/vision statements and goals should not simply be archived. They should be living documents that are reviewed regularly and revised as the program develops and changes.

Flexibility and Openness to Change

Even when schools do take the necessary time to plan and prepare for dual language programs and create mission and vision statements and goals, there still are challenges. As programs develop, administrators and teachers need to remain open and willing to be flexible and make needed changes. To make good decisions, it is important to have ongoing professional development, drawing on experts in dual language, and to read recent research about dual language programs (Howard et. al. 2018; Soltero 2016; Escamilla et al. 2014; Hamayan, Genesee, and Cloud 2013; Beeman and Urow 2013; Thomas and Collier, 2012; Lindholm-Leary and Hernandez 2011). The following example helps to illustrate the importance of flexibility and openness to change.

Omaha, Nebraska ◆ Nebraska, like many other states in the country's heartland, has experienced a huge growth in its Spanish-speaking population in recent years. Jobs in agriculture, the meatpacking industry, as well as a growing service industry have attracted new immigrants from states like California, Texas, and Florida. In many cities and small towns, the immigrants have settled in concentrated areas, and this has created Spanish-speaking neighborhoods.

In some areas of Nebraska, schooling for the children of these newcomers became a serious concern around the late 1990s, especially for administrators and teachers in schools in the rapidly changing neighborhoods where immigrants were settling. Two schools in Omaha Public Schools (OPS) heavily impacted by the changing demographics hired two principals interested in meeting the needs of Spanish-speaking students. The districts also recruited some key leaders with dual language experience from other states. The schools decided to start dual language programs.

Administrators and some teachers who would be involved in the two-way program went to the National Association of Bilingual Education conference and attended sessions on dual language, sharing what they learned with one another and others back at their school sites. The administration and faculty were open to new ideas and worked together, guided by their new knowledge and those with dual language experience. As a result, the programs they developed and implemented in 2000 had very positive early results.

Even with careful planning and a solid base of support, the early dual language programs faced challenges, and teachers and staff had to remain flexible and open to change. They made a constant effort to recruit qualified bilingual teachers and to ensure that all the teachers in the school understood the program and supported it. Administrators often had to travel outside of the state to recruit teachers. In addition, the teachers in the two-way program admitted they sometimes felt alienated from other teachers in the school. In one of the two schools implementing a dual language strand, teachers worked in pairs with an English-side teacher and Spanish-side teacher. When these pairs did not get along, an amicable divorce had to be negotiated.

Other school personnel also caused issues. It soon became apparent that the office and custodial staff needed to be educated about the program when they began complaining and making negative comments. Program leaders made a point of including these staff members in orientation meetings and often consulted about how the new program impacted them. The orientations also led to better relations with parents and teachers who did not teach in the dual language strand.

The dual language program has expanded considerably since 2000 when the first two schools enrolled emergent bilinguals in kindergarten. When we last worked with these schools, dual language extended through the third grade, and administrators were already beginning to consider moving dual language into middle school. This, of course, meant more planning and more change.

In September 2016, a featured article in The *Omaha World-Herald* reported that Omaha Public Schools (OPS) now has dual language programs in ten schools, enrolling about 2,800 students in grades kindergarten through 12 (Duffy 2016). The teacher featured in the article had been a student in the dual language middle school program of the district, and two other teachers in the district are also products of the district's dual language programs. As the article explains, "Parents in some parts of Omaha have been clamoring for dual-language programs at their schools to foster multiculturalism at an early age and to improve student performance" (1). As the program continues to grow and to move to more parts of the district, there will be the need to help the stakeholders in those areas understand dual language. At each step of the way, there will be a need for openness to change and flexibility.

A Multilingual Ecology

The fourth whole-school essential is based on the work of Ofelia García and the research team (García and Kleifgen 2010) at City University of New York (CUNY). Through the New York State Initiative for Emergent Bilinguals (NYSIEB), García and her researchers work with struggling schools in New York to help them improve their programs for bilingual students. Schools have to agree to two nonnegotiables: Bilingualism is to be seen as a resource in educating the students, and the whole school needs to support a multilingual ecology.

This second nonnegotiable, the support for a multilingual ecology, is not always evident in dual language schools. In schools with a multilingual ecology, the home languages of all the students should be visible everywhere, including on signs outside the school, in the hallways, in the cafeteria, and in the gym as well as in classrooms. In dual language schools, materials should be available in both languages, and student projects in both languages should be displayed as well as bilingual student-made posters. Both languages should be used and encouraged not only during class time but also outside the classroom in the office, during recess, and during specials including music and P.E. Figure 3.1 shows an example of a permanent visitor sign at Cedar Brook dual language school. Figure 3.2 shows an announcement for an upcoming parent orientation on the dual language program.

Figure 3.1. Visitor Sign at Cedar Brook Elementary School

Figure 3.2 Parent Orientation Announcement

In Highland High School Tom, the principal, has observed that creating a multilingual ecology is becoming easier as more Spanish resources are available and new technology supports better translations. As he explains, "We are methodically working through the school, adding signage in both languages and making sure that every document we send home is translated into English and Spanish." Figure 3.3 shows a bilingual sign outside one of the high school classrooms doors at Tom's school.

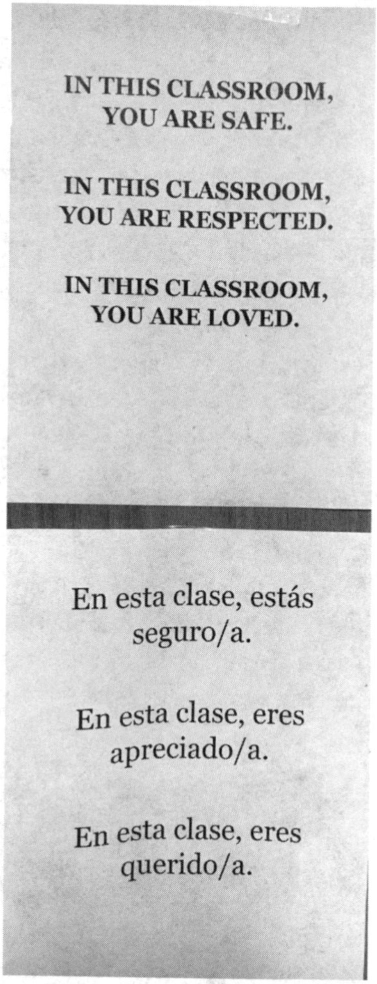

A multilingual ecology goes even farther than having two languages visible. García, Ibarra Johnson, and Seltzer (2017) argue that there should be evidence of the home languages of all the students attending a dual language school. So if the school is a dual language Spanish/English school and some students' home languages are Arabic, French, and Somali, there should be some acknowledgement of those students' home languages in the environment as well. Because we live and learn in a global, multilingual society, all students' languages should be recognized, even though Spanish and English might be the languages of instruction.

García, Ibarra Johnson, and Seltzer (2017) have developed a checklist for promoting an ecology of multilingualism. In addition to signs and student work that reflect students' languages, the authors suggest a number of other ways schools can develop a multilingual ecology. For example, a family member from each of the language groups at the school could compose a short welcome message in their language to send home with the home language survey. Students who speak languages other than English could work together to create a multilingual PowerPoint or a short video that emphasizes the value of bilingualism. Teachers can ensure that students have access to Internet translation programs or translator pens. These are just a few of the ways that schools with dual language programs can promote a multilingual ecology.

IN THIS CLASSROOM, YOU ARE SAFE.

IN THIS CLASSROOM, YOU ARE RESPECTED.

IN THIS CLASSROOM, YOU ARE LOVED.

En esta clase, estás seguro/a.

En esta clase, eres apreciado/a.

En esta clase, eres querido/a.

Figure 3.3 Bilingual Safe Sign

Academic and Social Equity and Equal Status for Both Languages

The fifth whole-school essential for dual language is that all those involved in the school must be committed to academic and social equity and the promotion of equal status for both languages. In her dissertation, Sugarman (2012) interviewed dual language teachers and administrators from a variety of dual language schools to look at equity in Spanish/English dual language classrooms. In her conclusion, she explains why equity is so fundamental to dual language programs.

> Equity has a meaning that is unique to dual language because this type of program is intended to challenge power structures by raising the status of the language spoken by minority students and giving value to their linguistic expertise, and by making school responsive to and relevant for minority students. (217)

Key Points for Achieving Equity ◆ Developing a program that provides equity in academics, social status, and language status is extremely difficult. Yet equity issues cannot be ignored if the goals of dual language, including high academic achievement for all, development of bilingualism and biliteracy, and demonstration of positive cross-cultural attitudes and behaviors, are to be achieved. It is also important to distinguish between equity and equality here for this discussion. Equity, especially in the education of diverse students, is giving all students what they need to be successful. It is adopting practices that lead to equal outcomes for diverse students. Equality is treating everyone the same. Treating students equally aims to promote fairness, but it can only work if everyone starts from the same place and needs the same help to reach their goals.

This last point is especially important when we consider dual language education. Although students in two-way dual language programs may all be learning in a language they do not understand in addition to further developing their home language, students do not all necessarily come from the same socioeconomic backgrounds or have access to the same support systems. Giving all students the same supports, treating them equally, and expecting equal outcomes is not a realistic expectation.

For her dissertation, Sugarman drew on work she had already been involved in with others in the creation of the first edition of the *Guiding Principles for Dual Language Education* (Howard et al. 2007). She pulled out key ideas for equity in dual language classrooms and presented these to teachers for her research. These key points, adapted from Sugarman (2012), are listed below.

1. There is cultural and linguistic equity in the classroom and school.

2. Instructional materials in both languages reflect the student population in the program and encourage cross-cultural appreciation.

Equity in Dual Language Programs

Principal Jeff Post explains the different factors he considers to ensure equity in his dual language programs.

3. Whether the dual language program is a whole-school program or a strand within a school, signs and daily routines (e.g., announcements) reflect bilingualism and multiculturalism.

4. Language, including academic language, is developed equally in both languages.

5. Student grouping provides opportunities for students to learn from one another.

We also would add a sixth point that really draws on all of the above points.

6. Teachers take a *juntos* stance and support a translanguaging *corriente* throughout their teaching. (García, Johnson, and Seltzer 2017)

This challenging list of key points to promote equity in dual language programs can serve as a checklist for personnel in dual language schools. We discuss each point and provide examples from schools we have worked with.

Cultural and Linguistic Equity ◖ According to Sugarman (2012), full implementation of cultural and linguistic equity would mean that teachers, administrators, and students "work together to create a learning environment where all linguistic and cultural groups are equally valued and respected" (172). This would include, of course, all ethnic and linguistic groups in the school. We discussed earlier how students in Spanish/English dual language programs may include a mix of ethnolinguistic backgrounds.

Researchers have investigated how students from different backgrounds feel in dual language programs and how they perform academically. Lindholm-Leary and Howard (2008) found in their research and a review of the literature that diverse students who were not either English-speaking Anglos or native Spanish speakers in a two-way program did well in Spanish/English dual language programs.

> In several different studies of TWI [two way immersion] students from three ethnic groups . . . results showed that students from Euro-American [French, German, Polish etc.], Hispanic, and African-American and Asian-American (though there were few such students) backgrounds all benefited from the TWI program. This was true regardless of the students' social class backgrounds, though middle-class students typically outperformed lower-class students. (190)

Anberg-Espinosa (2008) researched the experiences and perspectives of African-American students in Spanish/English two-way dual language programs. Interviewing teachers, administrators, students, and parents, she found that students in her study, though they had experienced some negative feedback at times from peers about their racial backgrounds, generally were happy in their program, felt included, and were proud of becoming bilingual. African-American students were successful in the program, but did need extra language supports.

Woodley (2015) conducted research in a newcomer high school in New York. About 90 percent of the students were from Spanish-speaking countries, and there was a small Spanish/English dual language program. Woodley focused her study on the students who were not Spanish speakers. About 10 percent of the students were Muslims who spoke a variety of languages including Arabic, French, Fulani, Wolof, and Kotokoli. She observed these students, led discussions with them, and conducted in-depth interviews with individual students. The teachers in this school were accustomed to working with Spanish-speaking Christian background students. At times, in the classes that were not part of the dual language strand, the teachers gave explanations in Spanish to help the Spanish-speaking students. However, the Muslim students who spoke other languages reported that they felt discrimination at the school and did not feel that they belonged there. In this case, not all students received equitable treatment, even though the teachers were well intentioned.

Educators in dual language programs are generally well prepared to work with cultural and linguistic diversity and make special efforts to support it. The teachers in the school Woodley studied did support the Spanish-speaking students at the school, but they did not know how to work with students who spoke other languages and came from very different cultural and religious backgrounds than the Spanish-speaking students. As Woodley's research shows, it is challenging to achieve full cultural and linguistic equity in schools when students come from multiple linguistic, cultural, and ethnic backgrounds.

Many teachers in dual language schools are able to foster equity for all students, as the following examples show. Carolina, a dual language French/English teacher in New York, had students from several different countries in her classroom. Besides keeping a map of the world where students' pictures were pinned around the map with yarn connecting to their countries of origin, Carolina posted words and key concepts students were studying in English and French. When the class studied land forms in geography, Carolina and the students created a poster with pictures, and French and English cognates, including *mountains* and *montagnes* and *valleys* and *vallées*, and posted it in the classroom. With the help of her Korean, Mandarin, Arabic, and Spanish speakers, and using the Internet, Carolina was able to also include the key words from each of those languages on the poster.

Jeff, the Texas principal we discussed in Chapter 1, who has both a two-way and one-way dual language strand in Cedar Brook Elementary School, described a schoolwide multicultural festival held at his school.

> Last year students and teachers worked to create a multicultural festival. During this time, students and teachers studied the language, customs, traditions, foods, and values of their own or of another culture. Students created artifacts to share with other grade levels and classrooms and the parent community in a culminating event that brought the community into the school. The work toward the festival was done both inside and outside of the classroom.

Tom, at Highland High School, has worked to help all his staff understand the importance of equity in his school. Through professional development and readings including Singleton's *Courageous Conversations About Race: A Field Guide for Achieving Equity in Schools* (Singleton 2015), he helps his faculty confront issues of equity. When asked about equity at his school, he responded with vigor:

> This is huge. With our staff we are working hard to offer many professional development sessions on equity. We are teaching staff how to engage in courageous conversations about race (using Singleton's model).

In different ways, Carolina, Jeff, and Tom are leading their schools toward full implementation of cultural and linguistic equity.

Equity in Materials ◗ Equity in schools goes beyond promoting culture and language. Dual language schools must also strive for equity in providing materials in both languages, and those materials should be of equal quality. Equity in materials is one facet of creating a multilingual ecology. This does not mean that materials students read in one language should be exactly the same as materials studied in the other. In fact, when studying a topic, students should frequently read related, but not necessarily the same, materials in the two languages to deepen their understanding.

So when studying weather, students might read a book in English about the water cycle and rain and how thunder and lightning occur and one in Spanish about *inundaciones* (floods) and what causes them. What is important is that the quality of the materials should be equal. That is, if the books in English have colorful illustra-

Promoting the Value of Bilingualism

Principal Vivian Pratts explains how she promotes the value of bilingualism in her one-way dual language program.

tions and clear charts, but the books in Spanish have few illustrations and small print that is difficult to read, then there is no equity. When there are big books, colorful posters, and CDs available in English, but only teacher-made materials in Spanish, there is no equity.

If translated materials are not sensitive to students' cultural backgrounds, and students never see themselves or their cultures reflected in the materials, there is no equity. For example, if the Spanish speakers in the program come primarily from Puerto Rico, and the stories are set in Spain or Mexico, then the materials do not reflect the students' backgrounds. In addition, if some well-known stories have been translated from English to Spanish, there should be equal numbers of well-known Spanish stories translated from Spanish to English.

Although it takes more time and effort to find materials in Spanish, for example, than in English, there are materials available, and teachers should be provided both the time and financial resources to acquire these materials. Materials and other resources to support content learning are more difficult to find for dual language programs in other languages such as Korean, Chinese, and Arabic. In cases such as these, it is important that teachers be given release time and outside personnel such as first language aides to help them create materials or look for online resources.

A final point about resources concerns library resources. When a school commits to dual language, there must be a commitment to build a library of resources in both languages. When visiting Spanish/English dual language schools, we always ask to see the library. In too many cases, even when the dual language program is a whole-school program, the number and quality of books, magazines, and CDs available in English far outnumber the resources in Spanish. It is important that librarians, administrators, and teachers work together to increase the percentage of quality materials in the non-English language in school libraries. In fact, there should be materials available in the home language of all the different linguistic groups represented in the school.

Edgewood Elementary, a one-way dual language school in the same district as Jeff's in Texas, has built a beautiful library that has a welcoming atmosphere and many books in both English and Spanish. The principal, Vivian Pratts, and her librarian have worked hard to ensure that students and teachers find the library a welcoming place that encourages reading in both languages.

One especially creative way the librarian at Edgewood involved the school in reading award-winning books in Spanish and English was to create a "book tasting" setting in the library. To promote these books, she set several tables elegantly as one does in a four-star restaurant. Each table had high-quality plastic silverware, several plates at each setting for different courses, and bright blue tablecloths. Next to the napkin at each place setting was a menu of the selected books. There were different menus for each grade level. The librarian expected that by reading the menu and previewing the books, the students were more likely to select and read books from the collection. After a weekly library visit, students and teachers ordered books from their grade's menu. This popular activity involved both teachers and students and increased use of the library's resources.

Signs and Daily Routines Reflect a Bilingual and Multicultural Focus ◗

Besides considering instructional materials, it is important to consider the visual landscape of the school. We discussed earlier the importance of the school supporting a multilingual ecology, the second nonnegotiable insisted upon by the researchers with CUNY-NYSIEB (García and Kleyn 2016). Even when a dual language program is only a strand within a school, there should be evidence of a multilingual and multicultural focus in the halls and in the languages heard during the day around the school. Announcements should be made in both languages of the dual language program, and signs in the halls and outside the school should be in both languages. In fact, multilingual signs should reflect all the home languages of the students in the school.

If a school has an alternate "language of the day" routine, there should be signs in evidence on classroom doors (Figure 3.4). When possible, the language of the day should be used as students and teachers pass in the halls and during specials. These daily routines should be accepted and respected by all in the school, including teachers and students who are not in the dual program.

There is a caveat about signs. It is important to consider both the language and the content of signs posted around the school. Tom, the Highland Park principal, related that he did an equity walk around the school with other administrators to look at the posted signs. Although there were a number of signs in Spanish, they all reflected a deficiency attitude toward Spanish speaking students. For example, there were signs giving a number to call for students with a drug problem and signs for

Figure 3.4 Language of the Day Sign

students who were struggling academically or who were looking for a job. Tom and his team made sure to replace these signs with signs that reflected a positive view of Spanish speakers.

Equal Attention Is Given to Academic Language Development in the Two Languages ◆ In both one-way and two-way dual language programs it is important to develop high levels of oral and written proficiency in two languages. However, this is difficult to accomplish. Too frequently, the Spanish language is not valued in the same way that English is. In dual language programs teachers and administrators are aware that student test scores in English are more important than Spanish scores, and that may result in program design and teaching practices that give more value to English than to Spanish. In addition, English is the language of power in U.S. society, so it is especially important to emphasize the other language of instruction..

Furthermore, some people assume that certain languages are inherently better than others. Yvonne remembers a conversation she had with some monolingual English-speaking friends who actually told her that "there is no great literature of importance written in Spanish." These misinformed friends had an impression that somehow Spanish was an inferior language. For all of these reasons, dual language programs have to work to give equal status to the two languages. Tom explains how he and his staff work on this at his high school:

> We are also taking active steps to help our staff understand that we need to elevate the status of Spanish (as a minority language in this country) as a legitimate academic language. This process takes a lot of time, but our administrative team is committed to it so we have accepted this as a standard part of all our work. We are all committed to this.

In the upper grades there are concerns about finding teachers who can model academic language, especially in the non-English language. We are often asked by administrators of Spanish/English programs if we could recommend good bilingual teachers whose academic Spanish and content knowledge would allow them to teach in upper elementary, middle school, and high school. Many districts hire teachers from Spain, Mexico, or other Spanish-speaking countries. These teachers may have academic proficiency in the non-English language, but they may lack the pedagogical training that prepares them to effectively teach in U.S. schools. In addition, because of issues with immigration status, these teachers are often short term, and by the time they become accustomed to the approaches and curriculum in this country and begin to teach effectively, they need to return to their homeland. Although sometimes these hires have been successful, they often result in inadequate instruction for the non-English component of a dual language program.

Colleges of education are beginning to provide programs for dual language settings and are recruiting bilingual teachers in languages including Spanish, Cantonese, Mandarin, Korean, and Hmong, but many more programs are needed. As dual language education grows, the supply of teachers who have both academic language in the non-English language and pedagogical knowledge becomes more critical. Without equally well-qualified teachers in the two languages, it is very difficult to achieve equal development of academic language proficiency in the two languages.

Hamayan, Genesee, and Cloud (2013) provide teacher tips for valuing and using both languages equally. These include being aware when instruction moves from the language of instruction to the other language and if one language is used for expressing affection and rewards and the other for discipline. Teachers should keep a balance of visuals in the two languages across classrooms and make sure that textbooks and classroom libraries have adequate numbers of books in both languages. If specialists or parent volunteers come into the classroom, there should be an effort to be sure that the balance of the support instruction is maintained. Materials created for the program and by the teachers and students should be published in both languages.

Grouping for Equity ◗ When considering issues of equity in dual language programs, teachers need to consider not only how they group students in the classroom but how to promote natural interaction outside of school as well. However, these outside interactions are often overlooked. Freeman (1996) studied the successful Oyster Bilingual School's dual language program in Washington, D.C. Although the school had shown academic success and received awards for excellent education, the school's plan included the aim "to promote social change by socializing children differently from the way they are socialized in mainstream U.S. educational discourse" (558). Freeman found that despite this goal and the commitment by administrators and teachers, students outside the classroom formed traditional social groups and divisions.

Teachers, then, need to consider how they group students and try to encourage students with different languages and social backgrounds to interact inside and outside the classroom. Sugarman (2012) reported that in one of the dual language schools she was studying, the staff noticed the students worked together in class but self-segregated during recess and at lunch. Native English speakers did not interact with their native Spanish-speaking peers. In their planning the teachers organized games for the playground. They also had bilingual pairs work together frequently in class. When the native English speakers realized that their native Spanish-speaking peers knew things they did not know and were able to help them, they saw their peers differently. By the end of the year the teachers noticed improvement in the amount of voluntary interaction both inside and outside the classroom.

At another school when an Anglo parent who put her child in a two-way program was interviewed, she admitted that at first, her daughter came home saying, "The Spanish-speaking kids don't know any English." But soon her child came home saying, "But, you know, they really know Spanish!" This type of respect building is an important by-product of a dual language program that fosters equity.

Teachers Take a *Juntos* Stance and Support a Translanguaging *Corriente Throughout Their Teaching* ◈ One of the key tenets of dual language education has been to keep the two languages separate. This has been important both to give students adequate comprehensible exposure to both languages as they are learning content and to avoid concurrent translation, an ineffective approach to learning. Concurrent translation occurs when a teacher says something in one language and immediately translates it into the students' home language. The problem with this approach is that students listen only to the language they understand better. As a result, they do not acquire the second language.

As we discussed in Chapter 2, dual language programs divide language use for instruction in a variety of ways. When divided by content in a Spanish/English program, the instruction in math might be in English during certain grades, or for a

Translanguaging to Compare the Sound of J in Spanish and English

In another lesson, Sandra Cordúa uses the translanguaging strategy of contrasting the sounds of the letter J in Spanish and English to build metalinguistic awareness with her kindergarten TWDL students.

semester, or a week. It is assumed, then, that instructional materials and teaching and interactions would be in English during that time. It does not, however, mean that there would be no place for translanguaging strategies to support learning for Spanish speakers.

It is useful to consider language use in dual language programs at both a macro-level and micro-level (see Figure 3.5).

At the macro level, the program level, it is important for teachers and students to use the target language for instruction. Teachers make the input comprehensible for the nonnative speakers of the language being used and teach content in that target language. Texts and other resources as well as interactions are in the language of instruction.

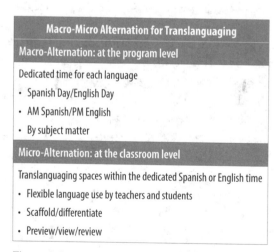

Macro-Micro Alternation for Translanguaging
Macro-Alternation: at the program level
Dedicated time for each language • Spanish Day/English Day • AM Spanish/PM English • By subject matter
Micro-Alternation: at the classroom level
Translanguaging spaces within the dedicated Spanish or English time • Flexible language use by teachers and students • Scaffold/differentiate • Preview/view/review

Figure 3.5

However, at the micro-level teachers support students who are learning in a second language in a variety of ways. They employ different pedagogical strategies to make the input comprehensible. One of these is the use of the students' home language. Teachers plan ways to draw on students' first language strengths as they teach in the students' second language. They use translanguaging strategies as a scaffold in teaching both academic content and academic language.

A good example of effective translanguaging comes from Sandra Cordúa, a kindergarten teacher in Jeff's two-way program at Cedar Brook. We observed her teaching her students about forming possessives in English using apostrophe *s*. She made a two-column chart, and using objects from around the room, including students' possessions, compared the formation of the possessive in English and Spanish. She began her chart with *La mochila de India* in one column, and in the opposite column she wrote, *India's backpack.* Then she continued with other students. She used this translanguaging strategy to help her students understand the differences in syntax and orthography for the possessive in Spanish and English. Figure 3.6 shows Sandra's chart.

When teachers take a *juntos* (together) stance (García, Ibarra Johnson, and Seltzer 2017), they hold three beliefs about inclusiveness and equity. The first is that

Figure 3.6 Lesson on the Possessive in Spanish and English

students' language practices and cultural understandings include those they bring from their homes and communities as well as what they adopt from school. These are brought together (*juntos*) and are considered and valued in the classroom and school. The second is that students' families and communities are valuable resources and should be included in students' education. The third is that classrooms must be democratic places "where teachers and students *juntos* co-create knowledge, challenge traditional hierarchies, and work together towards a more just society" (50).

The translanguaging *corriente* that we discussed in Chapter 2 is also a key part of equity as classrooms and, in fact, whole schools support translanguaging in strategic ways to help students learn language and academic content. Using their full linguistic repertoire students "make sense of their complex world and identities" (García, Ibarra Johnson, and Seltzer 2017, 21) when the flow of students' dynamic bilingualism, the translanguaging *corriente*, is evident throughout the school.

Equity in Sum ◆ Equity in schools is difficult to achieve, and, despite a commitment among dual language advocates to academic and social equity, all those involved in dual language programs must constantly keep issues of equity at the forefront. This is not a new concern. In her study of Oyster Bilingual School in Washington, D.C., Freeman (1996) found that despite the efforts of the personnel to create an environment of equity, constant attempts needed to be made to fight the wider societal values and the movement toward the status quo. Race and social class had strong influences on social grouping even at this school. In addition, responses from teachers in the two-way school she studied often showed that teachers, without being aware of it, held lower expectations for language-minority students. Despite the teachers' best intentions, these expectations were evident in their teaching.

In her article addressing concerns of equity in dual language programs for Spanish speakers, Valdés (1997) asked whether "hispanophone children acquire native-like academic Spanish" (416). She pointed out that some dual language teachers themselves lack high levels of academic Spanish and so have difficulty modeling the academic register for students. Valdés also questioned whether there was true equality in the value placed on developing bilingualism for both groups of students in dual language programs. Often schools do not assess Spanish language proficiency, and even when schools or districts do assess academic achievement in Spanish, those scores are essentially ignored in any overall assessment of students' achievement. As Hernandez (2017) points out in her case study of a dual language school, "the native Spanish-speaking sutdents are regularly over tested in their second language and designated incompetent when unable to perform at a level the native English-speaking students are not expected to reach in Spanish" (145).

Valdés also pointed to the fact that the progress English speakers in two-way programs make in developing Spanish is often highlighted, but the English development of Spanish speakers is basically ignored. Programs for parents often feature Anglo children displaying their Spanish skills but seldom highlight native Spanish speakers speaking English. "For minority children, the acquisition of English is expected. For Mainstream children, the acquisition of a non-English language is enthusiastically applauded" (1997, 417).

Perhaps one of the most disturbing of Valdés' concerns is that two-way programs may be giving future advantages to already privileged monolingual English-speaking children by making them bilingual. She explains that in the past "skills in two languages have opened doors for members of minority groups" (1997, 419). However, in successful dual language programs, all students become bilingual. Valdés' point is that the one advantage language-minority children might have may be usurped by English speakers who become bilingual.

Valdez, Freire, and Delavan (2016) discuss a disturbing trend in dual language that encourages the implementation of dual language programs that have the underlying purpose of giving the privileged monolingual English-speaking children the power that Valdés was concerned about. Valdez et al. reviewed the dual language programs developed and controlled by the Utah State Department of Education and concluded that those programs represent what they call a "global human capital framework" rather than an "equity/heritage framework." The Utah programs are aligned with the interests of the privileged groups and give them more privilege rather than helping to equalize power imbalances among social groups by revitalizing heritage languages and giving language-minority groups access to language and enriching curriculum.

The authors studied the growth of dual language in the state since 2006. They reviewed the demographics of the areas where dual language programs have been implemented. They discovered that the new state-supported dual language schools are located in areas that are wealthier and whiter than dual language programs that were established earlier. As a result the new programs serve more privileged students.

One-way programs, meant to serve communities with large numbers of speakers of a language other than English and help them acquire English and maintain the home language, are being replaced in Utah by a kind of one-way foreign language program where privileged white students learn another language and English in classes with a few speakers of that second language.

Of concern to Valdez et al. is that the Utah dual language model is now being adopted in over ten states with Delaware and Georgia explicitly emulating Utah's model. In these dual language programs, the goal of equity for language-minority students is being lost. Equity in dual language is indeed critical. It is essential that dual language programs be designed to promote equity in all aspects of the program.

Parent Education and Support

A final whole-school essential is parent education and support. No dual language program can succeed without parent participation from both language groups. At the beginning of the implementation of a dual language program and continuing through the years, schools should provide parents with information about what dual language programs are, their goals, and the theory and research supporting them.

Often, English-speaking parents enrolling their children in a dual language program are eager for their children to become bilingual because they see the benefits for their future and may also see the importance of their children gaining cross-cultural understandings. However, they seldom understand language acquisition and often have concerns about their children missing out on instruction that children in English-only settings are receiving. In addition, when English-speaking children beginning the program complain they can't understand the instruction in a language other than English, parents may want extra support for their children and often complain they can't help them with their homework if they don't speak the language themselves.

Parents of children who speak a language other than English may be pleased that their children are going to develop and become literate in their home language, but they may be worried about whether their children will learn enough English if the children are spending time learning in their home language. Many parents are convinced that "more English equals more English" and fear their children will never learn English if they are also instructed in another language. In addition, although a dual language program may be optional in a two-way school setting for English-speaking parents, it may be the only option for parents of language-other-than-English students, so it is especially important that these parents understand the benefits for their children.

For all of these reasons, schools need to provide education in language acquisition, dual language education, and the research supporting them. Even then, questions often arise from parents, and teachers and administrators alike must be able to answer them. Tom Koulentes at Highland Park High school explains that he and his faculty have had to address parents' concerns about their children's college readiness and test scores. To help educate parents and students about academic, social, and career benefits of bilingualism, Highland Park has formed a Dual Language Parent Advisory Committee and a Dual Language Student Advisory Committee

Showing the Value of Two Languages

Principal Jeff Post explains how his school highlights the use of both Spanish and English.

that meet regularly throughout the school year and provide input into the program. When asked about parent education and support, he gave us this response:

> Parental education and support is super important. In our community, if our parents who have political and social capital (for us, our white, middle-class parents) don't understand and buy into this program, we will get limited support from our school board. If our Latino parents don't understand why this program benefits their children, they will pull their children out and put them in monolingual English programs. Therefore, we are conscientious in all the communication efforts we are making with our parents. We started a Dual Language Parent Advisory meeting. Meetings occur three times a year and are attended by the dual language/English language coordinator and the principal. At each meeting, we speak half the time in Spanish and half the time in English. We have translators available for any parent to use. We use each meeting to explain dual language research to parents and discuss how we are turning this research into specific actions. In addition we ask parents for input about ways the program can support the students' education and social needs. Parents give us great feedback. When we come back for the next meeting, we are always sure to show parents how we used the feedback they gave us at the last meeting; this builds great trust that the thoughts they have are being heard and valued.

Programs like the one Tom has created are critical to the whole-school success of both one-way and two-way dual language programs. This last whole-school essential goes hand-in-hand with the other essentials we have discussed. All school personnel must understand the program. All parties involved, including parents, should help form a vision/mission statement. Once a program is implemented, there must be openness and flexibility because change is inevitable. Equity should be at the forefront of all decisions, and there should be parent education and support. All of these whole-school essentials need to be in place to form a firm foundation for the dual language program.

Chapter Overview

In this chapter we discussed whole-school essentials. When dual language programs incorporate these practices, the programs are more successful and can better meet the needs of all the students.

To begin, all administrators at the district and school levels, all teachers at the school including teachers who are not teaching in the dual language program, the support staff, parents, community members, and the students must understand and support the goals and benefits of the program. Without a solid understanding of the benefits, none of these stakeholders can fully support a dual language program. Because it takes several years for test scores of second language learners to reach national norms in English, this understanding and support is especially important so that the program will not be abandoned if it does not produce instant success.

To build understanding and support for a dual language program, it is essential to develop a mission/vision statement. This statement should be jointly created by representatives of the different groups who are stakeholders in the program. The statement can be relatively simple or more complex. Writing a mission/vision statement enables stakeholders to decide what their expectations are for the program outcomes.

Any new program will need to be revised as it is implemented. For that reason, it is essential that administrators and teachers be flexible and open to change. Although the vision/mission statement provides a framework, it is a living document, and as the program develops, the vision/mission statement may need to be updated to reflect current understandings.

A fourth essential is for the school to exhibit a multilingual ecology. García and Kleyn, (2016c) list this as a nonnegotiable. In schools with a multilingual ecology, the home languages of all the students should be visible everywhere. In schools with a dual language program, the two languages should be evident in the office, the halls, and the classrooms. In addition, languages of students whose home language is not one of the two program languages should also be visible in the school environment.

One of the most important attributes of a dual language program is an emphasis on academic and social equity and equal status for both languages. This is a difficult goal to attain, as Valdés (1997) points out. We list several key points for achieving equity. These include cultural and linguistic equity in the classroom, equity in instructional materials, student grouping that promotes equity, equity in language use and academic language development in two languages, and taking a *juntos* stance to support a translanguaging *corriente*.

Parent education and support are also essential for any dual language program. When parents understand theories of second language acquisition and bilingual education, they can better support their own children who are in the program and the program itself. Key understandings are that development of the home language promotes the development of an additional language and that academic concepts gained in one language transfer to the second language.

Reflect and Apply

1. The first whole-school essential deals with understanding and supporting the goals and benefits of dual language programs. We provided examples of programs where this essential was not present and others where it was present. Discuss these examples with a partner. Have you observed similar examples, positive or negative, in your school or in schools you are familiar with?

2. In this chapter we discuss several equity issues for dual language. What are these concerns? Have you seen any of these issues in dual language programs you know about in your community? In pairs or small groups make a visual showing what equity issues you have seen or experienced. Include what you see as some solutions. Prepare to share this.

3. Look around a dual language school. Does it have a multilingual ecology? Take pictures around the school that show examples to share with others. Discuss.

4. It is critical that dual language programs find qualified bilingual teachers and have support materials in both languages. What is your school or a school you are familiar with doing to hire qualified teachers and find materials in both languages? Take some notes on these essentials and prepare to share them.

5. In a dual language program where you teach or where you have observed, how are parents included and supported? Be prepared to discuss.

4

Administrator and Administrator/Teacher Collaboration Essentials

For a bilingual dual language program to succeed, knowledgeable administrators must fully support the program. In addition, administrators and teachers must collaborate to ensure that certain procedures and practices are implemented in the dual language program. In this chapter, we begin by outlining the essentials for administrators. Then we explain a set of essential practices for administrators and teachers working together.

Administrator Essentials

Whether the dual language program is implemented schoolwide or is a strand in the school, strong administrative leadership is critical for the program's success. The school site principal must be knowledgeable about dual language education and committed to the program. This means that there must be an investment of time and energy on the part of the principal. In many schools, a resource specialist has direct responsibility for the day-to-day operation of the program. The principal and the specialist form a team, and each person takes on some of the duties involved in establishing and maintaining a successful program. Howard et al. (2018) point out the importance of establishing a leadership team. They caution that "effective principals may be moved to a new post by the district administration. If a program relies on one person for leadership, even the most successful program can collapse if that leader is drawn away. Shared leadership through a leadership team can provide higher stability and sustainability for the program" (12). Without the support of the administration, a dual language program is not apt to succeed, but when administrators are committed and involved, dual language programs thrive.

There are several administrator essentials in the following list that we propose based on our experiences in schools. Each of these points is important and we have seen that in successful programs, these are in place.

- Promote the value of bilingualism throughout the district and school
- Stay current on research, theory, and practice to make informed decisions
- Ensure that some administrators and program specialists are bilingual
- Provide an on-site specialist for teacher support
- Provide and participate in ongoing professional development through consultants, school visits, and conferences
- Provide books and other resources in both languages
- Provide time for teachers to plan together
- Monitor to ensure consistent planning, curriculum implementation, and classroom organization
- Provide positive feedback

Promote the Value of Bilingualism Throughout the District and School

Although it might seem obvious that administrators should value and promote bilingualism, we include this essential because we have seen schools where teachers and parents might be enthusiastic about a dual language program, but the administration including superintendents, principals, and/or other administrative leaders were not fully committed to dual language and were even antagonistic toward bilingual education and dual language. In at least three districts where we have worked, including a small rural school district, a large district including both rural and urban schools, and a large urban district, lack of understanding of the value of bilingualism and dual language education has threatened or actually led to the elimination of the program.

The first example comes from a small, rural district along the border of Texas that implemented a dual language program in one of its schools. The commitment and passion of the principal for the one-way dual language program, the transfer of her enthusiasm to her teachers, and the support from faculty at a local university made the school so successful that it received state and national acclaim. This success led to pressure to open other dual language schools in the district. However, the superintendent and some of the central office administrators were skeptical of the program, and some were opposed to any form of bilingual education. Bilingual directors hired by the district were not well prepared for their positions and got little support from the superintendent and other central office administrators. The result was that the district eliminated dual language programs and now only offers transitional bilingual education.

In another larger district along the Texas border with both rural and urban schools, several schools implemented whole-school one-way dual language programs to meet the needs of the large Hispanic population in the area. Students were successful in these programs that extended K–12. Graduation rates were high and graduates went on to college.

Because of the success of dual language, a superintendent was hired who was knowledgeable about dual language and a known advocate. He proposed making all schools in the district dual language. However, the school board and some district-level administrators were opposed to this, especially when some community members who did not understand bilingual education worried their children would not learn English. Despite the success of the dual language programs that had been implemented, the lack of support from community members and district administrators eroded the plans for expanding dual language in the district. A key advocate for dual language who worked in administration in the district and did research on the success of the district programs finally moved to another district to do the work he believed in.

The final example of what happens when bilingualism is not valued comes from a large urban district. The Hispanic population in the district was served both by one-way and two-way dual language programs, depending on the neighborhood populations. As students reached middle and high school, serious problems arose. Many middle and high school principals did not see the value in continuing the development of bilingual education and refused to cooperate with central office bilingual staff members who were trying to help set up programs for the students feeding into these upper grades. These administrators were so resistant that they refused to attend mandatory principals' meetings if the topic was bilingual or dual language education. Without administrative support, the dual language programs could not be continued in the secondary schools.

These examples are negative ones, but, unfortunately, not that uncommon. Before any program can be successful, school and district leaders at every level must support dual language and see the value in developing students' bilingualism. There are many positive examples of district-level administrators, principals, and resource specialists who are knowledgeable about and committed to dual language education.

In his district, Tom knew he needed to promote the dual language program at the high school level. He understood his community and what the parents saw as important for their students.

> The middle class parents in our community want their children to take classes at our high school they believe will provide their children competitive advantages for admission into the nation's most selective colleges and universities. For many of these parents, the child's continuation in dual language is often sacrificed in order to enroll their child in honors/AP courses the parent believes have more value to a college admissions process. In order to keep our DL students enrolled in our high school courses, and in order to keep our Superintendent and Board of Education in support of allocating resources to dual language courses, we had to educate our community about the value that being bilingual, biliterate and bicultural has in the 21st-century economy.

In order to help parents see that bilingualism was key to their children's future, Tom's school hosted a community screening of the film *Most Likely to Succeed* (Whiteley 2015) and also educated families to review the Framework for 21st Century Learning, created by the Partnership for 21st Century Learning that we referred to in Chapter 1 (www.P21.org). He explained that the film and the Framework make the case that schools need to help students develop skills to compete in the new digital and global society and this includes strong social and cross-cultural skills. These skills, the "4 Cs" are: critical literacy and analysis, creativity, communication, and collaboration. Tom explained how he drew on these resources to build support for his dual language program at Highland High School:

> We helped our community understand that a well-designed dual language program was the perfect vehicle for teaching students critical literacy, cross-cultural communication and cross-cultural collaboration. We worked hard to help our community understand that our dual language students' proficiency in these skills, in addition to their bilingualism, would be seen as an asset by colleges and prospective employers. By positioning

Administrators Stay Current on Research, Theory, and Practice

Principal Jeff Post describes how he visits classrooms, reads, meets with consultants, and attends conferences to stay current in dual language theory and practice.

Administrators Stay Current with Research and Theory

Principal Vivian Pratts explains how she has stayed current with bilingual research and theory through her studies in a doctoral program in curriculum and instruction with an emphasis in bilingual education.

our advocacy for dual language firmly in the desire to provide our students an economic advantage in the emerging global economy, we gained greater support from our Board of Education and parents.

This example and those we provided of Jeff and the principal in Omaha in Chapter 3 show the importance of having knowledgeable administrators who are committed to their programs. National and state bilingual conferences offer many sessions on dual language, and dual language conferences are held all over the country from New York to New Mexico to California. These conferences attract not only dual language teachers but also many administrators who understand and value bilingualism and want to learn more to make sure their dual language programs are successful.

Stay Current on Research, Theory, and Practice to Make Informed Decisions

For a dual language program to succeed in a district or in a school, administrators—especially school principals and other on-site school administrators—must understand current research, theory, and practice in bilingual education and in dual language education in particular. If administrators do not understand the research and theory that support bilingual programs, they cannot make good decisions about how to develop a successful program. Knowledgeable administrators are instructional leaders who can work with their teachers to implement practices consistent with current research on bilingual programs.

Research on translanguaging is a good example of this. In the past, dual language research and models have called for a strict separation of languages at all times. However, as we explained in Chapter 2, new theory drawing on sociolinguistic and neurolinguistic research promotes carefully planned, strategic implementation of translanguaging strategies in classrooms to promote both academic language acquisition and content learning. If principals do not know about new understandings, such as translanguaging, they cannot promote and support best practices as they work with their teachers.

Ensure That Some Administrators and Program Specialists Are Bilingual

In dual language programs, administrators are in constant contact with bilingual people, including parents and community members who may speak only the language other than English (LOTE) taught in the program. The model that a bilingual administrator provides is extremely important. We have observed several Spanish/English dual language schools with only monolingual English-speaking administrators. In these schools the administrators are not able to communicate effectively with some parents, community members, or students. Parents who do not speak English need administrators who can answer their questions or respond to their concerns. In addition, it is difficult for monolingual administrators to evaluate teachers who teach in the language other than English, participate in planning for the non-English curriculum, or judge the quality of the materials being used in the parts of the program that are taught in a language other than English.

When asked how he assures that his administrative team at Highland Park High school is bilingual or moving toward bilingualism, Tom explained what he does:

> We are encouraging our administrators and program specialists to get their EL certification (they advance on our pay scale), to take dual language professional development (we pay for this), and to learn Spanish (we offer classes for educators after school on our campus). We believe it is most important for our team to understand the value of bilingualism, biculturalism, and biliteracy, as well as the methods schools employ for achieving these goals. Even if a person isn't fluent in another language, if they understand why it is important and how to achieve it, they can work with their monolingual limitations to help create bilingual kids.

We would agree with Tom that even when educators are not fluent, if they have had a language learning experience themselves, they better understand a dual language program and the students in it.

Jeff, the principal at Cedar Brook, has made extra efforts to become bilingual and to show that he values bilingualism. He wrote:

> I think the best way for me to promote the program is by having my own children educated there. Both of my girls are a part of the TWDL program at Cedar Brook and have found much success in acquiring the Spanish language. I have also committed to becoming bilingual and am able to communicate with parents in both languages, which encourages cultural inclusivity. We want parents to feel comfortable in the school and excited about their children's education!

Jeff's commitment to becoming bilingual serves him well in communicating with parents. He also sets a good example for his teachers of the importance of bilingualism. In addition, when he monitors classes given in Spanish, he can provide better feedback.

There are programs in languages other than Spanish, including Hmong, Cantonese, Mandarin, and Arabic, where it is difficult to find bilingual administrators, but there must be key well-prepared resource staff members who are bilingual to support the principal. Although there are dual language administrators who promote and value bilingualism and understand research, theory, and practice but are not themselves bilingual, we would suggest that monolingual administrators make an effort to learn some of the non-English languages and that they have an assistant administrator who is bilingual in the languages of the program.

Although teachers in dual language programs must be certified, in some instances the speaker of the language other than English hired to support the principal in a semi-administrative role is an aide without proper educational background and credentials. In an inner city middle school where we worked, the neighborhood had a large influx of Arabic-speaking Muslim students. The students had been refugees. They had been through traumatic experiences and had needs well beyond learning English and succeeding academically. Many of the parents had also been traumatized and were having difficulty adjusting to life in this country.

This large school had one Arabic-speaking resource person who was helping all the Arabic-speaking parents and students on a part-time basis. Although she meant well and wanted to help everyone, her only preparation for the job was that she spoke Arabic, had a Muslim background herself, and had finished high school in her country. She had no background in counseling and no preparation in bilingual education.

The school, desperate for someone who could communicate with the parents and students, hired her. She was given many responsibilities, including counseling students and placing them in appropriate classes as well as working with parents. The principal was relieved to have found her and gave her decision-making authority that should only have been given to a credentialed educator. A better approach would have been to conduct a search for someone with both the language skills and the professional training for the position.

Provide an On-Site Specialist for Dual Language Teacher Support

Principals and district-level administrators are extremely busy and attend to many different kinds of issues from finance, to discipline, to personnel issues. Although they should support dual language and understand it, by themselves some administrators cannot provide teachers with guidance for the day-to-day implementation of dual language in their classrooms. For this reason, there should be a designated dual language specialist on the school site to work with teachers.

For example, in Spring Branch Independent School District (ISD), Karina, who got her MA in bilingual education and was an excellent dual language teacher, recently became a vice principal at her dual language school, Pine Shadows Elementary, in the Spring Branch ISD. Her former co-teacher is now a literacy specialist for other teachers. With their practical expertise as well as Karina's academic background, both are now able to provide dual language teachers at her new school support in planning, program implementation, and lesson delivery.

In some districts, there is an ELL specialist who may work with one or several schools. This specialist can help teachers in a dual language program with strategies for second language teaching. However, an ELL specialist may not have expertise in bilingual education and with strategies for bilingual classes, so a better option is to have a dual language specialist. This person should be able to model lessons in two languages and support teachers in either teaching English or teaching the other program language to bilinguals. Whatever model of support is available, there should be someone who can provide regular support to dual language teachers and help monitor the program.

Highland Park High School (HPHS) has a full-time English language development/dual language (EL/DL) coordinator on site. His job is to organize the English as a second language and the dual language programs, advocate for student/family needs, and provide professional development to all HPHS staff members about how to support the language, academic, and socioemotional needs of bilinguals. This position is an official administrative assignment. As Tom, the principal, explains, "The EL coordinator is an official administrative position who sits on our school's Administrative Council with other department chairs and school directors. The coordinator also supervises and evaluates EL/DL teachers." In addition to the coordinator, HPHS is adding instructional coaches who must be skilled in supporting EL/DL students in classrooms, freeing the coordinator to work with teachers to meet the needs of all their students.

Although the EL/DL coordinator at HPHS has important responsibilities in the program, Tom explains that his role as principal is key:

> It is critical that the building principal be an active proponent of dual language education and be conversant in the unique needs that these programs present to a school. At HPHS, the principal leads a weekly "dual language Friday" meeting, where the EL/DL coordinator, as well as the assistant principals, gather for ninety minutes to discuss the state of our dual language program, identify areas that need support, and plan school-wide professional development for the program.

In schools where no one supports them, dual language teachers often find themselves isolated and may adopt teaching practices that are not consistent with the program model that has been adopted.

Provide and Participate in Ongoing Professional Development Through Consultants, School Visits, and Conferences

Professional development is an important component in the implementation and development of any dual language program. The model developed for New Caney Independent School District near Houston, Texas, offers a good example of effective professional development. Sandra Mercuri works directly with Dr. Pascual Yacovodonato, the District's director of bilingual, ELL, and migrant students. The model that Sandra has developed with Pascual works well because all those responsible for the dual language strands in the district's ten elementary schools receive support.

Before starting professional development sessions, Sandra and Pascual meet with the district's curriculum team to align their work in implementing dual language with other district initiatives. Sandra offers three types of professional development sessions: one for teachers, one for ELL/bilingual specialists and team leaders, and one for administrators. For teachers, she focuses on different strategies and the theory behind effective dual language practice. With specialists and dual language team leaders, Sandra presents the same content as in the sessions for teachers but also includes discussion about how to coach teachers in implementing the strategies. In the sessions with administrators—principals and assistant principals—Sandra provides background on what the teachers and specialists and team leaders have been working on, to promote a common language among the groups. A key goal of these sessions is to ensure that administrators use what Sandra refers to as "a dual language eye" when they observe classroom strategies teachers use or when they evaluate environmental print around the room. Administrators are thus able to en-

Long-Term Professional Development

Principal Jeff Post explains how he provides professional development for the teachers in his dual language programs, especially through consultants who work long-term with the administration and the teachers.

Supporting Professional Development for Teachers

Principal Vivian Pratts explains how she supports her teachers through professional learning communities, collaborative planning, conferences, and consultants.

sure that teachers are implementing effective practices in developing language and content in both languages.

Pascual also provides opportunities for Sandra to visit dual language classrooms and coach teachers directly. These visits are done in teams that include the director, the ELL specialists serving the school, and the consultant. During the debriefing with the teachers, all members of the team are present. In this way, they can also contribute to the discussion. For the specialists the debriefing is a modeling session on how to coach teachers for dual language implementation. In some schools, administrators also come to the observation, debriefing, and coaching sessions. This practice will continue to be encouraged to ensure long-term change and success.

At Highland High School Tom ensures that his faculty are given multiple opportunities for professional development. For example, Cheryl Urow, an education specialist from the Illinois Resource Center, provided a "Teaching for Biliteracy" workshop based on the book she co-authored with Karen Beeman, *Teaching for Biliteracy: Strengthening Bridges Between Languages* (Beeman and Urow 2013) for all the staff. The workshop had representatives from every department in the school attending. As Tom explained, "Having a large portion of the staff experience these types of trainings together is crucial for helping to get a critical mass established that you can build off of."

Supporting school visits is another powerful way that principals and district-level personnel can support dual language programs. Successful dual language programs can serve as models for schools that are just beginning a program or are looking for ways to improve one. It is especially important that principals and other administrators as well as bilingual specialists and teachers participate in these visits. When a principal can observe firsthand how another principal is supporting a dual language program, it serves as an inspiration as well as an example. Talking with other administrators and asking questions at the school site of a successful program can help principals or even a district superintendent understand what needs to be done to create a successful program at home.

Conferences can serve as professional development too. The conference should be carefully chosen, and principals and other administrators should attend along with teachers. The principal of the Omaha, Nebraska, dual language program we discussed earlier found funds to have a teacher at each grade level in his dual language program attend the national La Cosecha dual language conference. He also attended along with his school dual language specialist.

Before the conference, the principal and his specialist reviewed the conference program with the teachers. One person was assigned to each session that had the potential of informing the group. Each day the entire group met at lunch and dinner and shared what they had learned. Attending this conference served as excellent professional development for all who participated and was the beginning of the formation of a team at the school who became advocates and leaders for the dual language program.

Besides the staff development sessions that Tom supports on his campus, he and his team look for professional development opportunities across the state and nation. Tom's faculty follows a procedure similar to that of the Omaha group when they attend conferences. Tom commented:

> Each year we send a team of 4–10 staff members to La Cosecha. Our staff members are strategic when they visit a conference. They set specific areas of focus, and they meet to share what they have learned. Upon returning to school, staff will share the information they have learned with others.

Provide Books and Other Resources in Both Languages

A good administrative team also makes sure that teachers are provided with the necessary resources. Too often the resources in English are adequate, but there are not enough appropriate resources in the second language. As we discussed earlier, this not only limits learning in the minority language but also sends students the message that English is the valued language. For example, schools should have equal numbers of DVDs, CDs, and books in English and in the second language of the program, and the books should be equally attractive. If English books are glossy hardbacks and the second language materials are black-and-white photocopies, students get the message that the school does not value languages other than English.

A principal who started a Spanish/English dual language program in the Midwest was committed to giving students access to equitable materials in both Spanish and English. He wrote grants with his bilingual specialist to specifically fund a bilingual resource center at his school. The specialist worked with teachers to identify the topics of curriculum units in social studies, science, and language arts. Then, at meetings they looked together to find and order materials that would support those units of study in both English and Spanish. These were organized into thematic packets, and a library assistant was assigned to help teachers locate materials they needed for different content area subjects. In addition to these book sets, the principal directed the bilingual specialist to build a library of big books in Spanish that was comparable to the large numbers of big books the school already had in English.

In an MA-level course on biliteracy that both Sandra and Yvonne taught for dual language teachers, they asked teachers to work in groups to create a unit of study and support it with a variety of literature and content books in Spanish. They encouraged the teachers to use online resources as well. When teachers presented their units of study on topics like *Reciclaje* (Recycling), *La selva tropical* (The Tropical Rain Forest), *Los Organismos y como los organismos dependen uno del otro* (Organisms and How They Depend Upon One Another), *Tejas en el pasado* (Texas and Its Past), and *Mitos y leyendas* (Myths and Legends), they shared rich resources including literature and content books, magazine articles, and songs and readings taken from online sites. These projects showed the teachers that there are resources available, but almost all of them reported to their professors that for their everyday teaching they rarely have time to find these resources, and the schools where they teach have not gathered or organized the resources.

Although there are many books, DVDs, and other resources available in Spanish, it is more difficult to find materials in other languages, such as Chinese, Arabic, or Korean. In these cases, administrators need to make special efforts to search out materials. One approach is to locate other dual language schools with the same non-English language and share ideas and sources for finding books and other materials. Through networking, schools with Chinese/English or Korean/English programs can pool resources to improve and make available the quantity and quality of books and other materials, including those found online. The search for materials should

Providing Resources in Both Languages

Principal Vivian Pratts explains how she acquires funding and finds resources in both languages.

begin when the program is being developed, because without adequate resources, it is difficult for teachers to build a rich curriculum.

Provide Time for Teachers to Plan Together

To be effective, all teachers need time to plan. In dual language this is doubly true. In dual language programs with one teacher for each language, those teacher teams need a regular time for weekly planning. In addition, they need at least a brief time each day to check with their partner. In programs where a bilingual teacher teaches both languages, there still needs to be time for that teacher to meet with others at the same grade level to ensure that there is consistency in curriculum across the grade level.

Dual language teachers need to review content standards for their grade level and plan units of study that meet the needs of their students learning academic content and literacy in two languages. Principals of dual language programs should provide weekly time for teachers to meet. One strategy is to provide an early release schedule so teachers can meet in pairs or teams to plan together. However, too often this time is used to have teachers attend trainings or mandatory meetings. Administrators need to prioritize and protect planning time. When bilingual specialists or consultants can be available to support the planning, the time is most efficiently used.

Administrators can also help teachers find the time they need for collaboration by providing release time during scheduled inservice days when students are not there or by providing substitutes so groups of teachers can work together. Some very creative administrators occasionally arrange the school schedule so that different groups of teachers can meet while students go to their specials (P.E., music, art, and the computer lab).

In New Caney ISD, a district we discussed earlier, curriculum is planned with teachers and administrators working together. Pascual worked with Sandra, their

Providing Time for Teachers to Plan Together

Principal Jeff Post explains how he provides time for teachers to plan both vertically and horizontally.

dual language district consultant, to develop planning guides for grades kindergarten and 1. Then the kindergarten and first-grade dual language teachers, with support from Pascual and Sandra, began using the guides to write integrated lesson plans. Now the second-grade planning guides are being completed, and the plan is for the third-grade dual language teachers to develop planning guides for next year. Pascual continues to support his teachers as they carry out this important work for the dual language program. Without administrative support, teachers could not complete this important task. Providing planning and problem-solving time is important and is one way that administrators can show teachers they are valued.

Tom, the high school principal, explains how he has organized planning for his dual language program:

> Our school has a weekly collaboration time that teachers use to plan. We have found, however, that it is necessary for us to offer quarterly retreats where the dual language teachers in different subjects are able to meet with one another to discuss content and language objectives. We provide the teachers a substitute, and they take a professional development day to work together on curriculum coordination.

When administrators like Pascual and Tom schedule regular times for short- and long-term planning, teachers can develop and deliver a consistent and well-thought-out curriculum to their students.

Monitor to Ensure Consistent Planning, Curriculum Implementation, and Classroom Organization

Administrators play an important role in monitoring all aspects of a dual language program to ensure consistency throughout the program. Dual language programs must follow a curriculum that is consistent with bilingual education theory and best practices and that all teachers understand and can implement in their classrooms. Because dual language programs require teachers to apply specific strategies and to teach both language and content in classrooms where about half the students are learning in a second language, it is critical that principals understand what to look for when they observe classrooms, give feedback, and provide support to help teachers follow best practices. Because principals have many responsibilities, bilingual resource specialists or consultants can help fill this role and provide the support that ensures a dual language program is consistently implemented.

Soltero (2016) points out that teachers need mentors and instructional support. She encourages peer observations so that teachers can learn from one another, and she explains that there should be someone to help teachers as they plan. Teachers also need help in finding appropriate ways to assess students. When teachers have questions, they need someone to ask. Although a consultant can assist with many of these things, there needs to be a person at the school site to work with teachers consistently on these and other issues. A bilingual resource specialist can fill this administrative role.

Provide Positive Feedback

Everyone involved in a dual language program works hard and gives extra time and effort. Excellent administrators find several different ways to positively reinforce the good work that their teachers and other staff members are doing. The administrators compliment the staff members publicly in many settings, including at faculty meetings, school board meetings, parent meetings, or meetings with community members and university faculty. Some administrators write notes to teachers who have made an extra effort. When reporters from local newspapers come to gather information about the dual language program, good administrators make sure that the teachers are also interviewed and featured. However, perhaps the most meaningful support comes from daily encouragement that includes details about specific things that the administrator has noticed teachers and specialists doing.

Vivian, the principal of Edgewood Elementary School, a one-way dual language school in Spring Branch, Texas, is much beloved, and for good reason. She finds ways to show how much she appreciates her teachers every day. She encourages them, supports them when they need something, and knows about their personal needs and concerns.

She often shows her caring with food, providing lunch for everyone after faculty and staff have worked especially hard on some project. Birthdays are celebrated by sharing a cake, and when visitors come to campus, Vivian compliments teachers as she brings visitors into their classrooms and points out projects students are involved in and the excellent work the teacher is doing. She shows her teachers that she notices their efforts and that she appreciates them.

Monitoring in a Dual Language Program

Principal Vivian Pratts discusses how she monitors her OWDL program.

Monitoring in a Dual Language Program

Principal Jeff Post describes how his team at Cedar Brook Elementary monitors and evaluates their dual language programs using a set of non-negotiables.

Of course, it is not only teachers and resource specialists who need support. When administrators compliment clerical and custodial staff and occasionally take them to lunch, these staff members feel appreciated too. They come to see their work as critical and take a personal pride in the dual language program. The atmosphere that they help create is evident when anyone enters the school.

Finally, and perhaps most important, good administrators encourage the students in the school. They take an interest in the students, both native English speakers and native speakers of other languages. Rather than simply disciplining students when they catch them doing something wrong, good administrators take the time to talk to and joke with students informally in the halls or at school events, such as fairs and sports events. They learn students' names and learn something about their personal lives. This is especially important in dual language programs because students need to feel their program is special and that they are the key to making it that way.

One particularly poignant example comes from a now retired principal at a dual language school on the Texas/Mexican border. This was a 100 percent free lunch school because of the poverty of the area. In Texas, there is strong emphasis on standardized tests. Third-grade testing is especially critical. The third-grade teachers and students had worked on test-taking strategies and everyone was nervous on test day.

The principal brought the students gifts that she had bought using her own money. Every third-grade child received a stuffed animal to hug as he or she took the test. The principal explained to the children that she knew they had worked hard, and she wanted to show them that she knew they were all going to do the best they could. She appreciated their hard work, and she had confidence that they would do well. In fact, the students did very well, and on the day the results came in, to show her appreciation for all their hard work, the principal treated all the teachers to lunch!

Everyone in effective dual language schools works hard and is dedicated to what he or she is doing. But because there is so much to do, to understand, and to keep track of, people can get discouraged. Administrators must also be the cheerleaders, the people who show that every person's hard work is appreciated. When teachers, staff, and students know their work is valued, they work harder and do so willingly.

Administrator/Teacher Collaboration Essentials

As the section on the essentials for administrators makes clear, administrators must support teachers in every possible way. This, however, can only happen in a situation where the administrator and teachers collaborate to implement the program, respond to parents, and promote the program. In well-implemented dual language programs, administrators and teachers form a team that is focused on the academic success of the students. Listed below are essentials for administrators and teachers in dual language programs.

- **Collaborate for consistency in the dual language program**
- **Respond to parental concerns and needs**
- **Include parents from both language groups in program planning and implementation**
- **Promote the dual language program to parents, the school board, and the community**
- **Display a passion for the program, the students, and the families**

Collaborate for Consistency in the Dual Language Program

First, it is crucial in any school that administrators and teachers work together to plan and implement a consistent program. This requires a unified approach to curriculum development and literacy teaching. In addition dual language school administrators and teachers need to collaborate to make decisions about changes in how the two languages are allocated. The following sections provide examples of how teachers and administrators can work for consistency in dual language programs.

Cedar Brook Elementary ◆ In Chapters 1 and 3, we gave examples from Jeff, the principal at Cedar Brook School in Spring Branch, Texas. Jeff's school has both a one-way and a two-way dual language program. He explained that he and the teachers collaborate at the campus level as they meet in teams to determine their needs, goals, and opportunities for making improvements. He wrote, "Over the past seven years, I have met with campus leaders, dual language teachers, district directors, parents, and consultants to receive feedback on best practices for implementation of both one-way and two-way DL programs."

Jeff reported on some examples of how he worked collaboratively with teachers and others to improve the dual language programs at his school. The one-way program at his school is a 50/50 model with different subjects taught in each language. Three years ago, principals were given the option to change the language of instruction for specific subjects in the one-way program to increase English language development. Jeff worked with his teachers to develop a plan for the language of instruction that would meet the needs of both teachers and students. In this program, language arts is taught primarily in Spanish, but to increase English proficiency, thirty minutes of English language arts was added starting in second grade. This was a decision made jointly by Jeff and the teachers.

In the two-way 90/10 dual program, Jeff and his teachers decided that because science was being taught in English, the students needed exposure to science content vocabulary in both Spanish and English, so they continued to teach science in English for kindergarten and first grade and then teach science in Spanish in second and third and in English again in fourth and fifth. Jeff commented that he and the teachers felt that this would prepare the students better for middle school science, which is taught in Spanish in the district's two-way programs. These decisions were made collaboratively to meet the needs of both the teachers and the students at Cedar Brook.

Consistency extends beyond general program planning. Dual language schools often develop a list of nonnegotiables for classroom practices that all teachers follow. Jeff listed a number of nonnegotiables that he and his teachers at Cedar Brook have agreed on. See the following list.

Cedar Brook Nonnegotiables

- Organize bilingual pairs.
- Implement preview/view/review to avoid concurrent translation.
- Color-code environmental print using blue for English and red for Spanish.
- Ensure students have access to text/literature in both languages.
- Use sentence stems in all content areas to facilitate oral and written response.

Administrators Support Teachers

Principal Jeff Post explains how he supports the teachers personally and professionally at his school.

- Mirror classrooms when appropriate.
- Create sight word walls in Spanish and English.
- Post word banks to include cognates.
- Provide visual supports such as anchor charts.
- Display student work samples in both languages.
- Develop and post content and language objectives for multiple content areas.

This is an extensive list, and Jeff noted that they are further along on consistent implementation of some nonnegotiables than others, but they are working toward mastery every day.

Edgewood Elementary ◗ Edgewood Elementary is the one-way dual language school in Spring Branch ISD where Vivian is the principal. Sandra worked as a dual language consultant with Vivian and teachers to revise the one-way 50/50 program to include more English literacy in early grades. First, Vivian, Sandra, and the teachers created a new schedule for the pre-K to grade 2 classes so that teachers could provide language arts in both languages rather than only in Spanish. See Figure 4.1. In this schedule they alternated language arts and social studies in Spanish and English in the mornings with English instruction in these subjects on Tuesdays and Thursdays and Spanish instruction Monday, Wednesday, and Friday. They also incorporated some language arts in English with science in the afternoons.

After the first semester of implementation teachers found the revised schedule too hard to follow. Vivian and Sandra then met with the teachers to discuss the advantages and disadvantages of the new plan. The teachers said they were familiar

	Monday	Tuesday	Wednesday	Thursday	Friday
7:35–7:45	10 Announcements	10 Announcements	10 Announcements	10 Announcements	10 Announcements
7:45–8:00	15 Community Circle	15 Community Circle	15 Community Circle	15 Community Circle	15 Community Circle
8:00–8:45	45 Language Arts/SS	45 Language Arts/SS	45 Language Arts/SS	45 Language Arts/SS	45 Language Arts/SS
8:45–9:35	50 Specials	50 Specials	50 Specials	50 Specials	50 Specials
9:35–10:45	70 Language Arts/ SS cont.	70 Language Arts/ SS cont.	70 Language Arts/ SS cont.	70 Language Arts/ SS cont.	70 Language Arts/ SS cont.
10:45–11:10	25 Math	25 Math	25 Math	25 Math	25 Math
	35 *Lunch*	35 *Lunch*	35 *Lunch*	35 *Lunch*	35 *Lunch*
	30 *Recess*	30 *Recess*	30 *Recess*	30 *Recess*	30 *Recess*
12:10–1:15	65 Math	70 Math	65 Math	70 Math	65 Math
1:15–2:00	45 Science/LA	55 Science/LA	45 Science/LA	55 Science/LA	45 Science/LA
2:00–2:15	15 Metalinguistic Awareness		15 Metalinguistic Awareness		15 Metalinguistic Awareness

Figure 4.1 Revised Edgewood K–2 Schedule in September 2016   KEY: Spanish ☐ English ▨

with the research on simultaneous biliteracy, that they could develop more metalinguistic awareness, but the main disadvantages that teachers voiced were that there would be too many switches between languages and that they did not have time to organize units of study and organize resources. Edgewood teachers Gladys Baez, Marietta Del Riego, and Yadira Roel expressed their concerns in the following way:

> We used this schedule at the beginning of the year, but we stopped using it because it was difficult for us to plan and implement. It was hard to follow it accurately, because we did not get used to alternating every day. In addition, although our school has enough resources, we had a difficult time collecting particular resources and materials we needed in both languages every week. It was difficult to maintain a sequence in our delivery of instruction.

Together, Vivian, Sandra, and the teachers listed their needs. They would need to adjust to the new framework, use everyone's expertise, ensure fidelity to the 50/50 model, and develop a plan for how to implement the plan. To do this, they would need more training on language support and language development practices, such

	Monday	Tuesday	Wednesday	Thursday	Friday
7:35–7:45	Announcements	Announcements	Announcements	Announcements	Announcements
7:45–8:00	15 Community Circle	15 Community Circle	15 Community Circle	15 Community Circle	15 Community Circle
8:00–8:45	45 Language Arts/ SS	45 Language Arts/ SS	45 Language Arts/ SS	45 Language Arts/ SS	45 Language Arts/ SS
8:45–9:35	Specials	Specials	Specials	Specials	Specials
9:35–10:45	70 Language Arts/ SS cont.	70 Language Arts/ SS cont.	70 Language Arts/ SS cont.	70 Language Arts/ SS cont.	70 Language Arts/ SS cont.
10:45–11:00	15 Metalinguistic Awareness/Oral Language	15 Metalinguistic Awareness/Oral Language	15 Metalinguistic Awareness/Oral Language	15 Metalinguistic Awareness/Oral Language	15 Metalinguistic Awareness/Oral Language
11:00–11:10	10 Math/LA	10 Math/LA	10 Math/LA	10 Math/LA	10 Math/LA
	35 *Lunch*	35 *Lunch*	35 *Lunch*	35 *Lunch*	35 *Lunch*
	30 *Recess*	30 *Recess*	30 *Recess*	30 *Recess*	30 *Recess*
12:10–1:30	80 Math Content	80 Math Content	80 Math Content	80 Math Content	80 Math Content
1:30–2:15	45 Science/LA	45 Science/LA	45 Science/LA	45 Science/LA	45 Science/LA

Figure 4.2 Re-revised Edgewood K–2 Schedule in November 2016   KEY: Spanish ☐ English ▨

as preview/view/review and bridging across languages. They also would need access to additional online resources. Following this meeting, Vivian, Sandra, and the teachers revised the framework for instruction and made clear plans for how they would implement it. This involved planning units and collecting resources. The revised plan included the integration of English language arts in both math and science. The teachers are currently developing interdisciplinary units of inquiry based on the new framework, still true to the program model, but adjusted to the needs of the teachers and the students. See Figure 4.2.

As this example shows, administrators, consultants, and teachers need to work together over time to make adjustments to curriculum plans so that an effective curriculum can be implemented consistently.

A Rural Dual Language School ◆ A final example of collaboration for consistency comes from a rural border dual language school where we did research and also supervised student teachers. The school had a 100 percent Hispanic student body as well as teaching staff and administration. In addition, 100 percent of the students qualified for free lunch and breakfast. All the teachers and administrators were committed to helping their students succeed and were committed to the one-way dual language program at the school.

Planning days were provided at the school so that teachers could do horizontal planning across classes at each grade level and vertical planning across grade levels. This planning ensured that curriculum was coordinated across and within grade levels. Faculty and administration also met together to problem solve. When a teacher noticed that ten third-grade students were not doing well on standardized tests in English, the principal called a meeting of the kindergarten and first-grade teachers to study the cumulative folders of those children to determine whether early instruction and support was lacking. They asked us as university faculty, the region's bilingual director, and student teachers assigned to the school to be part of that meeting. They invited everyone to give input.

A review of student records showed that the struggling students had not received adequate literacy development in Spanish before starting their English literacy program. Throughout the meeting, the principal insisted that the problem had to be solved. She admitted, "We haven't always done things correctly, but that is going to change." The group decided to increase the number of sections of Spanish literacy instruction at the school. The administrative team also sat down with third-grade teachers and discussed with them concerns about the academic Spanish of the third graders. They all talked together about how to support students to give them access to grade-level Spanish content in the core subjects.

Several teachers at different grade levels were asked to provide tutoring to the struggling students. These tutoring sessions supported these students in reading in their home language, Spanish, as well as in English. As a result of these extra sessions, the students made remarkable progress. Through this kind of collaboration between administrators and teachers, the program was strengthened and support for students was provided more consistently.

Respond to Parental Concerns and Needs

A second essential for both administrators and teachers is that they should respond immediately to parent concerns. For example, a first-grade student whose home language is English and who is in a 90/10 two-way program where most of the instruction is in Spanish may feel overwhelmed and may tell his parents he doesn't like school or doesn't want to attend any more. When these parents come to the school, both administrators and teachers need to explain the rationale for the program and the steps that are being taken to help make the instruction understandable for the student.

At the rural border school we described above, a room at the school was reserved specifically for parent workshops and meetings with parents. Parents could come to this room at any time to have coffee and talk over any problems their children were having. The principal realized that many parents lacked the benefits of schooling themselves and needed help with parenting. She provided workshops for parents with a skilled bilingual facilitator who helped parents develop parenting skills through role-plays and examples that were relevant to them.

At one school in Washington, English-speaking parents of several kindergarten and first-grade students came to school because they were concerned that their children did not like school and felt lost. The principal and the teachers met with the parents, and it was determined that the teachers would send home a weekly newsletter in English explaining what they would be teaching in Spanish the following week. For example, if the students were studying magnets, the teachers explained the activities they had planned for the children. They also included in the newsletter a few key words in Spanish and English that they would use including words like *imán* (magnet), *atraer* (attract), and *repeler* (repel). In this way, English-speaking parents could explain to their children what they would be doing in school before they engaged in the activities. Teachers also included the topics of books they would be reading so parents could read books to their children on those topics or discuss those topics with their children in English. In this way, parents could provide a kind of preview for their children and help them with the Spanish instruction.

Like the dual language school in Washington, other districts have found that sending home information to parents is valuable. A school district just outside San Antonio, Texas, makes it a point to send assignments home in both Spanish and English to dual language parents. In addition, they publish a monthly newsletter for families in both languages, highlighting accomplishments of students in both languages.

Spanish-speaking parents may be concerned because they believe the acquisition of English is important for their children to succeed academically, and they can't understand why the teacher is using so much Spanish. Administrators and teachers must be able to explain why the development of the students' home language promotes the acquisition of English and academic competence. They need to find ways to explain this because it seems logical that more English would result in faster acquisition of English. And they need to provide an explanation that is clear and not too theoretical. It is particularly helpful if they can point to specific examples of English

Responding to Parents' Concerns

Principal Vivian Pratts explains how she responds to Spanish-speaking parents' concerns about their children learning English in a OWDL program.

Responding to Concerns of English-Speaking Parents in TWDL

Principal Jeff Post discusses how he and the teachers respond to concerns of English-speaking parents of students in the TWDL program.

Promoting a One-Way Dual Language Program to Spanish-Speaking Parents

Principal Vivian Pratts discusses how she meets with Spanish-speaking parents who do not want to enroll in the OWDL program and explains to them the benefits of bilingualism for their children.

learners who have succeeded and are proficient in English because their first language was well-developed. Administrators and teachers must work together to meet these concerns and to present a unified message to parents.

Jeff and the teachers at Cedar Brook respond to parent concerns in needs in several ways. Jeff commented:

> Parents will often have concerns that need to be addressed when their students are part
> of a dual language program. This usually occurs when a student struggles with learning

> a second language and the parents don't have the resources to help. Through Dual Language Parent Orientations, we share pertinent information and resources and also encourage parents to reach out to teachers on a regular basis with questions and to receive support. We also meet in parent-teacher conferences to respond to individual needs.

Having dual language parent orientations and encouraging parents to reach out to teachers on a regular basis with questions are two ways that Jeff and the teachers at Cedar Brook respond effectively to parent concerns and needs.

Include Parents from Both Language Groups in Program Planning and Implementation

In addition to responding to parents' concerns, administrators and teachers should work together to include parents from both language groups in program planning and implementation. At Cedar Brook both Spanish-speaking and English-speaking parents are involved in different ways as the program develops. There are monthly parent coffees. During these meetings Jeff and the teachers share news about the program and respond to questions from parents. Both Spanish-speaking and English-speaking parents participate in these meetings. Jeff noted that many of the two-way parents have been a part of the Campus Improvement Team over the years and have provided feedback that has helped the school make positive changes.

Parents' concerns are allayed when they are involved in program development and implementation. It is important for parents from both language groups to be equally involved and to have an equal say in program decisions. Otherwise, they may not understand and support the program. The greatest success occurs when bilingual administrators and teachers conduct the meetings bilingually rather than directing the meeting using English and then having the information translated for parents of students who speak languages other than English.

It is important that one language not be privileged over the other. In some cases, schools have held separate meetings for the two language groups, but this can lead to misunderstandings. The goal is for parents from both groups to have equal opportunities for input, and this can best be done by bringing the two groups together so they can learn to work together to build a program that benefits the children from both groups.

Promote the Dual Language Program to Parents, the School Board, and the Community

Parent meetings should also include school board members and other community members. These are opportunities to explain and promote the program. When all the stakeholders are involved, there is a much better chance that the program will succeed and will be sustained as it is implemented and developed. By show-ing that bilingual dual language programs are the best educational model for both language-majority and language-minority students, administrators and teachers can build the support they need to establish a successful program.

Cedar Brook promotes their dual language programs in many ways. The dual language programs at Cedar Brook are open to students from any attendance zone in the district. For this reason, school personnel spend time promoting this choice program as an opportunity for parents. Jeff wrote:

> We create a flier early in the fall to advertise campus tours and site visits, orientation sessions, and our district's Choice Festival. Parents are encouraged to complete the Common Application online and follow the timeline to participate in our campus lot-tery the following spring. We also make sure to send out emails, make phone calls, and post messages on Twitter to remind parents and get the word out about our school's language program.

In addition, Jeff has found ways to inform school board members and the district superintendent about the program. He explained:

> Each year I host tours of Cedar Brook Elementary with one or more board members. During this time, I share with them the great things that are happening in our school regarding second language acquisition. I take them on classroom visits and answer any questions they may have. Also during the year the superintendent connects with staff members for a "state of the district" address during one of our faculty meetings. Before the meeting I send him highlights of the best practices occurring on campus, many dealing directly with our dual language programs. In this way we stay connected with and provide updates to our board of trustees and superintendent.

Like Jeff, Tom, the Illinois high school principal, works to promote his program with the school board. He described what he does at his school:

> We have worked very hard to help our school board understand the importance of our dual language program to our overall student achievement. It is very easy for educators, let alone lay people, to think that dual language is only about language acquisition. We have been explicit that dual language is so much more than language; it is about a child's identity, culture, and overall academic achievement. In the past two years we have made three presentations to our board of education about elements of our dual language pro-gram. In addition, in my reports to the board, I frequently highlight different parts of our dual language program so that the board members know this program exists as a unique, and wonderfully successful, aspect of our school. Finally, we have invited our board of education members to observe some of our dual language classes so that they can see firsthand the power these programs have upon our students.

Promoting the Dual Language Program

Principal Jeff Post describes how he works to promote the dual language programs at Cedar Brook Elementary to recruit students.

Pine Shadows Elementary School, which is in Spring Branch ISD, also promotes the dual language program to parents. Karina, a vice principal, explained to us that this year there were four parent orientation events and that the school hosted the district School of Choice event so that parents could chose Pine Shadows Elementary's dual language program if interested. Parents are shown an informational PowerPoint that includes the two-way dual language program's expectations for parents, the difference between a 50/50 and a 90/10 model, and key points about second language acquisition. After the presentation, parents who have had a child in the program talk about their experience in the school and the two-way dual language program. At each orientation parents are given a school tour and classroom visits in different grades so parents can see how the program looks at different grade levels. As Karina told us, "This has been a great way to promote not just the program but also the school."

Display a Passion for the Program, the Students, and the Families

Dual language programs are a departure from the norm for schooling both language-majority and language-minority students. Most schools provide all English instruction for students who meet proficiency standards in English. Schools also offer bilinguals specialized programs, such as English language development, structured English immersion, or transitional bilingual programs. However, the idea of offering a long-term bilingual education program for all students with the goal of developing high levels of bilingualism, biliteracy, and cross-cultural understanding is new to many teachers, administrators, parents, and community members.

For a bilingual dual language program to succeed, the administrators and faculty and staff must share their enthusiasm for the program with both the students in the program and their families. Students may be confused about why they are being instructed for at least part of the day in a language that is new to them. Parents whose home language is English may need to be convinced that the dual language program will help their children achieve high levels of academic proficiency in two languages and that the time spent acquiring Spanish or Mandarin or some other language is not time taken away from learning academic content and academic English. Parents whose home language is not English must be convinced that their children will learn English and will be successful academically, even when instruction for part of the day is not given in English.

It is common for administrators and teachers to have informational meetings to recruit students and then to orient parents and students new to dual language. However, in addition, at a minimum there should be a meeting at the beginning of every school year to inform parents about recent trends and research in dual language education and to remind parents of their commitment to dual language for their children. For example, translanguaging and its role might be explained to parents with examples of how it is used to draw on their children's full linguistic repertoires. In addition, a reminder could be given to parents that developing biliteracy takes time and patience. Administrators might also suggest that parents should look for opportunities for students to practice and use the second language outside of school, providing some suggestions such as participating in community special events, visiting grocery stores in different neighborhoods, watching engaging videos in the second language, or checking out books in the other language at the public library.

In whatever settings where administrators and teachers meet with parents and community members, they have to go beyond logical explanations and show their own conviction and passion for the dual program. When this commitment is clear, enthusiasm spreads through the school and to the community the school serves.

Vivian Pratts and her faculty at Edgewood Elementary School provide a good example of displaying a passion for the program, the students, and the families. In the spring of 2016, Vivian was chosen the district's elementary principal of the year by her peers. The criteria for the award include concern for all staff and students and the ability to inspire both of these groups, ability and willingness to work cooperatively with all staff and administrators, proven drive to initiate and implement effective strategies supporting continuous improvement in student performance, ability to work with diverse community groups and all district stakeholders, proven desire for continuous personal and professional growth, and ability and willingness to make meaningful contributions to education.

Vivian, who is completing a doctoral program in bilingual education, has continuously inspired her staff to work with her to develop the best dual language program possible. Together, she and her teachers have accomplished many things. The school has student academic success rates that are among the highest in the district. Vivian and the teachers work closely with parents and the surrounding community. She makes a point of showcasing the excellent work of both teachers and students. In all these ways, Vivian fulfills the criteria of the award. When interviewed, her comments show her passion and that of her teachers.

> I believe that when administrators take care of their teachers, the teachers will in turn do a great job meeting all the needs of their children and improving student achievement. Teachers and students inspire me. Their resiliency, passion and commitment make me want to give them 100 percent each and every day. (SBISD 2017)

Chapter Overview

In this chapter we discussed administrator and administrator-teacher collaboration essentials. When dual language programs incorporate these essential practices, the programs are more successful and can better meet the needs of all the students. Administrators are key to any school program. First, it is essential that administrators value and promote bilingualism. Knowledgeable administrators can take the lead in advocating for the program with district personnel, school boards, community members, parents, teachers, and students. This requires that administrators develop a good understanding of second language acquisition theory and bilingual theory and practice including new research.

It is also essential that some administrators and program specialists are bilingual. A bilingual administrator, even when his or her proficiency in the second language is low, has more credibility than a monolingual administrator of a bilingual program. Program specialists should have fairly high levels of proficiency in both languages to work well with parents and teachers. Every dual language program should have an on-site specialist who can provide teachers with the support they need. This person's main role should be to work with teachers to develop curriculum, find resources, and implement best practices for bilinguals.

Research on effective dual language programs and practices continually evolves. For that reason administrators should provide and participate in ongoing professional development for teachers and other support personnel. They can do this by bringing in consultants, making school visits, and attending conferences. It is especially important that administrators participate in this professional development so that they can better support their teachers as the teachers implement new strategies or develop new curriculum.

Dual language teachers need books, videos, and other resources in two languages to teach effectively. Administrators should provide these resources. They also need to provide time for teachers to plan together. In many dual language programs, there are pairs of teachers, one for each language, and these teachers need to plan together. Even when one teacher provides instruction in both languages, that teacher needs to have time for planning with other teachers on the grade-level team. Without a designated time for planning, teachers cannot deliver coordinated curriculum.

Finally, it is essential that administrators monitor to ensure consistent planning, curriculum implementation, and classroom organization. By monitoring the different aspects of the program, dual language administrators can help teachers use best practices. Although this may involve pointing out areas that need change, it is also important that administrators provide positive feedback and let teachers and other staff members know what they are doing well, not just what they need to improve on.

In addition to administrator essentials, we discussed several essentials that apply to administrators and teachers working together. These include collaborative planning for the development and implementation of all aspects of the program; building a good understanding of bilingual theory and research; working for consistency in program planning, classroom organization, and literacy instruction; responding to parent concerns; and finding ways to include parents in program planning. Furthermore, administrators and teachers should work together to promote the dual language program to parents, the school board, and the community. In addition, both administrators and teachers should display their passion for the dual language program and promote it with parents, the school board, and community members.

Reflect and Apply

1. Which of the administrator essentials do you consider to be most important? Provide an example of why this is so important. Is there another essential that you think should be added?

2. We have shared some of the positive things that Tom, Jeff, Pascual, Vivian, and other administrators have done to help their dual language programs succeed. Choose a couple of examples that impressed you and explain why you chose them, applying the examples to your own school or to a dual language school you are familiar with.

3. We described administrator and administrator-teacher collaboration essentials, giving examples at several different schools. What kinds of things that are being done at the schools we described would you like to see being done

in the dual language program where you teach or where you have observed? If you do not know a dual language school, visit one and then use what you learn to answer the question.

4. How do administrators and teachers in your school or in a school you have observed respond to parent concerns?

5. We said that one essential for teachers and administrators is to display a passion for the program, the students, and the families. What examples of this have you seen in your dual language school or in one you have visited?

Teacher Essentials

In this chapter we discuss several teacher essentials. Without well-prepared teachers, no bilingual dual language program can succeed. We begin by describing examples of the different kinds of teachers we have worked with or observed in dual language programs. Then we explain a series of essentials for any teacher in a dual language program.

Teachers in Dual Language Programs

Everywhere we have traveled across the country, administrators and specialists working in dual language programs have talked to us about the importance of finding quality teachers. Because all three authors have been involved in teacher preparation programs specializing in preparing dual language bilingual teachers, we are often approached by administrators eager to recruit our students. In many areas, the emergent bilingual population has grown rapidly, and there is community support for the establishment of dual language programs, but it is difficult to find qualified bilingual teachers.

Our own experience has been primarily with teachers and teacher candidates who speak Spanish, and because the overwhelming majority of dual language schools teach English and Spanish, we draw our examples from Spanish and English teachers in dual language programs. However, we recognize that there are also teachers with similar characteristics to the teachers we describe here who teach in Mandarin, Korean, French, and other dual language programs, and the characteristics of the teachers we describe here apply equally to teachers in programs where the language other than English is not Spanish.

In the following sections we describe several teachers who are currently teaching in or preparing to teach in Spanish/English dual language programs. Some of these are immigrants with academic language proficiency in Spanish. Others are teachers whose home language is Spanish but who lack academic Spanish proficiency. Some teachers in dual language programs teach the English side of the program. They have academic English proficiency and should have some competence in the language other than English taught in the program.

Before discussing teacher essentials, we give examples of these different types of teachers and also identify the supports they need to succeed. Because the teacher and the teacher's language proficiency are crucial to the success of any bilingual dual language program, those involved in establishing or maintaining programs need to carefully consider the characteristics of their teachers and the supports they need. Figure 5.1 lists characteristics of teachers in dual language bilingual programs.

Immigrants with Good Academic Preparation in Spanish

Immigrants whose home language is Spanish, who have been educated in their own country can provide a good model of academic Spanish. These immigrants come to the United States for a variety of reasons. Some come with family or to join family living here. Others come in search of fulfilling the American Dream. Still others arrive because they have married a U.S. citizen, or they come for other reasons and then marry here. Some are educators by profession, but many are not. Francisco, Juan Carlos, and Marcela serve as examples of immigrant teachers with good academic preparation in Spanish who are teaching or have taught in dual language classrooms.

Francisco ◖ Francisco came to the United States from El Salvador with his brother to reunite with his mother when he was fourteen. Although he was from a small

Teacher	Strengths	Challenges
Immigrants with academic language proficiency in Spanish	Academic language proficiency in Spanish	May need citizenship papers, work permits, or teacher certification May not be familiar with U.S. schools May have limited English proficiency
Teachers whose home language is Spanish who lack academic language proficiency in Spanish	May relate well to their bilingual students and may be familiar with U.S. schools	May lack academic proficiency in Spanish or English May have difficulty completing certification program
Teachers whose home language is English who have some proficiency in Spanish	May provide a strong model of academic English May show an interest in learning Spanish	May not be able to communicate with their Spanish-speaking students, especially at lower grades

Figure 5.1 Teachers in Dual Language Programs

village, he did attend a local rural school. He loved learning and developed a good level of academic Spanish. He was determined to get an education and a good job in the U.S.

Francisco went from a small rural school in El Salvador to a large inner-city high school in the United States where he was mostly lost. Although he had English as a second language (ESL) classes once a day, he struggled in the all-English classes most of the time. Because he was literate in Spanish and had a good academic background, he managed to get enough credits to graduate by studying hard. After high school, Francisco, who was an excellent soccer player, was recruited by a local private university and admitted provisionally.

The first year at the university was overwhelming. The reading load in English took him hours to get through, and he considered dropping out. Fortunately, his soccer coach visited his home and spoke to Francisco and his mother about the importance of persevering. With the help of counselors, tutoring, and English-speaking peers, he improved in all his coursework and graduated with a B average.

After graduation, Francisco entered the fifth-year teacher education program to become a bilingual teacher. Since then, he has taught first, second, and third grades in a transitional bilingual education program, English-only program, and dual language programs. He recently moved to the San Francisco Bay Area and is teaching third grade in a one-way dual language program. He continues to read books in Spanish to maintain his academic proficiency in the language. He loves his teaching and is especially committed to helping his Latino students see the importance of school and the power of being bilingual.

Juan Carlos ◆ Juan Carlos had always dreamed of becoming a teacher in the United States. He studied both music and elementary education pedagogy in Chile and taught there for fifteen years. When a pastor friend in California offered to sponsor him if Juan would lead the music ministry at his Spanish-speaking church, Juan Carlos jumped at the chance.

After four years, Juan Carlos was hired by the Los Angeles Unified School District to teach in Spanish in a first-grade dual language classroom in inner-city Watts. He had good success with his students, but his English was very limited, and he could not pass the exam for teacher credentialing in California.

However, Juan Carlos did not give up. He knew Spanish-speaking teachers were needed in this country. He found another ministry job in Omaha, Nebraska. Once in Nebraska, he explored the idea of teaching there. He found an advocate in the district ESL coordinator who needed fluent speakers of Spanish to teach in the newly begun dual language program. Juan Carlos got a provisional certificate and a contract in a dual language classroom. When passing state certification became a problem, district officials gave him release time to study and provided tutoring. Juan Carlos summarized his experiences:

> Challenges? Frustrations? Many!! The school district did their part and I really value and appreciate that, and I believe I did my part too. Teaching in the United States is an honor for me as a Latin American teacher. It is amazing the amount of resources available for teachers. My last memory as a teacher in Chile is forty-five students in my classroom, no paraprofessional, and a piece of chalk in my hand as the only supply.

Marcela ◆ Marcela was born in Colombia and educated at a university there where she received a degree in modern languages. After graduation, because of her English proficiency, she taught second grade at the American school in Bogotá for four years. She had always wanted to study in the United States so she applied to an elementary education program in Missouri where she had made some contacts from her work at the American school. After graduating from the teacher education program in Missouri, Marcela moved to California and completed an MA degree in teaching English to speakers of other languages. There she met her future husband.

After completing her MA, Marcela and her husband moved to Wichita, Kansas, where the school district was looking for bilingual teachers for a new dual language program. Although she was well prepared academically with degrees from two U.S. universities and had teaching experience in the American school in Bogotá, Marcela found the paperwork required to get her teaching credentials to be extremely complex. In addition to studying for and passing the state teachers' exam, she need-ed translated transcripts from Colombia and even letters from previous professors. After meeting all the requirements, she taught for several years in a dual language program in Wichita. When she and her husband decided to move to New Mexico, Marcela discovered that she would not meet the New Mexico state requirements for teacher credentialing. As a result, she returned to teaching in Wichita in a newcomer program.

Francisco, Juan Carlos, and Marcela had to overcome hurdles to teach in the United States. Their own learning experiences in their countries were with traditional teaching approaches, but here they were expected to teach using a student-centered approach. They faced difficulties in getting credentialed and passing exams for which they lacked background knowledge. Francisco and Juan Carlos had studied almost no English before coming to this country, so they struggled to pass coursework and take tests in English. Juan Carlos and Marcela had to do extra paperwork to meet creden-tialing requirements in the United States.

Considerations When Hiring Teachers from Outside the United States

Francisco, Juan Carlos, and Marcela provide examples of the challenges and adjust-ments immigrants make to teach in this country. When hiring teachers from other countries, administrators should consider a number of issues. The teaching approach in dual language must be learner centered and should be inquiry based. These ap-proaches are quite different from the past schooling experiences of many immigrant teachers. The relationship between teachers and students is also different in the United States from practices in other countries, and immigrant teachers may need help in adjusting to these differences. In addition, the entire school system is differ-ent. Newcomers need mentors to help them understand and adjust to a new way of teaching and learning.

Having these teachers teach in English can also be a consideration. At a recent bilingual conference, a dual language specialist approached Yvonne after she pre-sented a talk on translanguaging. The specialist explained she was struggling with the mentoring of a teacher recruited from Mexico who was constantly switching to Spanish during designated English math time. Although the specialist understood that translanguaging and using Spanish to scaffold instruction might be appropri-ate, the constant falling back into Spanish was not providing students with enough instruction in English. Both the specialist and Yvonne determined that the teacher's academic English in math was the issue. They discussed strategies for this teacher to be certain the students had understood such as using a preview in Spanish, a view where there were more hands-on activities and structured group work in English, and a review in Spanish. Another option would be to use another teacher for the math instruction. Although recruiting teachers for their academic Spanish ability can be useful, accommodations might need to be made if these teachers are also expected to teach in English.

There is one last concern that may arise when schools hire newcomer native Spanish speakers. Sometimes teachers recently from another country who come from upper-middle- to upper-class families in their native countries are not accustomed to working with children of lower socioeconomic status or with parents with little or no educational background. Those teachers need some sensitivity training to help them appreciate and value their students and empathize with them, their families, and their needs. This includes sensitivity to the variety of the language the children speak. It is important that the children learn academic Spanish, Mandarin, or Korean, but at the same time not be made to feel that the variety of that language they speak at home is inferior.

Teachers Whose Home Language Is Spanish Who Lack Academic Spanish

Francisco, Juan Carlos, and Marcela had all developed proficiency in academic Spanish. Although the road to good teaching positions in dual language programs was not smooth for them, their strong background in Spanish helped them succeed. However, some bilingual teachers and teacher candidates have developed conversational proficiency in Spanish but lack the academic Spanish proficiency they need to become successful teachers in a dual language program. Irma and Kari are good examples of teachers who lacked Spanish academic language proficiency.

Irma ◖ Irma came to the United States from Mexico when she was three. Her family moved to a farming community in California. She spoke only Spanish at home, so she entered kindergarten as a monolingual Spanish speaker. Irma lost most of her ability to communicate effectively in Spanish because she was schooled entirely in English. No supports for emergent bilinguals were provided during her early schooling, and Irma struggled through middle and high school as a long-term English learner. As she approached high school graduation, no one at her school encouraged her to further her education, so she went to work in the fields and later in a fruit-packing plant.

While working at the packing plant, she regained conversational Spanish by speaking Spanish with her coworkers. Because she had a high school diploma, Irma eventually applied to the local school district and became a bilingual aide. She related very well with the bilinguals in her class because her own experiences were so much like theirs. When she heard about a program designed to help bilingual para-professionals get their teaching credential, she decided to enroll in college. Although it took her several years, and she struggled academically, she eventually graduated from the local junior college, enrolled in the local university, and earned her BA degree.

Irma entered a teacher education program that prepared dual language teachers. She studied Spanish at the university and learned to read and write Spanish. She was not fluent, but she continued to refine her Spanish abilities by working with the bilingual students in her classroom.

Irma represents a large group of Spanish speakers in this country who have lost or nearly lost their first language. She developed conversational Spanish and some proficiency in academic Spanish, although her Spanish literacy skills were not strong. After being hired as a bilingual teacher, Irma still needed to work to improve her academic language proficiency in both Spanish and English. At the same time, she served as a good role model for her bilingual students because her background experiences were much like theirs.

Kari ◆ Kari, although of Latino background, grew up speaking only English in a middle-class neighborhood. Because she had relatives in Spain, she decided to study Spanish in high school and college. Her Spanish classes, however, focused on grammar and did not give her either the conversational or the academic Spanish she really wanted. Kari traveled twice to study in Barcelona, Spain, where her family members lived.

When she returned from her second trip, Kari decided that she wanted to teach emergent bilinguals and use the Spanish language she was regaining. Preparing herself to teach in a two-way bilingual education program seemed to be the best way to do this. During her student teaching experience Kari was placed in a dual language classroom where she was able to use and further improve her Spanish.

Kari, unlike Irma, developed strong academic competence in English in school. When she got to high school and wanted to develop her heritage language, she had the underlying competence in English to help support the acquisition of a second language. At the same time, she had to seek out opportunities to improve her Spanish. She was fortunate that she had Spanish-speaking family in Spain. Her study in Spain helped her develop both conversational and academic proficiency in Spanish. Both of these kinds of proficiency are necessary for teaching in a dual language setting.

Evaluating Teachers' Language Proficiency

States generally have tests for Spanish language proficiency for teachers. However, even for Spanish, the exams in some states only assess candidates' conversational skills. An increasing number of dual language programs are now being offered in languages other than Spanish, such as Mandarin, Korean, Arabic, and Hmong. Some states do not have exams for these languages.

Some teachers or future teachers may speak Mandarin, Korean, Arabic, Hmong, or another language as their home language and have good conversational proficiency in that language. However, they could lack academic proficiency because their schooling has been in English, and they have had few opportunities to develop academic language in their home language. For that reason, it is important for administrators in dual language programs to search out standardized tests that assess candidates' ability to read and write academic texts in the language they will be teaching. The American Council on the Teaching of Foreign Languages (ACTFL) is a well-respected organization that provides tests in a number of languages.

Teachers Whose Home Language Is English Who Have Some Proficiency in Spanish

The teachers we have discussed to this point are all either bilingual in Spanish and English or native Spanish speakers who have at least some proficiency in English. Many dual language programs, however, include teachers whose home language is English and who have at least a receptive knowledge of Spanish. These teachers can pair with a proficient Spanish teacher in a program where there are two teachers for each group of students, an English-side teacher and a Spanish-side teacher. Gloria provides an example of this kind of teacher.

Gloria ◆ Gloria took a few Spanish classes in high school and college. It was her church work with Latino youth, however, that convinced her that she wanted to teach English learners. Gloria saw how even her minimal knowledge of Spanish helped her reach the Spanish-speaking young people more personally. That experience motivated her to become a teacher. She knew that she lacked the ability to teach in Spanish, but she entered the dual language teacher education program to learn theories and strategies to work more effectively with bilingual students and to provide the English instruction in two-way bilingual dual language schools.

Throughout her teacher education program, Gloria demonstrated her commitment to Latino students. She took an intensive summer seminar to improve her Spanish skills, and she forced herself to use Spanish to make presentations in her education classes. Her coursework and her efforts helped prepare her to better meet the needs of her emergent bilinguals. Although she does not have an adequate level of academic Spanish to teach content in Spanish, she can support her students as she teaches in the English side of a dual language program.

In programs such as a Hmong/English program, the English-side teacher would find it much more difficult to develop even beginner-level proficiency in Hmong, and there would be fewer opportunities to study the Hmong language. However, as we discuss in the next section on teacher essentials, teachers who are monolingual English speakers should make an effort to learn some of the home language of their students, even if it is only some words and phrases. They should view both themselves and their students as emergent bilinguals who are developing proficiency in two languages.

Teacher Essentials

In the sections that follow, we discuss teacher essentials. Like administrators, teachers need to understand bilingual theory and practice. Some additional essentials relate specifically to teachers. Teachers need to have appropriate levels of academic proficiency in both languages used in the program. They must also accept and build on the language varieties that students bring to school while modeling academic language. Teachers in dual language settings must be able to work collaboratively with others in planning curriculum. Finally, teachers must work together to find and share resources. When teachers plan and share together, they expand the potential for student learning. See the following list for these teacher essentials.

- **Understand bilingual theory and practice**
- **Have appropriate levels of proficiency in the two program languages**
- **Recognize and appreciate language variation and model academic language**
- **Collaborate to plan curriculum**
- **Collaborate to find resources**

Understand Bilingual Theory and Practice

It is important for teachers to understand bilingual theory so that they can implement practices consistent with current research. In Chapter 2 we reviewed some of the key theory and research that teachers should understand. This includes the research by Cummins (1979) that shows that languages are interdependent and that what is learned in one language can transfer to a second language because there is a common underlying proficiency. García (2009) argues that we should think of bilinguals as having one complex linguistic system rather than two interdependent systems with a common underlying proficiency.

The theories of both Cummins and García point to the importance of teaching for transfer and drawing on all the linguistic resources of bilinguals. Teachers can use translanguaging strategies, such as studying cognates or comparing and contrasting grammatical structures in two languages. They can also use a student's home language as a linguistic scaffold to make input in an additional language more comprehensible (García and Kleifgen 2010; García and Kleyn 2016).

Cummins (1979), Collier (1989), and others have also conducted research to show how long it takes for a student to reach grade-level norms on standardized tests of reading and math in a new language. Most emergent bilinguals develop conversational proficiency in a new language in about two years, but it takes from five to seven years to develop academic language proficiency and score at grade-level norms on standardized tests in a new language.

This knowledge can help teachers develop reasonable expectations for student progress. Bilinguals in dual language programs generally make excellent progress in acquiring a new language. However, because they start school with little or no proficiency in one of the languages, they generally do not meet grade-level norms for native speakers until fifth or sixth grade. For example, students whose home language is English would not be expected to read, write, and discuss academic texts in Spanish during their first years in school. In the same way, native Spanish speakers would not develop grade-level academic English proficiency for several years. Knowing this, teachers can adjust their expectations while still providing rigorous, comprehensible instruction in both languages so that all students make steady progress.

Teachers also need to know what strategies have been successful with bilinguals to inform their instructional practices. Based on his research, Cummins (2000) distinguished between conversational fluency and academic language proficiency. Conversational language is context embedded and cognitively undemanding, and academic language is context reduced and cognitively demanding.

Teachers in dual language programs should teach using language that is cognitively demanding while still being context embedded. By doing this, they make academic content comprehensible. In dual language programs, and especially in two-way programs, it is essential that teachers make the instructional language comprehensible at all times. Whether teachers are teaching in English, Spanish, or another language, many of their students will not be native speakers of the language, so unless the teacher uses appropriate sheltering strategies, students will not develop academic content knowledge or academic language proficiency.

Fang (2004) has shown that academic language contains the technical vocabulary of the content areas, and it is abstract, authoritative in tone, and lexically dense. Lexically dense texts have more content packed into each sentence than conversational texts. Furthermore, each content area organizes texts in different ways. For example, in science students read and write procedures and procedural accounts. In language arts students read narratives and biographies and write persuasive essays. In social science and history they read and write reports and explanations. These are different genres. Gibbons (2014), Brisk (2015), and others have shown how teachers can teach students to read and write the genres of the academic language register.

When teachers develop a thorough understanding of second language acquisition and ESL methodology, they can choose effective teaching approaches, and they can explain why they teach the way they do. It is important for teachers to be informed and to keep up with current approaches. When teachers understand bilingual theory and research, they can communicate better with parents. They can explain why the student is being taught in two languages and the time it takes to develop proficiency in two languages. Parents have many concerns when their children are in dual language programs, and teachers need to be able to explain the theory and research-based practices in a way that makes sense to parents. In this way, teachers help build the parental support that the dual language program needs.

Have Appropriate Levels of Proficiency in the Two Program Languages

Although bilinguals are not perfectly linguistically balanced as we discussed earlier, the second essential is that teachers should have appropriate levels of proficiency in the two languages used in the program. For example, in a Spanish/English program where a bilingual teacher provides instruction in both languages, that teacher should have a high level of academic language proficiency in both Spanish and English. Francisco, the teacher we described earlier, developed academic Spanish proficiency before coming to the United States and by continuing to read, write, and teach in Spanish since coming here. By attending high school and university in this country and teaching for over twenty years in English as well as Spanish, he has developed a high level of academic English as well. He provides a good model of academic Spanish and English for his first third graders in the 50/50 one-way program at his dual language school.

We realize that this is one of the most difficult essentials to achieve in dual language programs. Research shows that people do not become competent bilinguals in a short period of time. It takes five to seven years, depending on different factors, for someone to be able to achieve at grade-level norms on academic tests of a second language (Collier 1989; Cummins 1979). Often, aspects of a second language, such as pronunciation or command of idioms, may never be completely mastered. Because developing high levels of academic language proficiency is so difficult, nonnative speakers face a challenge in teaching academic content in the language, especially at the upper grades.

Yvonne provides a personal example. She has been studying Spanish since high school. She majored in Spanish at the university she attended and has lived in Colombia, Mexico, and Venezuela. Still, she knows she has an accent when she speaks Spanish. When she teaches her biliteracy course at the university in Spanish, it takes more energy than when she teaches in English, and she does not always feel confident. She realizes some of her syntax is not nativelike, and she sometimes lacks certain technical vocabulary because her academic studies of this subject were primarily done in English.

Native Spanish speakers in this country may also struggle with Spanish. The authors have all lived in the Rio Grande Valley in South Texas, ten miles from the border with Mexico. The community is very bilingual. In stores Spanish is spoken as often as English. The local university is 91 percent Latino, and Spanish and English are heard in the halls and classrooms. Still, English is the language of power, and students who have spoken Spanish with families and friends often have had little formal schooling in Spanish. Dual language programs did not exist when they were younger. When local students decide to study bilingual education and get a bilingual credential to teach in dual language settings, one of their biggest hurdles is gaining the academic Spanish they need. They are proficient users of Tex-Mex, but to teach academic content, they must be able to read, write, and speak academic Spanish.

In some dual language programs, schools have chosen a model in which teachers are hired to teach in only one language. Teachers work in teams. One teacher teaches in English and the other in the non-English language. In these cases, it is important that both teachers have at least receptive knowledge of the other language of instruction. This is critical for teachers in the earlier grades. As Howard et al. (2018) explain, "A teacher who does not understand the students' native language cannot respond appropriately to the children's utterances in that language." In this case, comprehensible input as well as linguistic equity in the classroom may be severely impaired. Even a basic knowledge of Spanish can help the teacher communicate with emergent bilinguals and implement basic translanguaging strategies, such as the use of cognates. Gloria provided an example of a teacher in a dual language program teaching in English but with enough Spanish to understand her Spanish speakers and support them using translanguaging strategies.

In programs where the non-English language is not Spanish but Arabic, Japanese, Chinese, or Korean, it may not be possible to find English-side teachers with some competence in the non-English language. However, the English-side teachers should make an effort to learn to understand some basic words and phrases in the language, especially when they teach in lower grades. They can make the students their teachers and ask them how they say things like "I want a drink of water" or "Can I use the bathroom?" Both the students and their parents appreciate the efforts teachers make to learn a little of the students' home languages.

Recognize and Appreciate Language Variation and Model Academic Language

There is a reverse side to concerns about teachers having language competence. Native Spanish speakers teaching in a dual language program are sometimes not tolerant of the Spanish dialects their students speak. McCollum (1999) documents how Spanish-side teachers in a two-way program criticized students' local Spanish dialect. This caused students to reject their native language and turn to English. In the same way, English-side teachers may not value the dialect of English that some of their Latino students speak. Tex-Mex, for example, may be considered "broken English" by some teachers.

Cummins (1996) points out that schools are places where students "negotiate identities." Because a student's home language is a central component of his or her identity, it is important to recognize how the student communicates in his or her home and community. One goal of translanguaging pedagogy is to develop students' identities as bilinguals. Using strategies that draw on students' full linguistic repertoires contributes to their socioemotional development. One goal of education is to help students develop what Schleppegrell (2004) terms the "language of schooling." Students need these registers to succeed academically. Academic language development should build on the linguistic resources students bring with them.

Teachers should model and teach academic language, both oral and written. At the same time, they should validate the language variety students speak and use that as a base for building academic language. Yvonne watched one teacher work with Spanish-speaking children to help them understand that *Stá bueno* used by local Spanish speakers to mean *OK* or *fine* is all right in informal conversation, but another way to say *OK* that is more academic and more appropriate to use with elders, including teachers, is *Está bien*.

Another example of recognition and acceptance of students' language comes from Pérez' (2004) description of the San Antonio schools. The teachers required strict language separation in their classes, but their emergent bilinguals were accustomed to translanguaging. It was the common language practice in their bilingual community. Although some teachers simply rejected any use of the home language, others began to draw on the home language as an effective pedagogical strategy. In some classes, for example, teachers chose to read books that included instances of both Spanish and English, and they encouraged students to make purposeful use of their full linguistic repertoire as they wrote. These teachers viewed their students' language as a resource and attempted to develop that resource by showing students effective ways to use two languages in their writing. In the process, they validated the local language practices that both students and teachers often used and also introduced students to an academic use of drawing on two languages in literature.

One way teachers can help students develop academic language while validating the language variety they speak is through a strategy called *rephrasing* or *recasting*. Teachers begin with a response from a student and then restate the response in more academic language. This may require several turns. Zwiers (2014, 66–67) provides a good example of a teacher using rephrasing as she helped a student develop the topic and title for a report:

1. Teacher: So what's the topic?
2. Student E: People lookin' at daily life things?
3. Teacher: Yes, how archeologists study . . . let's use the word artifacts.
   How archaeologists study artifacts to . . .
4. Student E: Find out.
5. Teacher: What's a better word? What do you do in school?
6. Student E: Learn?
7. Teacher: Let's put that for the topic: "How archaeologists study artifacts in order to learn about daily life in the past?" Why do they study artifacts? In order . . .
8. Student E: In order to learn about the past? (66–67)

In this example, the teacher affirms the student's answer and rephrases it, using the word *archaeologists* instead of *people* and then introduces the technical term *artifacts*. Next, she provided an oral sentence frame, "How archaeologists study artifacts in order to . . ." When the student responded with the conversational phrase, *find out*, the teacher asks for a more academic term. Then the teacher models a complete sentence that includes both academic vocabulary and syntax that can serve as the topic and title of the student's report.

Often, teachers correct a bilingual's pronunciation or choice of vocabulary. However, even when students are asked to correct their language, they seldom begin to incorporate the corrections into their speech or writing. Rephrasing takes a different approach because the teacher affirms student responses and then models how the idea could be expressed using academic vocabulary and grammar. Rephrasing requires that teachers take the time to help students acquire academic language, but this process is more effective than the usual practice of correcting students.

When teachers recognize and appreciate the language variety that students speak and also help them develop the academic registers of schooling, they build their students' linguistic resources. Students whose home language is English come to school with a variety of conversational English and need to develop both oral and written academic English. The same is true for speakers of Spanish, Mandarin, or Japanese. In dual language programs teachers begin with the variety of the language that students have acquired in their homes and neighborhoods and then use this language to help them build the oral and written registers of academic language.

Collaborate to Plan Curriculum

Dual language teachers need to understand curriculum, know how to plan, and collaborate with other teachers. We want to emphasize the word *collaborate*, because in effective dual language schools, teachers work well together. Many times teachers work in teams with an English-side and Spanish-side teacher. It is especially important that these teachers have a regularly scheduled time to meet for planning and for discussing the progress individual students are making in each language.

Even when one teacher provides instruction in two languages, the teacher must collaborate with other teachers at that grade level to provide a consistent curriculum. Teachers must also work with their colleagues across grade levels to ensure that the curriculum builds logically from one grade to the next. In many schools, the dual language program is a strand. As a result, at each grade level some classes are for dual language students and some are for students in the all-English program. Dual language and all-English class teachers need to plan together to ensure that there is a consistent standards-based instructional plan for all students. In addition, when dual language and all-English teachers plan together, there is a better understanding of both programs. This breaks down any barriers that may build up when the dual language strand is seen to be a special program with a different curriculum than that of the all-English classes.

At the rural border school we described earlier, teachers met in grade-level teams to plan horizontally. Teachers at each grade level met during scheduled work days and over lunch to coordinate themes and to ensure they were covering standards and teaching to the state-required benchmarks. In many schools, the schedule includes one early dismissal day each week. Teachers can use the time after the students leave to meet and plan within and across grade levels.

Teachers should meet to solve particular problems at their grade level. In Chapter 4 we described third-grade teachers who met with the principal and specialists to discuss how they could help raise the level of the academic Spanish their students were acquiring. We also explained how teachers worked together with Sandra and Vivian to revise the one-way 50/50 program to include more English literacy in early grades at Edgewood Elementary School. The teachers reworked and revised the schedule until it reflected what they thought would work best for them and their students. The teachers at Edgewood provide an example of both horizontal and vertical planning. Teachers at the same grade level looked at the revision horizontally for their grade level but then worked vertically at other grades to be sure the program would be consistent across grade levels. In both these schools teachers collaborated to solve problems and improve instruction for the bilingual students.

Collaborate to Find Resources

Teachers should also collaborate to find resources. Especially in new programs, finding resources for teaching around units of inquiry and teaching content in the language other than English can be a problem. Rich resources are available in Spanish, but it is more difficult to find resources in some other languages. When teachers in dual language programs work together, the job of locating resources is not so overwhelming. The librarian can help, but if the program is new, the librarian may not be accustomed to looking for resources in languages other than English. Resources can often be found at state and national bilingual and dual language conferences. If a few teachers from a school go to these conferences, one of their responsibilities can be to look for such materials. Teachers can also find resources by checking the Internet. Publishers have increased their production of books in a variety of languages because of the demand from dual language schools, and more materials are available each year.

Earlier we described the school in Omaha where the teachers worked with the librarian to gather resources in Spanish and English. First, they established the units of inquiry that the teachers at each grade level would teach. Then they pooled their resources. For example, for the solar system unit, they collected the books, charts, models, and videos they might use. The librarian purchased large plastic bags with handles, and for each unit, she placed all the Spanish materials in one bag and all the English resources in another bag. She labeled the bags and arranged them so that teachers at each grade level would have easy access when they taught the unit.

After gathering these resources, the teachers took an important second step. They agreed on the order that each teacher would follow in teaching the units. In this way they avoided the problems they had had in the past when all the teachers at a grade level planned to teach the same unit at the same time. Rather than spreading resources for a unit across three or four teachers, by rotating the order of teaching the units, all the resources were available for each teacher when she taught the unit.

As teachers gathered new resources for the unit, they added them to the bags in the library, and over time they were able to expand and update all the materials.

Chapter Overview

We began this chapter by discussing the different kinds of teachers in dual language programs and the challenges they face. Native Spanish speakers teaching in dual language programs, if they are immigrants, may need support in completing their education and in obtaining work permits and state teaching certification. They also need to adjust to American schools and to a new culture. Some native Spanish speakers lack academic Spanish and need to increase their oral and written academic Spanish proficiency. Native English speakers who teach in Spanish must build their Spanish proficiency as well. Furthermore, teachers who teach in just one of the languages in the dual program need to develop at least basic competency in the other language. Teaching is never easy, and teaching in a dual language program carries additional challenges depending on teachers' backgrounds and their proficiency in two languages.

We concluded this chapter by outlining essentials for dual language teachers. Teachers in a dual language program need to have appropriate academic language proficiency in both languages. They should recognize and appreciate language variation and build academic language competency in two languages. Furthermore, dual language teachers need to collaborate in planning and in finding resources in two languages. Teachers in effective dual language programs we have visited or read about demonstrate all or most of these essentials, and they constantly work to improve their language proficiency and their teaching abilities. They work together to improve their programs by refining curriculum and locating needed resources in two languages.

Reflect and Apply

1. Consider a dual language teacher you know. How would you categorize the teacher (refer to Figure 5.1)? What specific strengths does that teacher have and what are the teacher's challenges?

2. How does that teacher display the teacher essentials listed in this chapter? Write a short case study of the teacher and evaluate the teacher referring to each of the essentials.

3. Where have you found resources for teaching in languages other than English? Make a list of useful sources that you can share with others.

 # Curriculum Goals, Planning, and Implementation Essentials

In an era of standards and accountability with high-stakes standardized assessments, it is easy for the goal of curriculum to become achieving good test results. However, this approach for students who are learning in two languages is inappropriate. Research consistently has shown that it takes five to seven years for emergent bilinguals to reach national norms on standardized tests of reading and math in English (Thomas and Collier 2012). Because students in dual language classrooms still need to meet standards as they acquire another language, it is important to engage them in meaningful activities as they learn academic content in two languages rather than simply teaching to the test. As Howard et al. (2018) state, "There is a substantial and consistent body of research over the past several decades indicating that successful schools and programs have a curriculum that is clearly aligned with standards and assessment and is meaningful, academically challenging, and incorporates higher order thinking" (32). In this chapter we first discuss curriculum goals. Then we explain essentials for dual language curriculum, planning, and implementation.

Dual Language Curriculum Goals

Traditional language teaching has focused on the domains of reading, writing, speaking, and listening as discrete language skills. Given the demands of literacy and disciplinary standards, instead of teaching the skills of these four domains separately, educators working with students learning language and content should examine the standards and integrate teaching the domains across the subject areas.

Van Lier and Walqui (2012) suggest a view of language and learning in schools as action-based learning.

> In a classroom context, an action-based perspective means that ELs engage in meaningful activities (projects, presentations, investigations) that engage their interest and that encourage language growth through perception, interaction, planning, research, discussion, and co-construction of academic products of various kinds. (4)

As students engage in these meaningful activities they learn language and the content of the subject areas.

Bunch and his colleagues (Bunch, Kibler, and Pimentel 2013) argue that educators should take van Lier and Walqui's stance of language as action:

> This stance is reflected in how we chose to address the ELA [English language arts] domains, focusing not on reading, writing, speaking, and listening as discrete language "skills" to be acquired, but rather on underlying practices highlighted by the Standards that are particularly related to one of the domains but ultimately involve the integration of all of them: engaging with complex texts to build knowledge across the curriculum; using evidence to analyze, inform, and argue; working collaboratively; understanding multiple perspectives; and presenting ideas. (26)

To take this stance, dual language curriculum should be organized so that bilingual students use their full linguistic repertoires as they translanguage and learn in school (García, Ibarra Johnson, and Seltzer 2017). These are active processes. Bilinguals do not learn language or content through repeating forms or memorizing facts or by being restricted to using one language at a time as they learn. Instead, curriculum should be organized so that bilinguals are active learners who work together to solve problems and answer essential questions using their full linguistic repertoires as they learn language and content.

Van Lier (2007) explains that although teachers must plan, there is a kind of continuum in planning for action-based learning that recognizes the tensions between planning to meet standards and allowing students and teachers to be creative and between establishing routines for a safe, predictable environment and creating an environment that encourages exploration and questioning.

The challenge, then, for dual language teachers is to plan curriculum for their students to help them meet required standards and, at the same time, actively involve their students in engaging activities that draw on their strengths, all their language resources, and their interests. This curriculum allows bilinguals to explore and question. The curriculum goals, then, should be the development of meaningful curriculum that helps students to learn academic content to meet the standards and to acquire and use academic language in the process. Figure 6.1 shows the elements of the dual language curriculum goals.

We have divided our discussion of curriculum essentials for meeting the dual language curriculum goals into two sections: curriculum essentials for overall organization and curriculum planning essentials. We describe each of these sets of essentials and explain why they are especially critical in dual language settings.

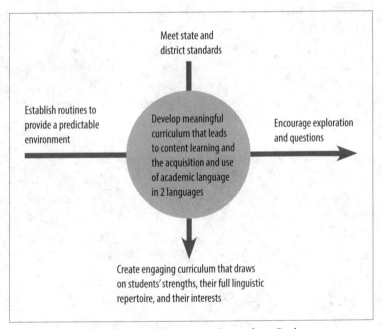

Figure 6.1 Dual Language Curriculum Goals

Dual Language Curriculum Essentials for Overall Organization

In dual language teaching, students learn language through meaningful content, and as they learn the content, they develop the academic language of school. As Bunch, Kibler, and Pimentel (2013) point out, language is developed "through meaningful and engaging activities across the curriculum" (6). The content they study should be standards based and organized around units of inquiry answering essential questions that engage students and draw on their strengths and interests. The following points outline the dual language curriculum essentials for overall organization.

- **Teach language and content drawing on different disciplines to develop academic language and academic content knowledge**
- **Organize curriculum around interdisciplinary units of inquiry based on answering essential questions**

Teach Language and Content Drawing on Different Disciplines to Develop Academic Language and Academic Content Knowledge

Teaching both language and content differs from traditional approaches to language teaching. Traditional approaches focus on the language itself and, as mentioned earlier, often separate the four domains of language—listening, speaking, reading, and writing. Traditionally, language teachers taught the grammar and vocabulary of the language by focusing on grammatical patterns, language forms, or functions of language such as apologizing or asking for directions (Freeman et al. 2016). As a result of traditional teaching, many students knew something about the language, but they often couldn't use the language effectively for communication. The standing joke was that someone learning language through drills and dialogues never could use the language because in real life no one ever gave them the first line of the dialogue.

In English as a second language (ESL) classes and in dual language programs in K–12 settings, students need to be able to understand and talk, read, and write about academic subjects. Learning about language doesn't help students learn language or learn through language (Halliday 1975). There are several benefits to teaching language through content. The following list outlines these reasons.

Reasons for Teaching Language and Content
- Students learn both language and content.
- Students learn the academic vocabulary of the different content areas.

- Teaching language and content keeps language in its natural context.
- Students have a real purpose for using language.

First, this approach is efficient. Students learn language, and at the same time, they learn the important academic content they need. Bilinguals do not have time to learn language first and then learn content later. Instead, they can learn language and content simultaneously. In addition, when teachers teach language and academic content, students acquire more than the everyday language they need for basic communication. They also acquire the academic vocabulary that is so necessary to read, write, and discuss academic texts.

Furthermore, as students study content they are exposed to the language of each academic subject area in a natural context, and they have a real purpose for using the language. For example, dual language students studying insects read interesting content books about insects in both Spanish and English, they observe insects in a class terrarium, and they keep journals in both languages about insects. They observe and make predictions about how long it takes a cocoon to become a moth and draw and graph the stages working together and talking about all they are learning.

In language arts the students read *La Mariposa* in Spanish and English (Jiménez 2000a, 2000b) and compare the part of the story where the caterpillar becomes a butterfly with their own observations. They discuss how the main character doesn't speak English well and is bullied but in the end is appreciated for his artistic talent. This kind of action-based learning (van Lier and Walqui 2012) that involves students in projects and experimentation as well as listening, speaking, reading, and writing provides an authentic and natural context for students to develop the academic language of science. Because the students are learning interesting academic content and are involved in projects and exploration, they have a real purpose for developing a second language.

In dual language settings, students are constantly involved in learning content in both their first language and a second language. Dual language teachers understand that action-based teaching across the disciplines will help students develop both language and content. The previous list summarizes the reasons for teaching language through academic content.

Organizing Curriculum Around Interdisciplinary Units of Inquiry Based on Answering Essential Questions

The second dual language essential for overall organization is to organize curriculum around interdisciplinary units of inquiry based on answering essential questions.

Howard et al. (2018) write that in addition to alignment with standards, dual language curriculum should be cross-disciplinary and project based:

> Another consideration related to curriculum is the use of thematic, cross-disciplinary, or project-based learning approaches. These approaches organize instruction and material across traditional subject-matter lines, typically involve projects that integrate learning across these subject areas, and are usually student centered. Research has demonstrated the effectiveness of these curricular approaches. (33)

This avoids what has been called the cha-cha-cha curriculum (Kucer, Silva, and Delgado-Larocco 1995, Freeman et al. 2016). In a "cha-cha-cha" curriculum students might study insects in science, different community workers in social studies, rhyming words in language arts, fractions in math, and *ea* words for spelling. The different content areas are not related. It is as though the teacher finishes one area, such as science, and then cha-cha-cha the teacher moves on to a new, unrelated subject. Emergent bilinguals often get lost in the transition, and by the time they figure out that the topic has moved from insects to community workers, cha-cha-cha, the teacher is moving on to a new subject. Because all students in dual language settings are learning in two languages, it is critical that teachers organize their curriculum in ways that make sense to their students.

The cha-cha-cha curriculum is more prevalent in upper elementary, middle schools, and in high schools because there is more departmentalization. In dual language programs, when different teachers teach different subjects and in different languages, it is very difficult to organize curriculum around interdisciplinary units of inquiry. Even when teachers who are part of a dual language program take the time to work together, there may be scheduling difficulties or difficulties in finding appropriate materials in both languages on inquiry topics. Within a particular subject, there may sometimes be thematic organization. For example, in language arts, students might be engaged in a unit on exploration. The reading selections and writing activities all relate to this unit of inquiry. However, the unit on exploration seldom is carried through into science, social studies, or math.

Developing Units of Inquiry Based on Essential Questions ♦ One way that dual language teachers can avoid a cha-cha-cha curriculum is to base curriculum around big questions such as "How does food get from the field to the table?"; "How does what we grow help us grow?"; or "How does the weather affect our lives?" Wiggins and McTighe (2005, 2011, 2012) argue that curriculum must deal with essential questions worth investigating. These are questions that do not have a simple answer. During a unit answering the question, "How does food get from the field to the table?" students would use literature and information from the various content areas to

build their understanding of plants and plant growth and transportation of products from the farm to the store. The unit might also include smart shopping and healthful eating. Students could use information from language arts, social studies, science, and math as they explore these related topics. Organizing around essential questions leads to an inquiry approach to education (Miles 2014; Freeman et al. 2016) and helps students make important conceptual connections across the disciplines.

Earlier we discussed teaching language and content in a unit based on insects that connected science and language arts. A unit of inquiry could investigate the relationships and interdependencies of insects and humans. Students could investigate questions like "How do insects depend on humans, and how do humans depend on insects?" or "How are humans and insects alike and how are they different?" The big questions help provide unity for the inquiry as students move from one subject area to the next.

For example, students studying how insects affect people could read a poetry alphabet book and create their own insect poems in language arts, study where different kinds of insects live for geography, learn about how insects serve people in social sciences, observe and keep insect journals in science, investigate how insects spread or prevent diseases in health, and calculate insect reproduction rates in math.

Teachers can foster inquiry and connect curriculum to state and federal standards by basing the essential questions on these standards. For example, a grade 1 science standard is to recognize ways that the appearance of animals changes as they mature. Often, grade 1 teachers include a unit on growth and change. Turning the topic of growth and change into a question such as "How do people and animals change as they grow?" helps focus the curriculum and connects it directly to the standard. This is a big question because it is complex and multifaceted. Students can investigate different aspects of growth and change. The inquiry also naturally leads into a study of life cycles.

To take another example, a fourth-grade social studies standard requires that students understand the impact of environment on culture. This standard can also be turned into an essential question, "How does where we live influence how we live?" Students can begin by studying the local community and then look at other communities that are different from theirs because of differences in the physical environment. A similar standard for secondary students studying world geography is to understand how geographic contexts and processes of spatial exchange influenced events in the past and helped to shape the present. In our multicultural society spatial exchange occurs as ideas, products, and even cultural traits spread from one culture to another. In dual language classes with students of different cultural backgrounds there is a constant exchange, and students adopt many ideas and, often, the cultural traits of their peers. Many standards, like this one, are recycled at higher grade levels so that students can build a deeper understanding of key concepts. At both fourth grade and tenth grade, though, students can approach the ideas through a focused big question.

Teachers can often include the literacy, literature, and math standards within questions based on social studies and science standards. It is important to spend time focusing on literacy and math skills, but they are best learned in the context of literature, social studies, and science. For example, students could read a novel or an informational text in literature or language arts about weather and climate change during a unit titled "How does where we live influence how we live?" They could record the high and low temperatures daily and then graph the results in science and math. Both literacy and math skills could be developed as students read and write about this essential question.

In a study on immigration, students could work to answer the big question, "Who belongs here?" They could discuss reasons immigrants came to the United States in social studies, look at immigration patterns and graph them in math, look at where immigrants have come from during different time periods as they study geography, and read biographies and autobiographies of immigrants in language arts. In political science in upper grades, the politics of immigration, refugees, and their effects on society could be investigated and discussed. In our present political climate, this big question, "Who belongs here?" is being debated. High school students can research this topic and carry out debates drawing on information they gather.

Tom and his secondary dual language team are beginning to work on interdisciplinary units based on essential questions at Highland High School. Individual courses are organized around big question units of inquiry. As the team members plan together, they are working toward making more connections across subject areas. However, as mentioned previously, this is a challenge in middle and high school and requires continuous planning.

Tom explained how a senior seminar course taught in Spanish in the dual language program forms, investigates, and answers critical questions:

> The entire course is built around asking questions and defending answers through solid argumentative and rhetorical skills. During the first semester, students spend significant time doing a group research project, and they come up with the questions about a topic they wish to answer. During the second semester, students do individual research projects (in Spanish) about a topic of interest. What's so cool about this is here is a college-level class (an official AP class) that students around the country take in English. Our students (heterogeneously mixed with diverse learners) are tackling this very rigorous curriculum in Spanish. I don't think any other school is doing this; the AP College Board is telling us they haven't heard of anyone else doing anything similar.

In another example at Highland High School, the entire freshman Patterns of World History course is centered on the topic, "identifying and challenging single stories." For the final unit this year, students did a project on youth activism after reading about the Middle East and Malala, the Pakistani girl who won the Nobel Peace prize for her advocacy for education for women and children around the world. Tom explained that for this project, "Students had to create a thesis, find information to defend their thesis, and then practice arguments with classmates." These essential issues are ones that students can become engaged with, and through their investigations, they read, write, and talk using academic language as scholars. Essential questions lend themselves to exploration of key concepts and help students develop both content knowledge and academic language. When teachers teach around big questions, students benefit.

Reasons to Organize Curriculum Around Interdisciplinary Units of Inquiry Based on Essential Questions

When teachers organize their curriculum around units of inquiry based on big questions, students learning both language and content benefit in several ways. The following list outlines the reasons for organizing curriculum around themes based on essential questions.

- Because students see the big picture, the English instruction is more comprehensible
- Content areas (math, science, social studies, literature) are interrelated
- Vocabulary is repeated naturally as it appears in different content area studies
- Because the curriculum makes sense, second language students are more fully engaged and experience more success
- Teachers can differentiate instruction to accommodate differences in students' language proficiency
- Through units of inquiry teachers can connect curriculum to students' lives and backgrounds

The Big Picture Focus Makes the Input More Comprehensible ◆ A focus on an essential question provides a context within which students can better understand instruction in a second language. In the same way that it's easier to assemble a jigsaw puzzle if we can look at the picture on the cover of the box, it's easier to make sense of individual lessons when we know they all focus on the same big question. Students engaged in the study of a question such as "How do animals and people change as they grow?" know that each lesson will relate to this topic. Because bilingual students have the big picture, they can make better sense of a math lesson taught in English in which two graphs compare the growth rate of two animals or of a science lesson taught in Spanish in which they study the stages of growth from a tadpole to a frog.

Content Areas Can Be Interrelated ◗ A second reason to organize around units is that teachers can help students make connections across subject areas. Students investigating a big question like "How does where we live affect how we live?" might do a tornado-in-a-bottle activity and learn about the conditions that cause tornados during science in Spanish or Chinese, locate areas where tornados have struck in the last year during geography (also taught in Spanish or Chinese), and read a story about a family preparing for a tornado in language arts taught in English. In their English math class, students could study charts showing where tornados most often form. They could study how meteorologists use data to predict the formation of tornados and the strength of the wind in different tornados. They could use weather data to predict the likelihood of a tornado touching down in their area.

In classes and schools that organize around inquiry units answering big questions, knowledge that students gain in one subject area in one language can be used in studying in another language in other subject areas. As they begin a new lesson, read a story, or write a report, teachers can also remind students of what they learned during math or science and make the connections more explicit.

When subject areas are interrelated through the focus on a big idea, students keep thinking and learning more about the essential questions they are answering as they move from subject to subject, language to language, or class to class. For example, looking at the concept of change, students could consider the big question "How does the world change and how do those changes affect our lives?" In science students might study the water cycle and the weather changes as a result of the cycle and look at the effects of weather such as a drought or severe thunderstorms. In language arts students might read a story and analyze how changing circumstances affect the different characters. In social studies students could study their community past and present and analyze the changes that have affected it. In math the teacher could have students look at different mathematical operations and how numbers grow larger or decrease as a result of the application applied.

In dual language classrooms, concepts related to math learned in English may apply in social studies or science studied in the other language. Students don't put what they learned in one context out of their minds when that lesson is over. The more subjects are interrelated, the greater the chance that emergent bilinguals will understand the instruction in English, in Spanish, in Korean, or another language. Basic concepts the students study about change during science in Spanish, for example, might connect when the big question is revisited during social studies in Spanish or language arts in English.

Vocabulary Is Repeated Naturally ◆ Maintaining the same topic by focusing on a big question also ensures that key academic vocabulary will be repeated naturally in the various subject areas and languages. In the past, teachers might have traditionally used repetition to help students learn vocabulary. A teacher might have the class or a student repeat a word or phrase as a way of improving pronunciation and memorizing the words. However, second language acquisition research has shown that we do not learn a new language through imitation and repetition. The problem with repetition is that it can become mindless, much like writing out each spelling word ten times. To acquire some aspect of language, like a word or phrase, students need to encounter it several times in meaningful contexts.

By organizing around units of inquiry in dual language, teachers provide the repeated exposure to meaningful language that students need in both languages. Rather than only hearing a word such as *temperature* in science class in English, dual language students might hear or see *temperatura*, a clear cognate, again during language arts in Spanish, in social studies in Spanish, and in math as they graph temperature changes in English. Because the subjects are interrelated, some of the same vocabulary comes up in each subject area, and this increases a student's chance of acquiring important academic vocabulary in both languages. Oftentimes, as with the example of *temperature*, the academic vocabulary includes cognates, and with the help of teachers, students make connections to both concepts and vocabulary across the different disciplines.

Even if the words for a concept are not cognates, with the presentation of similar concepts across content areas, students come to understand the vocabulary in both languages. So for example, as students read a short story in English about the effects of pollution on the environment of the Everglades and how characters and animals in the story are affected, they make connections as they read and discuss *el medio ambiente* (environment) and *la contaminación atmosférica* (pollution) that affect wetlands in science in Spanish. Because the topic of the inquiry "How do living things adapt and change in the environment?" is constant, students acquire the vocabulary of the central ideas as they study the different aspects of the inquiry.

Because the Curriculum Makes Sense, Students Are More Engaged ◆

Listening to someone speak a language we do not understand well is mentally tiring. Our brains naturally attend to things that make sense, so if a reading passage or a lecture is hard to understand, our attention turns to something else, something we can understand. For this reason, it is critical for dual language teachers to make the input comprehensible for all their students at all times. One way to do this is to organize around units of inquiry. Even when students don't fully understand the language of a new lesson, they know it is connected to the big question, so they stay engaged for a longer period of time. Especially when teachers encourage translanguaging and acknowledge the translanguaging *corriente* that is always present in a dual language classroom, they can help students connect what they know and understand about a topic in their first language to what they are learning in their second language. Later in this chapter we will explain the preview/view/review (PVR) translanguaging strategy that makes this point.

When teachers help students make connections, emergent bilinguals are more engaged, and this leads to both language development and increased subject matter knowledge. If students can stay focused on the lesson being delivered in a language that they are learning and make connections with what they already know, there is a greater chance that they will learn the concepts and acquire more of the new language. Curriculum organization based on interesting essential questions makes instruction more comprehensible, engages learners, and leads to greater academic success.

Inquiry Instruction Allows Teachers to Differentiate Instruction ◆ A fifth benefit of organizing around units of inquiry is that teachers can more easily differentiate instruction to meet the needs of emergent bilinguals at different levels of language proficiency. As long as all the students are studying the same topic, teachers can adjust assignments to suit the varied language proficiency levels of the students. For example, during a lesson in English based on the question "How does food get from the field to the table?" native Spanish speakers could read a picture book with limited text while native English-speaking students could read more challenging books on the topic. Students then could work together, speaking both English and Spanish, to demonstrate their understanding by making a flowchart or labeled drawing showing how food gets from the field to the table, and present their project to the class in English.

Later, in social studies in Spanish, Spanish speakers could help native English speakers negotiate the social studies text describing where crops are grown around the world and the geographic influences, including climate, on crop growth. Students could then work in heterogeneous groups to make a relief map, labeling the areas where certain crops can be grown, and write a group report in Spanish explaining what they learned.

Teaching Language and Content in a Lesson on Objects and Light

In his fifth-grade OWDL science class Francisco González introduces scientific terms and concepts for a lesson on objects and light. He reinforces key vocabulary using music.

Teaching the Term *Refraction*

Francisco González teaches a hands-on science lesson on refraction of light by having students work in groups followed by whole-class discussion to build academic vocabulary.

Big Question Units of Inquiry Allow Teachers to Connect the Curriculum to Students' Lives ◆ A final reason for organizing around units of inquiry based on essential questions is that this approach makes it possible to connect subject matter content with students' lives. Units of study based on big questions are universal. Animals and people everywhere change and grow. The weather affects our lives no matter where we live. Because the curriculum focuses on such big questions, teachers can connect key concepts with students' lives. In fact, bilinguals can often make important contributions to a class by giving examples from countries where they or their parents have lived or experiences they have had.

Discussions that occur during the "How does what we grow help us grow?" unit provide a good example. A student from the United States might eat cereal, toast, and juice for breakfast and a student from Venezuela might have *arepas* and *papaya*. Both students can draw on their own background experience as they learn how food gets from the field to the table. At the same time, the variety of examples coming from a class with students from different backgrounds expands the curriculum and enriches the learning experience for all the students in the class.

Organizing curriculum around big questions provides these six benefits for emergent bilinguals: (1) instruction is more comprehensible, (2) the subject areas are interrelated, (3) vocabulary is repeated naturally, (4) students stay more engaged, (5) teachers can differentiate instruction, and (6) teachers can connect curriculum to students' lives. In dual language schools, curriculum should be organized to teach language and content through interdisciplinary units of inquiry based on essential questions. We have explained what we mean by doing this, but it is equally important to help dual language educators understand how to go about planning for this type of curriculum.

Dual Language Curriculum Planning Essentials

There are five key steps to curriculum planning that teaches language and content and is organized around big question themes. The list below details these steps.

- **Develop long-term interdisciplinary units of inquiry based on big questions**
- **Develop short-term units supporting key concepts within the long-term interdisciplinary unit**
- **Designate a consistent, specific time for the long- and short-term planning**
- **Develop daily lesson plans connecting content objectives to standards and supporting content learning with language objectives**
- **In daily planning, consider classroom environment and routines, grouping, and translanguaging strategies such as Preview/View/Review**

Curriculum planning involves both long-term and short-term planning. Teachers need to be able to connect the content they will teach to standards and create an overall big question for their units. Then, to answer their big question, teachers look at short-term goals and create daily lesson plans that connect the content objectives they have identified to language objectives that will support students as they learn both the content and language of their theme.

Within the daily lesson plans, teachers consider how to group students and how to teach the content and support language development. They develop routines and incorporate translanguaging strategies that draw on the translanguaging *corriente* always present in dual language classrooms. The reading, writing, and discussion activities teachers use with students help them meet standards of the disciplines and answer the big question for the unit of inquiry.

Develop Long-Term Interdisciplinary Units of Inquiry Based on Big Questions

Long-term planning is critical for a unified curriculum. It is best done with the teachers who will be teaching the content, and when possible, with a school or district specialist and a curriculum specialist from inside or outside the district. Unless the different stakeholders are involved, important pieces of a unified curriculum may not be included. For example, teachers and specialists know that the curriculum should be aligned with the district's scope and sequence, and they are usually very familiar with this scope and sequence. District specialists and outside consultants are familiar with state and federal standards and research-based best practices. They can help teachers identify standards and key themes that fit within the scope and sequence required at different grade levels. Identifying units of study, then, that come from standards and are aligned with district requirements is a first step.

A group organizing curriculum first looks for a central theme for a unit of study and identifies an essential question, drawing on state required standards and district scope and sequences. We provide an example drawing on state content standards in Texas and California for the fourth grade. Both sets of language arts standards require students to compare and contrast information on a topic by reading different texts presented in diverse media and formats, and to integrate and evaluate what they read. Students then should be able to write informational reports framing a central question about an issue and present the information they have researched to a specific audience (TEA 2015, Kirst et al. 2013).

In content standards for both states, there is a focus on science and social studies/history of the state. One standard, for example, asks students to examine the impact of human activity and technology on the state and identify renewable and nonrenewable resources. In social studies students are asked to look at current political issues and social responsibility. Given the terrible storms that have affected California and Texas, the political arguments affirming or denying climate change, and the rich natural resources in both states, students could investigate the essential question, "How does what humans do affect our environment?" Science, social studies, and math standards can be incorporated into this big question topic, and students in dual language classrooms can find resources in English and the second language in books, pamphlets, and online.

Organizing Curriculum Around Big Questions and Subquestions

Yadira Roel, the First-Grade Bilingual Grade-Level Chair, explains how her team organizes curriculum around big questions and subquestions across content areas.

Develop Short-Term Units Supporting Key Concepts Within the Long-Term Interdisciplinary Unit

An essential question like "How does what humans do affect our environment?" can easily lead to subtopic questions that still connect to standards. Some subtopic questions to explore might include, "Have weather patterns changed in my state?"; "What do weather patterns tell us about climate change?"; "What arguments are there that there is no climate change?"; "What are the most important renewable and nonrenewable resources in my state?"; "How do we use renewable and non renewable resources?"; "How do our state's renewable and nonrenewable resources affect our environment?"; and "Who benefits from our renewable and nonrenewable resources?"

Questions such as these lend themselves to reading articles and then creating charts and graphs in math as students study weather patterns and chart or graph weather changes in their own areas. Students identify renewable and nonrenewable energy sources through reading texts and doing Internet searches. In the upper grades, students can refer to primary sources as they read arguments about how protecting some of our resources means fewer jobs for some and influences their state's economy. Students compile reports looking critically at the information they have and debate the causes of climate change and how humans affect it.

Designate a Consistent, Specific Time for the Long- and Short-Term Planning

The process of long- and short-term planning cannot take place unless there is a consistent, designated time set aside to do this. Teachers, specialists, and administrators are busy, and in schools there are constant distractions that come up and need immediate attention. Because of this reality, it is easy for good intentions about joint productive planning to be set aside for what seem to be more pressing matters. We mentioned in our administrator essentials that there should be time for teachers to plan together. For the kind of long- and short-term planning that is so critical in dual language settings, there must be a commitment from administrators, specialists, and teachers to set aside time.

Tom, at Highland High School, provides details about his "dual language Fridays" when his team meets to plan. He explains that his team meets often and regularly to work toward a unified curriculum.

> Each Friday afternoon for the past three years we have had "dual language Friday." From 1:30 to 3:00 PM I bring the EL/DL coordinator, assistant principals, and world language chair to my office, and we spend the time only talking about dual language implementation. These "dual language Fridays" frequently include teachers working in the program and representatives from districts sending students to our program. Topics for these joint meetings include curriculum development, course offerings, professional development sessions, and communication with stakeholders. In addition, "guests" talk about what they are experiencing, what they need for their continued development and/or success, professional development sessions, and communication with stakeholders.

The dual language Fridays are critical to keeping the dual language program at the forefront, and there is additional time set aside at Highland High for planning.

> In addition to dual language Fridays, our school has late starts every Wednesday morning where teachers have one hour of collaboration time to work with colleagues on curriculum, instruction, or assessment practices. On these Wednesday morning late starts we frequently bring our dual language staff together to coordinate our program.

Tom explains that time is also provided for long-term planning in thirty-hour summer workshops that the district plans and delivers. Dual language faculty and administrators have been brought together during these workshops to help design the dual language program and coordinate instructional approaches.

At Cedar Brook Elementary school, Jeff explains how teachers start with the Texas Essential Knowledge and Skills (TEKS) standards and plan based on them.

> Teachers plan together in teams at least one to three days per week, depending on the depth and complexity of the TEKS that are required for the coming week. Teachers look for connections and incorporate activities that will meet the standards. They unpack upcoming TEKS, share teaching strategies and ideas, and look at assessment data to plan for reteach opportunities.

In addition, over the past five years Sandra has worked with the dual language teachers at Cedar Brook as a dual language consultant. In this capacity Sandra visits the school, observes classes, coaches, and assists with curriculum planning. Sandra's work with curriculum planning leads teachers in the process of looking at the district's scope and sequence, connecting that to standards and identifying essential questions. Specialists in dual language like Sandra, who have expertise in bilingual education and curriculum, can help teachers understand how to go about long-term and short-term planning.

Develop Daily Lesson Plans Connecting Content Objectives to Standards and Supporting Content Learning with Language Objectives

We have discussed how curriculum should draw on standards and be organized around interdisciplinary units of study based on essential questions. However, besides learning curriculum content, students need to be able to understand, read, and write about that content using the appropriate academic language of the content areas. This is true for students being instructed in their home language, but it is perhaps even more important when students are learning content in a second language. For this reason, in dual language programs teachers develop both content and language objectives for each lesson.

Lesson planning begins by identifying content objectives. These are drawn from the standards and reflect key concepts students need for that content. So in a long-term science inquiry unit on plant growth and nutrition answering the question "How does what we grow help us grow?" a teacher plans a short-term unit on plant growth. One of her content objectives is to have students learn the steps of a scientific procedure. She has students plant seeds in a pocket garden and keep track of their growth as they conduct observations of their seeds. For one of her early daily lesson plans she might have students write the procedure for planting a pocket garden. A language objective would be for students to use the imperative form of verbs, such as *choose, moisten,* and *place*. A different language objective would be for students to use prepositional phrases to show location, such as *in the towel* and *under the table*. The teacher could use a sentence frame to scaffold this structure: "Place the seeds _____."

To develop language objectives, once teachers decide on the content objectives, they should ask, "What language forms and functions will my students need to discuss, read, and write about this content?" Teachers may choose one or two aspects of language to teach. Language forms can include verb endings, comparative forms, possessives, types of questions, punctuation, or descriptive adjectives and adverbs. In the pocket garden example, language forms would be the use of imperatives or prepositional phrases.

Students use language forms to carry out functions such as summarizing, describing, explaining, or comparing and contrasting. Another type of language objective might be for students to write a description using adjectives or to write a summary. Teachers should consider the function of the language students are using (describing, explaining, persuading) and then write language objectives focused on teaching the language forms students would need for these functions.

If the content objective in a language arts class is to write about a recent experience that includes an identifiable beginning, middle, and end, a language objective could be to use signal words to show time sequence such as *first, then, next*, and *finally*. Another language objective could be to use the correct form of regular past-tense verbs, because the description would be in the past. A third possible language objective would be to use descriptive adverbs to modify actions.

In a math class lesson, the content objective could be for students to order objects by length and to compare the lengths of two objects indirectly by using a third object. A related language objective could be to use the comparative and superlative suffixes -*er* and -*est* on one- or two-syllable adjectives, as in *longer* and *longest*. Another possible language objective could be to write sentences showing comparison, using the frame "_____ is shorter than _____." More advanced students could write compound sentences with a coordinate conjunction, following the pattern "A is shorter than B, but it is longer than C."

As a final example, the content objective for students in a social studies class could be to compare and contrast geographic features of an area. One language objective could be to write complex sentences with signal words showing contrast, such as "The western part of the state is flat; however, the eastern part is mountainous." A second language objective could be to use the correct form of present-tense verbs to agree with the subject, as in "The river *runs* south" and "The rivers *run* south."

An important caveat in planning language objectives is to avoid making the vocabulary of the content area the language objective. Content area vocabulary should *not* be considered a language objective. The technical vocabulary of the content area should be considered part of the content objectives. For example, in teaching the structure of an atom, a teacher will explain that an atom has *protons* and *neutrons* in the *nucleus* and *electrons* in the *orbital*. The italicized words are technical terms that a teacher would need to use in teaching the concept of atomic structure. These terms are labels for key concepts in science that need to be understood, so they should be listed under the content objectives not the language objectives.

Developing both content and language objectives is an important first step in teaching academic language and subject matter content. Many dual language

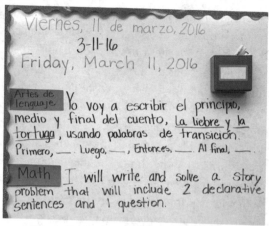

Figure 6.2 Language Objectives Posted in
Dual Language Classroom

classrooms we have visited have had content and language objectives posted in the room. Figure 6.2 shows a posted language objective for *Artes de lenguaje* (language arts) taught in Spanish and math taught in English. The *Artes de lenguaje* objective is for students to use signal words retelling the classic story *La liebre y la tortuga* (The Tortoise and the Hare) (Mlawer 2016). The language objective translates into English as "I am going to write the beginning, middle, and end of *La liebre y la tortuga* using transition words, *first . . . next . . . then . . . at the end.*" The math content objective is for students to write a story problem. The language objective is for students to use two declarative sentences and a question to write the math problem. Both of these language objectives make explicit the language forms students will need to carry out functions needed for the content objectives.

Planning Time for Teachers

Team leader Yadira Roel explains how at her school there is a specific planning time for teacher teams.

In Daily Planning, Consider Classroom Environment and Established Routines, Grouping, and Translanguaging Strategies Such as Preview/View/Review

Content and language objectives provide teachers with the content they should be teaching and help them consider their students' language learning needs. As dual language teachers plan their lessons, they also need to consider classroom environment and routines, grouping, and translanguaging strategies.

Classroom Environment and Routines ◖ One way to help students understand and be willing to take risks is to create an inviting classroom environment that supports classroom routines. Many dual language classrooms are set up in such a way that different sections of the classroom physically lend themselves to activities that are carried out there on a regular basis. Teachers may set up centers each day, assign students to centers, and then have them rotate through those centers. Sometimes the teacher's centers are organized around a content area and at others around literacy. Figure 6.3 shows one dual language teacher's centers chart. The chart shows the clothespins with students' names on them that help her organize who goes to which center first. The chart indicates centers for each day, Monday through Thursday.

Figure 6.3 Centros de Alfabetización—Literacy Centers Chart

All dual language classrooms should be places where students use language to learn academic content. Often, teachers organize students into small groups at tables to work on projects rather than having students sit in traditional straight rows. The physical classroom set up should promote language use as students work together to solve problems Figure 6.4 shows a fifth-grade science classroom at Edgewood Elementary School where students are working in small groups as they study circuits.

Rug time is a typical routine in lower grades. Lower-grade teachers often read a key book to students or introduce a key concept or project with students sitting on the rug. Rug time engages students as they sit close together on the floor, and it provides the opportunity for students to talk together. In Figure 6.5 these second graders at Cedar Brook Elementary School have written on their whiteboards, and this pair is now sharing what they wrote.

Upper-grade teachers also can use rug time for certain activities. In Figure 6.6 the students are listening to a song about circuits that their science teacher, Francisco González, always in his white lab coat, has written for them. They will learn to sing this song, which contains all the key concepts they need to remember about circuits. This fifth-grade science teacher at Edgewood Elementary School routinely gathers his students at the rug to discuss their science projects or to sing songs about science.

The total physical environment of a classroom, then, is important for learning and promoting language development. Figure 6.7, a picture of a one-way dual language first-grade classroom at Edgewood Elementary School, is an excellent example of this. Instruction is in both Spanish and English in this classroom and the print rich environment supports students as they learn in two languages. The classroom rug is located in front of the SMART Board screen and key vocabulary is displayed in both languages throughout the room.

Figure 6.4 Fifth-Grade Students Working on a Circuit

Figure 6.5 Rug Time Shared Writing

Figure 6.6 Fifth-Grade Rug Time

Figure 6.7 First-Grade Classroom

To the right on the front bulletin board the teacher has listed language objectives for language arts, math, science, and social studies. The first two objectives are the ones we showed in Figure 6.2. Figure 6.8 is a close-up of this side of the room. The Spanish language science objective is below those two objectives. The content objective is for students to draw and label the life cycle of a person, and the language objective is to describe it using transition words.

Looking closely at the left front of the room (shown in Figure 6.9), there are posters in English with discussion and classroom management words and math terms in English. Because math is taught mainly in English, the teacher has posters on place value, planes, flat shapes, and three-dimensional solid shapes. She also has cards posted to help the students talk about math concepts including *more* and *greater* and *equal* and *same*. This side of the classroom also has two book holders with a variety of content and literature books in Spanish and stuffed animals children can hold during center or sustained silent reading time.

The teacher's whiteboard moveable chart with sticky notes can be seen in the foreground. The teacher uses this for a variety of lessons. The chart can be easily moved around the room for small- or larger-group activities.

It is also important that the environmental print in a classroom reflects student work. In the dual language classrooms we have visited teachers post student work and projects around the room for everyone to read and reread. Figure 6.10 shows a fourth-grade project on the sun that a student completed at Edgewood Elementary. Figure 6.11 shows students' written responses to a reading. These second graders were writing about what they had learned about the main character (*Lo que aprendi de este personaje . . .*) in a story of an immigrant girl, Aiki, living in Michigan, whose grandmother comes to visit from Japan.

Figure 6.8 First-Grade Language Objectives

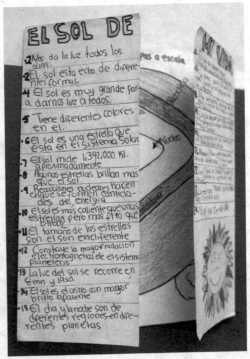

Figure 6.9 Close-up of Math and Book Corner

Figure 6.10 Facts About the Sun

Routines are important in any classroom and especially in classrooms where students are learning content in two languages. When students have an idea of what kinds of activities will take place, they are better able to follow the instruction and acquire language. It also is helpful to administrators and classroom visitors to know what is happening at different times during the day. Some dual language teachers post their schedules outside the classroom door. In fact, in some districts it is a nonnegotiable to have the daily schedule posted outside the door. (See Figure 6.12, Horario: Classroom schedule with times.) This enables administrators or others to know when the class goes to computers (*Computadoras*) if they are not in the classroom or to P.E. (*Educación física*), and at what times different content areas are being studied.

The figures we discussed showing the classroom environment reflect many important routines including centers; rug time; oral language development; and the daily schedule. Writers' workshop is another important routine to include.

Grouping ◆ In dual language classrooms, it is important to consider how students might be grouped to create optimal conditions for their learning. Howard et al.

Figure 6.11 *Lo que aprendí*

Figure 6.12 Horario: Classroom Schedule

(2012) state that, "Studies suggest that when diverse students work interdependently on school tasks with common objectives, students' expectations and attitudes toward each other become more positive, their academic achievement improves, and language development is facilitated by extensive interactions among native and non-native speakers" (520).

Group work also facilitates oral language development. Oral language development has been emphasized in recent curriculum standards for emergent bilinguals. In California's English Language Arts Anchor Standards students are asked to "participate effectively in a range of conversations and collaborations with diverse partners" and to be able to "present information, findings, and supporting evidence such that listeners can follow" (www.corestandards.org).

Zwiers (2011) has written about how classroom conversations should be structured to promote academic language during group or pair work. Careful grouping can help students meet oral language development standards. He suggests four key practices that promote academic language development, including being prepared for discussions, using appropriate body language, participating by taking turns, and making connections to what others have said. He provides descriptions of activities teachers can use to implement these practices. Teachers need to help their students develop oral language and participate effectively in group work, and these suggestions are good first steps.

In his blog, Wong (2016) lists "using group work strategically" first among his five fundamental strategies for bilingual learners. He emphasizes the importance of structuring groups carefully with both heterogeneous groups, so that students can communicate across languages and cultures, and homogeneous groups to allow for tailoring instruction to specific objectives.

Like Zwiers, Wong suggests that both structured and unstructured tasks give students different opportunities for language development. A structured task might involve completing a graphic organizer using specific academic language as students plan a project, and an unstructured task might be to discuss what students liked best about a book they just read.

Most one-way and two-way dual language classroom teachers we have observed are intentional about how they group students so that they can acquire both language and content. Often, they organize their students into bilingual pairs. In two-way programs, a native English speaker is paired with a speaker of the other language of the program. In this way members of the pair can help their partner, when instruction is in the language they are stronger in.

However, it is also sometimes important in two-way programs to put students of the same language group together. If at all times students are grouped with speakers of another language, they might never have the advantage of being challenged by their home language peers to develop more advanced vocabulary and syntax in their home language. In addition, when teachers have students in their classrooms who are not native speakers of the language of instruction, they are likely to simplify language rather than push all students to use advanced academic language.

De Jong (2002) describes how a two-way program in Florida decided to separate language arts instruction in fourth grade because Spanish-speaking students and some native English-speaking students were not at grade level in Spanish, especially in oral language. Each group had English language arts and Spanish language arts separately for a period of time. "The native Spanish speakers were appropriately challenged with literacy activities and rich class discussion in Spanish. At the same time, the grouping by language reduced the range of Spanish language skills, and this allowed Spanish instruction for the native English speakers to be targeted to their proficiency level" (14). The results were positive for both groups. This study has implications for pairing or grouping students. It suggests that teachers should sometimes group students in same language groups to fully develop their language proficiency in their home language or to provide more sheltered instruction for students working in a second language.

In one-way programs where students usually have varying degrees of proficiency in both languages of instruction, teachers often pair a student more proficient in English with another student less proficient in English during English instruction. During Spanish time, students who need more support in Spanish are paired with a stronger Spanish speaker. Figure 6.13 shows how one teacher in a one-way program uses clothespins with student names to organize and change around her pairs both for times when instruction is mainly in English and for times it is mainly in Spanish.

Teachers sometimes bring students together in small groups to work on specific concepts they know that students need help with. In Figure 6.14 this dual language specialist at Edgewood Elementary has formed a group with some fourth graders to work specifically on forming adverb clauses in Spanish. This sophisticated construction is important for the students who are developing high levels of Spanish proficiency.

During centers students have many opportunities to share and to learn from one another. Centers in upper grades usually have students working together on projects, like the students in science shown in Figure 6.4 working on their circuits. In lower grades students can be reading together at reading centers or working together on other kinds of projects. In Figure 6.15 two kindergarten students, grouped in a bilingual pair, are composing sentences in Span-

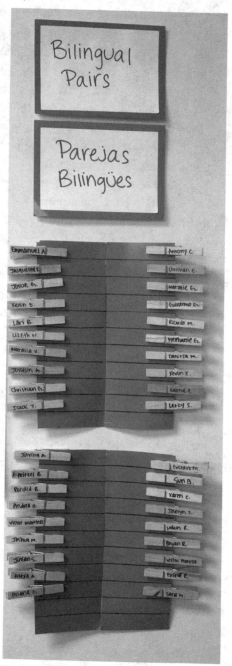

Figure 6.13 English and Spanish Bilingual Pairs

Figure 6.14 Small Group Working on Adverb Clauses

Figure 6.15 Kindergarteners Building Sentences in a Center

ish with blocks, drawing on their unit about fairy tales. They have read *Rumpelstiltskin* as a class, and their teacher is teaching them sophisticated verbs that appear in the story in both the present and the past tense, including *miente mintió* (lie, lied), *amenaza amenazó* (threaten, threatened), *promote, prometió* (promise, promised), and *adivine adivinó* (guess, guessed). As the children work together they teach each other and help each other put together sentences.

Writers' workshop is another opportunity for grouping pairs or small groups of students together to support each other's writing. When students can talk together about their writing and share it, their writing improves. With computer accessibility, shared writing becomes even more important. Figures 6.16 and 6.17 show pictures of students at different ages sharing their writing. In Figure 6.16 a bilingual pair of third graders in a one-way program is editing a shared writing piece. In Figure 6.17 two fifth graders are composing a poem on a computer.

Translanguaging Strategies ◆ Group work also promotes the use of translanguaging. Dual language teachers can and should strategically plan translanguaging in their classrooms. In this last section of the chapter, we explain some translanguaging strategies that can be effective in both one- and two-way dual language settings. We also describe in detail how preview, view, review can work effectively in dual language.

As we have discussed in earlier chapters, a translanguaging *corriente* is always running through dual language classrooms. Teachers can draw on that *corriente* to

Figure 6.17 Sixth Graders Composing a Poem on a Computer

Figure 6.16 Third Graders Sharing Writing

promote both language and content learning. It should be kept in mind that translanguaging should be strategic and carefully planned for a language or content learning purpose. Teachers should avoid concurrent translation where teachers or students are randomly moving back and forth between languages.

One strategy many dual language teachers use to increase students' academic vocabulary is to post word walls in different content areas that include words and phrases in two languages. Figure 6.18 is a math word wall that includes key vocabulary in English and Spanish. It contains math expressions students need to use as they talk, read, and write about math. Some of the pairs, such as *suma* and sum, and *resultado* and result, are cognates that students can draw upon as they learn. However, the teacher needs to help students recognize these cognates as they work.

Turn and talk offers another opportunity for strategic translanguaging. Teachers can group students in same language groups to discuss a particular concept. They can then report back in the language of instruction. Small-group work can also afford opportunities for translanguaging. For example, the group working on circuits could discuss what they learned about circuits in Spanish or English and report back to the class in English. If writing partners are paired by the same language, they can discuss what they are going to write about in their home language, and then support each other as they write their piece in the language of instruction. Writing partners can also be bilingual pairs, and they can use either language as they discuss what they will write.

If dual language teachers do daily news with their classes, they can allow students to participate using their home language. For example, if a teacher is doing the daily news in English, a student can contribute an idea in Spanish, and the teacher can write the idea in English. When finished, the entire class reads the daily

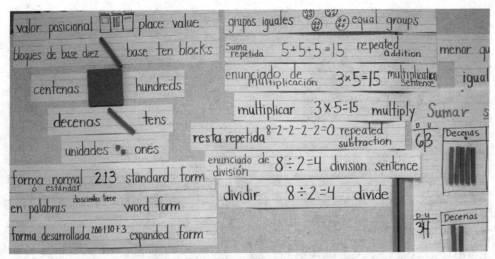

Figure 6.18 Math Bilingual Word Wall

news aloud, and the students who contributed in Spanish can see and hear their ideas in English.

Translanguaging offers an excellent opportunity for reviewing homework. When teachers assign the homework, they ask students to talk in same language groups to tell each other what the assignment is for the following day. In this way, there can be no excuses the following day that the students did not understand the homework assignment.

It is also important to encourage students and parents to discuss homework assignments in the home language. Even when an assignment is to be done in English for a Spanish-speaking child, discussing the assignment with his or her parents in Spanish helps to clarify it, and often parents can offer suggestions even if not in English. This holds true for an English-speaking child studying in a Spanish/English two-way program. Parents can quickly see if the child understands the Spanish assignment if he or she can explain it to them in English. Teachers in dual language classrooms might send home instructions in the child's home language even when the actual assignment is in the second language. That way parents understand what the child should be doing.

Preview/View/Review in Dual Language ◗ We have written about the power of preview, view, review (PVR) for students in both ESL and bilingual classes (Freeman and Freeman 2011; Freeman et al. 2016; Mercuri 2015). PVR can support learning both at the micro- and macro-levels in dual language classrooms. In traditional ESL classrooms the teacher, a bilingual peer, a bilingual cross-age tutor, a

Hands-On Lesson to Classify Objects

Francisco González uses hands-on group work to help students develop academic language and concepts as the classify objects.

Translanguaging Strategies

Students translanguage using both Spanish and English as they work in small groups during a lesson in English.

Bilingual Pairs

Dora Baxter organizes students into bilingual pairs for different activities in her TWDL preK class. Most pairs include a native English speaker and a native Spanish speaker.

---

bilingual aide, or a parent can simply tell the English learners in their home language what the upcoming lesson is about to provide a preview. A preview can also be reading a book on the topic or encouraging a discussion in the home language.

During the view, in an ESL class the teacher conducts the lesson in English using strategies to make the input comprehensible. With the help of the preview, the students can follow the English better and acquire both English and academic content. Finally, it is good to have a short time of review during which students can use their home language. Students who speak the same home language can meet in pairs or groups to review the main ideas of the lesson and then report back in English. Figure 6.19 outlines the traditional PVR technique.

Preview (home language)	View (English)	Review (home language)
If the English learners share the same home language, the teacher or a bilingual helper gives an overview of the lesson or activity in the students' home language. The teacher could give an oral summary, read a book, show a video, or lead a short discussion. If there are several language groups in the class, students could work in same language groups to answer a question and report back in English.	The teacher teaches the lesson or directs the activity in English using strategies for making the input comprehensible.	The teacher or the students summarize key ideas and raise questions about the lesson in their home language. Students can work in same language groups to do this and report back in English.

Figure 6.19 PVR in ESL Classes

Preview/View/Review

Yadira Roel talks about planning for preview/view/review.

PVR in dual language also helps students draw on their home language. At the micro-level, teachers can use a preview at any point in a lesson where they want to be sure students understand a key concept. For example, a teacher who is going to teach about the parts of a plant in Spanish can clarify in English for students that they will be studying the parts of the plant today. In addition, the teacher could ask a question about what students already know about parts of a plant and have the students discuss in their home language and report back in English. This preview helps students focus on the topic and makes the lesson in Spanish much more comprehensible. Students could turn and talk to a home language partner at the end of a lesson to summarize key concepts.

At the macro-level PVR requires more planning and organization. For PVR to be effective at the macro-level, teachers need to connect their curriculum thematically. In other words, the academic content areas must be interrelated so that the vocabulary and key concepts are reinforced when taught across the two languages.

Helping New Teachers Organize for Dual Language

Yadira Roel, team leader, explains how she helps new teachers organize the classroom environment to support bilingual students.

Buenos Días Song, Days of the Week Song, Months Song

Dora Baxter leads her preK TWDL class in routines including the songs Buenos Días, the days of the week, and the months of the year. She uses music and gestures to make the input comprehensible.

PVR at the macro-level makes use of translanguaging because both languages are used strategically over a series of lessons. A series of related lessons provide a PVR structure for optimal learning. During the preview, a lesson is taught in the home language. During the view, a related lesson, often in a different content area, is taught in the second language. Then in the review, there is still another related lesson, again perhaps in another content area, taught in the home language. Of course, this type of macro-level PVR only works when curriculum is organized around units of inquiry. The following is an example of how PVR provides a translanguaging strategy at the macro-level.

A teacher or a dual language team plans a long-term unit of inquiry answering a question we have discussed before, "How does the weather affect our lives?" During science taught in Spanish the students study how the seasons are caused by the Earth's rotation around the sun. They have a globe and use a flashlight to understand this concept, and there is discussion in Spanish about this. In addition, the students gather data on the temperature from day to day both inside and outside the classroom. These activities in Spanish are a preview for Spanish speakers because they provide some basic concepts and key vocabulary about weather and seasons.

Then, during English language arts, the students read a series of informational texts and poems about the seasons. They discuss these readings in English and then do an art project with fall leaves and write their own poem about a favorite season and its characteristics. This is the view part of the series of lessons for the Spanish speakers. It is also serves as a preview for English speakers for the next lesson to be taught in Spanish.

In social studies taught in Spanish, students investigate the question, "How does where we live affect how we live?" They look at climate in different regions and how that affects the types of houses people live in, the clothes they wear, and the crops that are grown there. They do Internet searches, and groups report the effects of climate in different parts of the world. For Spanish speakers this lesson serves as a review of the concepts studied in Spanish science and English language arts and also previews what is coming next in an English lesson in math. For native English speakers this Spanish social studies lesson is a view of what was previewed in English language arts as they read about seasons and weather in English.

In math taught in English, students, working in groups, take the information they gathered on the temperature over time, both inside and outside the classroom, and make graphs. Then in groups, students present the findings orally. This lesson serves as a view for Spanish speakers and both a review for English speakers and a preview of the Spanish language arts lesson that follows.

During Spanish language arts students read stories about extreme weather, such as hurricanes and tornados and how the weather affects the characters. They also read informational texts about what causes different kinds of weather. Figure 6.20

How the Weather Affects Our Lives				
Content Area	Science	English Language Arts	Social Studies	Math	Spanish Language Arts
Lesson	Seasons Earth's rotation Gather weather information	Read about seasons and weather poem project	Investigate how climate affects how we live	Graph inside-outside temperature report	Read stories about storms and fables
Language	Spanish	English	Spanish	English	Spanish
Spanish speaker	Preview	View	Review	View	Review

Figure 6.20 Macro-Level PVR for a Spanish Speaker   KEY: Spanish ☐ English ▨

Preview/View/Review

María Amaya introduces order of operations using PVR in English in her TWDL fifth-grade math class with a short video and group discussion. Then she continues the lesson during the view by giving instructions in Spanish for an activity.

shows how PVR works for a Spanish speaker during the unit. As we explained, this type of translanguaging strategy at the macro-level also provides a continuous preview view and review for the English speakers.

The advantages of this macro-level translanguaging PVR strategy is that concepts and vocabulary are continually reinforced as students move from one related lesson to the next. There is natural language development as students relate the concepts and vocabulary they learn in the connected lessons. Although this strategy takes careful planning, the learning rewards are great. What we described here is better suited for a 50/50 model of either one-way or two-way dual language instruction because the instructional time for each language is fairly equal.

Although this particular approach might be less effective in the initial stages of a 90/10 model, there is still potential for some use of this translanguaging strategy. If the instruction in English and the instruction in Spanish are related, then English-speaking students will get a preview and review in their first language of the content they are studying in their second language. For Spanish speakers, the instruction in English is the view, and the part of the day taught in Spanish provides both a preview and a review of the English lesson.

Because the English instruction time is so limited in a 90/10 model at the early grades, it is critical that teachers connect what they do in English with the topic of the Spanish instruction. In addition, because every lesson in either language is the view lesson for some students, teachers should make extra efforts to make the input comprehensible while still promoting high levels of academic concept development. In summary, then, in dual language programs with integrated, content instruction, students preview and review content in their home language and view content in their second language.

The key for teachers is to keep students engaged and to keep providing comprehensible input for all the students in a class, even when half of them are learning academic content in a second language. It is only when the input is comprehensible and the students are engaged that acquisition takes place. When curriculum has been previewed and reviewed in the students' first language it is more comprehensible and more interesting. Students are motivated to pay attention and want to learn.

Chapter Overview

In planning for and implementing curriculum, it is important to first consider the goal for the curriculum. This main goal should be to develop meaningful curriculum that leads to content learning and the acquisition and use of academic language in two languages. The curriculum must help students meet standards. It should be an engaging curriculum that draws on student strengths, their full linguistic repertoires, and their interests. It should encourage exploration into questions that matter. Because the students are learning in two languages, the curriculum must be understandable, and teachers should create a predictable environment with established routines.

There are two goals for the curriculum of dual language programs. Students in bilingual dual language programs need to learn content and acquire the academic language of both languages of instruction. By organizing around interdisciplinary units of inquiry, teachers can help students develop language and content as they make important connections across languages.

Curriculum planning should include development of both long-term interdisciplinary units of inquiry based on big questions and short-term units supporting key concepts within the long-term interdisciplinary unit. A designated time must be set aside for this type of planning, and the planning should involve both the teachers and curriculum specialists familiar with the dual language program. Beginning with the standards for the grade levels and the district programs of study, teachers and curriculum specialists draw out key concepts to develop long-term interdisciplinary units based on big questions. Within these long-term units, topics and questions emerge that support the key concepts and the big question or questions in the long-term unit.

Once the overall big questions and underlying topics are identified, individual daily lesson plans in the different subject areas should be developed based on the identified topics. Because the students are in bilingual dual language programs, not only content objectives but also language objectives should be developed in each lesson. The language objectives are developed by asking, "What language do students need to talk, read, and write about the content?"

The classroom environment should support the content instruction. Teachers should establish routines and group students in different ways. Translanguaging strategies that draw on students' home languages include bilingual word walls and cognate charts, opportunities for students to use the home language when working in pairs or small groups, and the use of preview, view, review (PVR).

Reflect and Apply

1. Look at a particular grade level you are teaching or would like to teach. Go to your state standards and review the standards in language arts, science, social studies, and math. Pick out a big question that would address a standard across these subject areas as we described in the chapter. Be prepared to share this.

2. Based on the big question, identify subquestions or themes that would fall under that bigger question. Share these ideas.

3. Look at the physical setup of your own classroom or a dual language classroom you visit. How is it organized? Does it support both language and content learning? List the pros and cons of setting up the classroom this way.

4. Consider the environmental print of your classroom or a dual language classroom you visit. What kinds of print are evident and in what languages? Does the environmental print support content and language learning? How?

5. Pick out content objectives that you might teach in a lesson in language arts, math, science, and social studies. What language do students need to be able to read, write, and talk about the content? Write a language objective for each of these content objectives.

5. Looking at the content and language objectives you have written, how could you implement a translanguaging strategy that would help students acquire both language and content?

6. We described PVR in detail at the macro-level. Can you think of a unit of study where you could use PVR? What are some ways the content in the different disciplines taught across languages could be connected? Draw out a plan using the table format in Figure 6.20 to share.

7 Biliteracy Essentials

Academic success depends to a great extent on students' ability to read and write a wide variety of texts. One important goal of enrichment models of bilingual education is for students to develop high levels of biliteracy. Biliteracy is now recognized through the Seal of Biliteracy. In 2011 California was the first state to pass legislation creating a Seal of Biliteracy. Presently, 23 states have adopted the Seal and 7 other states are in the process of adopting it. Students who demonstrate their biliteracy receive a seal on their diploma or are recognized by a separate certificate or award.

Biliteracy Essentials

In dual language programs students read and write in two languages to become biliterate. There are several essentials for developing effective dual language biliteracy programs. The following list outlines these essentials.

- **Base methods on a theory that views reading and writing as meaning construction**
- **Ensure a good match between theory and teaching methods**
- **Consider the choice of language or languages for initial literacy instruction**
- **Use translanguaging strategies to promote literacy transfer and biliteracy development**

The first two essentials are to base methods of teaching on a theory that views reading and writing as meaning construction and to ensure a good match between the theory and the teaching methods. Teaching methods should reflect this focus on constructing meaning when reading and writing in both languages. Howard et al. (2018) report that in their review of experimental research, August, McCardle, and Shanahan (2014) suggest that teachers use meaning-oriented approaches to literacy instruction because they "provide greater impact on reading comprehension than decoding-oriented approaches" (50).

In any dual language program, it is essential to carefully consider whether language arts should be taught initially in one language or two languages. This important choice is the third essential. Program developers ask such questions as, "If biliteracy is taught sequentially, which language should be introduced first?" The choice of language or languages for initial literacy instruction also may depend on whether the program is a one-way or a two-way program and whether it is a 90/10 or a 50/50 model.

A fourth essential is to use translanguaging strategies to promote the transfer of literacy between the two languages and to develop biliteracy. For example, in the Spanish language arts lesson on possessives that we described in Chapter 3, the teacher contrasted possessive structures in Spanish and English.

Base Methods on a Theory That Views Reading and Writing as Meaning Construction

The desired end result for any method of teaching reading is for students to be able to comprehend texts, and the end result for teaching writing is for students to create clear texts that communicate their ideas. As Beeman and Urow (2013) state, "The goal of all literacy instruction is to instill in students the ability to read and write

Works on Capitalization and on Adding Details to Create Tone in Writing

Teresa Batres works with her TWDL third grade on editing capitalization.

Teresa Batres reminds students of a book they read in English and discusses how authors create tone that readers can interpret using their five senses. She uses sentence strips to show how authors add details to show tone. Students work in groups to create to their own sentence strips and then present their writing to the class.

comprehensibly . . . Teaching students to read means teaching students how to comprehend text, and literacy instruction includes reading and writing" (88).

Skills-Based and Meaning Construction Theories of Reading ◆ Although all theories of literacy have comprehension, the construction of meaning, as the goal, one theoretical approach argues that teachers should begin by teaching discrete skills. This is the approach that August et al. (2014) refer to as a decoding oriented approach. Educators who hold this view believe that skills are the building blocks of comprehension in reading and clear written communication. Another approach keeps a strong focus on meaning construction during reading and writing and always presents skills in the context of meaningful reading and writing. These two theoretical approaches are often referred to as skills-based or meaning construction-based. Both theories have the same goal and include the same components, but the process of introducing and teaching the components differs, and the focus of instruction between the skills-based and meaning construction-based theories varies.

Skills-Based Approaches to Literacy ◆ With a skills-based approach, the emphasis is on developing skills needed for reading and writing. However, too much emphasis on skills during reading instruction can lead students to become word callers who can sound out words and read quite rapidly but still lack comprehension. As Beeman and Urow (2013) explain, "Sometimes teachers put so much emphasis on the elements of reading — the discrete word-level skills — that those skills become the goal" (88).

Similarly, in writing, too much emphasis on skills such as handwriting, spelling, and punctuation may result in students who can produce short texts that follow writing conventions but not convey much information. The emphasis on skills may also lead students to be very reluctant writers who fear making errors.

The Report of the National Reading Panel (NRP) (National Institute of Child Health and Human Development 2000) summarized studies that used scientific research methods with control and experimental groups randomly selected or carefully matched, careful data collection, and statistical analysis. All of the studies that were included were based on students whose home language was English. No English learners were included in the studies. The report identified five research-based components for effective reading instruction in English: phonemic awareness, phonics, fluency, vocabulary, and comprehension.

The Reading First initiative was a federal education program based on the NRP report. This initiative was mandated under the No Child Left Behind Act (2001) and administered by the Department of Education. Schools funded by Reading First were required to use methods based on scientifically-based reading research. *Put Reading First* (Armbruster and Osborn 2001) was widely disseminated as a guide to implementing appropriate methods of teaching reading in kindergarten through grade 3 based on the five component skills identified by the NRP. In *Put Reading First* the authors explain how to help students build skills needed to recognize words, read them fluently, expand vocabulary, and develop comprehension. Teachers across the country implemented this approach.

In classes that implemented Reading First reading skills students were taught beginning with phonemic awareness, the ability to identify phonemes in words. The second skill was phonics, the ability to apply the sounds associated with spellings to sound out words. Students also needed to build a bank of sight words. These are words like *of* or *one* that occur frequently but do not follow regular phonics patterns. In addition, students needed to learn how to break down longer words, using structural analysis to identify word parts, prefixes, and suffixes.

Through practice, students could apply these skills to identify and pronounce words rapidly. They practiced these skills to develop the ability to increase reading fluency. Reading instruction also included teaching vocabulary skills that students could use to identify word meanings. The belief was that when students could read words aloud, they could use oral language skills to comprehend what they read. This process could then be internalized and applied to silent reading. However, many emergent bilinguals became "word callers," students who could say the words but did not understand what they were reading.

Despite criticism of both the NRP report and the summary (Garan 2002; Coles 2000), *Put Reading First* shaped reading instruction in many U.S. classes, including dual language classes. An extensive review of the effects of the Reading First initiative was published by the Institute of Educational Sciences (2008). This report found that although more time was being allocated for reading instruction and basic skills had improved for many students, there were no significant gains in reading comprehension. The results of the Reading First Impact Study led schools to gradually move away from strict adherence to the Reading First approach because comprehension is the goal of literacy instruction.

Meaning Construction–Based Approaches ◗ Theories of literacy based on reading and writing as the construction of meaning keep the emphasis on comprehension and teach skills in the context of meaningful reading and writing. The model of reading that we advocate is a transactional, sociopsycholinguistic model. In this model, readers construct meaning as they transact with texts. The term *transaction* was proposed by Rosenblatt (1978), who argues that meaning is not in the text or in the reader. Instead, each text has a meaning potential, and readers use both cues from the text and their background knowledge to build meaning. Beeman and Urow (2013) also take a transactional approach. They explain that "Comprehension is a complex process that involves the successful interaction of three elements: the reader, the text, and the context in which the reading occurs" (90).

Goodman (1984) explains *transactions* with his theory of dual texts. There is the written text. In addition, "the reader is constructing a text parallel and closely related to the published text. It becomes a different text for each reader" (97). The reason that this mental text is different for each reader is that readers differ in their background knowledge and their purpose for reading. The concept of dual texts helps explain why we can read a text as an adult that we read years before as a child and get a very different meaning from the same written text. In addition, two people can read the same text and construct different meanings from it.

For Yvonne, the novel *Rain of Gold* (Villaseñor 1991), an epic romance story of two families from Mexico and the history of their coming to the United States, provides a clear example of Goodman's idea of dual texts. Her son-in-law, Francisco, came to this country at fourteen as an immigrant from El Salvador escaping poverty and war. *Rain of Gold* was for him "the best book I ever read! I could picture everything that was happening in my mind. It was like people I know and experiences I have had."

When Yvonne read *Rain of Gold*, she was fascinated. She loved the book because it represented so many of the students she had had over the years and it helped her to internalize the struggles, the passions, the contradictions she had encountered in the Mexican culture over the years. For one of Yvonne's Anglo students whose family had little contact with immigrants, it was a long, tedious book with "way too many details." He only read the book because it was assigned to him by a university instructor teaching a class in cross-cultural understanding. Each person read the same book, the same words, but the mental text each reader constructed was completely different.

The meaning construction-based theory is also *sociopsycholinguistic* because the reading process is social, linguistic, and psychological. It is social because the meaning we construct depends on our purposes for reading, the context, and on the ideas we develop from interacting with others. In fact, the mental text we create keeps changing as we talk about a book with others. We interpret and reinterpret what we read in part based on our social interactions as we clarify or deepen concepts presented in the text.

Reading is also a linguistic process and an individual psychological process. Readers use cues from three linguistic systems — graphophonics, syntax, and semantics — as they transact with texts. Graphophonics refers to the letters and sounds, syntax involves the order of words in a sentence, and semantics has to do with the meanings of words. All three linguistic cueing systems are used simultaneously when the focus is on building meaning from the text. Readers also use a series of psychological strategies as they read. They sample the text using visual cues and their knowledge of how letter patterns correspond to sounds, make predictions based on their developing understanding of the text as well as their knowledge of word and syntactic patterns, and make inferences to fill in missing information. They confirm or disconfirm and correct their predictions and integrate their new understanding with what they previously understood. Through this process, they construct meaning as they transact with texts.

Writers use a similar process as long as they remain focused on constructing a meaningful text to communicate ideas. They have a purpose of communicating a message in written form. They draw on their knowledge of graphophonics, syntax, and semantics to produce a written text. They revise their text in response to feedback from readers.

Research Supports a Meaning Construction–Based Theory of Literacy ◖

Studies on eye movements during reading and research from miscue analysis lend support to the transactional sociopsycholinguistic theory. Although these studies are not based on "scientific research" (studies with control and experimental groups randomly selected or carefully matched, careful data collection, and statistical analysis), they are empirical studies of students conducted as they read meaningful texts.

Skills-based approaches put an emphasis on developing phonemic awareness and phonics skills. However, to apply phonics rules, readers have to look at each letter. The eye movement studies conducted during the last 100 years have shown that readers do not visually sample every letter of every word (Paulson and Freeman 2003). Instead, the brain directs the eyes to gather necessary information for making and confirming predictions during reading. When readers pause to fixate words, information is sent to the brain. When the eyes are moving between fixations, the brain receives no information. The eye movement studies show that readers fixate about two-thirds of the words in a text. No reader fixates every letter of every word.

In addition, proficient readers fixate the important content words, especially the nouns and verbs that provide needed input for meaning construction. Content words are fixated about twice as often as function words, such as conjunctions and prepositions, by good readers. Eye movement data support the claim that readers selectively sample a text to get the information they need to make and confirm predictions.

One assumption of those who take a skills-based approach is that because skills are central to proficient reading, poor readers are students who cannot decode words well and instead rely more on context during reading. Kucer and Tuten (2003) conducted research to test the claim that less proficient readers rely more on context and that more proficient readers make better use of visual information to recognize words automatically. They examined the miscues of twenty-four proficient adult readers who were advanced graduate students. During oral reading, a miscue occurs when a reader omits, substitutes, or inserts a word.

Students Identify Words That Begin with J

Sandra Cordúa teaches a lesson to build metalinguistic awareness for her kindergarten TWDL students using a strategy to help them identify words beginning with the letter J.

The proficient readers in the Kucer and Tuten study relied more on context and less on graphophonics (sounds and letters) than beginning readers do. Kucer and Tuten conclude that "the readers relied most heavily on story and sentence meaning and syntax, made partial use of graphics and sounds and produced miscues that made sense" (2003, 290). In contrast, as other miscue data have shown, younger, less experienced readers rely more heavily on graphophonics and less on the other cueing systems, syntax, and semantics. Kucer and Tuten write that the results "cause us to question early reading programs that rely heavily on the teaching of graphic and sound (phonic) strategies, especially in isolation, as well as programs that promote 'balance'" (2003, 290).

Kucer and Tuten's study was with native English speakers. Freeman (2001) analyzed bilingual students' eye movements and miscues during reading. All four of her bilingual readers made miscues that had high or some graphic similarity about 95 percent of the time. These same readers had much lower scores for syntax or semantics. Thus, this miscue data show that these bilingual students, like the less experienced readers in the Kucer and Tuten study, relied more heavily on graphophonics than on syntax and semantics. Students learning to read in a second language, like those in Freeman's study, need strategies that help them focus on constructing meaning by relying more on syntactic and semantic cues than graphophonic cues and by making greater use of the key content words in the text. To a great degree, though, these abilities develop through extensive reading in the new language with a focus on meaning.

Ensure a Good Match Between Theory and Teaching Methods

In dual language programs, the methods for teaching reading and writing must match the meaning construction–based theory we have discussed in the previous section. A gradual release of responsibility model keeps the focus on constructing meaning and teaching skills in context. This model provides a balanced literacy program.

Gradual Release of Responsibility ◗ In effective dual language programs teachers follow a gradual release of responsibility model of reading and writing (Pearson and Gallagher 1983). The model is based on Vygotsky's (1962) research on learning. He proposed that learning is a social process. What we can first do with help, we can eventually do independently when we receive support from a more experienced person. The support is what Bruner (1985) calls *scaffolding*. In bilingual classes, teachers scaffold instruction to enable emergent bilinguals to read and write independently.

Vygotsky explained that people have what he called a zone of proximal development (ZPD). This zone is the developmental area slightly beyond our current ability level. Instruction should fall within this zone. If instruction is too far beyond our current level, we cannot use it, and if it is at or below our level, we do not improve. If I play tennis with someone who is at or below my level, I probably won't improve my game, and if I play against a professional, I won't get any better. I need to play against someone who is slightly better than I am.

Krashen applies these ideas to language acquisition. He claims that language acquisition occurs when learners receive comprehensible input that is slightly beyond their current level, what he calls $i + 1$. That is input plus one. If the input is at $i + 0$, we do not acquire because it is at our current level, and if the input is at $i + 10$, we do not acquire because it is too far beyond our level. This is the same concept as Vygotsky's ZPD. If a teacher uses simplified oral language and texts with advanced students, they cannot improve their academic language proficiency because they are not challenged. On the other hand, if a teacher assigns an advanced text to a beginning student, the student cannot improve because the input is not comprehensible.

Effective instruction involves gradually releasing responsibility from the teacher to the student. At first the teacher performs the task, and the student observes and begins to engage with it. Then the teacher helps the student perform the task. Gradually, the teacher removes the support and releases the responsibility so that the student can complete the task independently. Figure 7.1 shows how the gradual release model is applied to literacy instruction.

Figure 7.1 illustrates how teachers can gradually release responsibility for reading and writing. Instruction moves from teacher support, the area above the diagonal line, to student independence, the area below the line. As the figure shows, responsi-

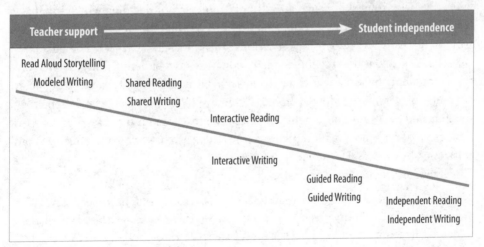

Figure 7.1 Gradual Release Model

bility for reading and writing rests at first entirely with the teacher. The teacher models reading by reading books aloud or telling stories. Read-alouds and storytelling model for students how texts are structured and introduce the academic vocabulary and syntax of written language. The teacher models writing by engaging students in language experience as students dictate stories or information that the teacher writes, projecting the writing so all the students can see her writing. Then she and the students read back what has been written.

During the next stage, the teacher and students take joint responsibility for reading and writing. In shared reading teachers often use big books so all the students can see the text. She tracks the text as she reads, and students chime in on predictable repeated sections. During shared writing, the teacher and the students jointly construct a text that the teacher scribes. Interactive reading and writing may be done with the teacher or with peers. For example, the teacher may read a text and have students echo what she reads. She may stop at certain sections so the student can continue the reading, and then the teacher may come back in. Interactive reading is often done in bilingual pairs with one student assisting the other during the reading. During interactive writing the teacher may sit with the student and help as needed as the student writes, or two students may work together on developing a piece of writing.

For guided reading and writing the teacher may begin by presenting a minilesson to illustrate a particular skill or strategy. In guided reading the teacher sits with small groups of students who all have a copy of the text. Students take turns reading to practice certain skills, such as predicting or using context to infer the meaning of unfamiliar words. In guided writing the teacher works with a small group to help them with specific writing skills, such as writing a good lead or deciding where to break a text into paragraphs. During guided reading and writing, the students take responsibility to read and write, focusing on certain skills under the teacher's guidance.

The final step is for students to read and write independently. There should be a time for independent reading and writing each day. Independent reading leads many students to continue reading at home. Cullinan (2000) in her article "Independent Reading and School Achievement" reviewed the research on the effects of independent reading on school achievement. Her article was part of a national study commissioned by the U.S. Department of Education.

Cullinan reached this conclusion:

> The amount of free reading done outside of school has consistently been found to relate to growth in vocabulary, reading comprehension, verbal fluency, and general information (Anderson, Wilson, and Fielding 1988; Greaney 1980; Guthrie and Greaney 1991;

Taylor, Frye, and Maruyama 1990). Students who read independently become better readers, score higher on achievement tests in all subject areas, and have greater content knowledge than those who do not (Krashen 1993; Cunningham and Stanovich 1991; Stanovich and Cunningham 1993). (3)

Despite research showing the benefits of independent reading and support from teachers and administrators for independent reading, only about a third of teachers and administrators polled in a national study find time to allow independent reading in school. The April 26, 2017, *Edweek* blog reported on a survey conducted by Scholastic (Loewus 2017). The survey of 3,700 teachers and more than 1,000 principals found that 94 percent agree or strongly agree that students should have time during the day to read a book of their choice independently, but only 36 percent of the teaches say they are able to make time for independent reading. For this reason, it is especially important for teachers who follow a gradual release model to include independent reading each day.

Independent reading should include digital print as well. Teachers need to instruct students on how to search for texts online, how to choose texts, and how to read online texts without becoming distracted. Students also need more opportunities to use computers in class to access online texts. As Liana Heiten (2016) reports in an *Education Week* article:

> According to survey data from the 2015 National Assessment of Educational Progress, only about 1 in 10 4th graders use computers to access reading-related websites on a daily basis or nearly every day at school. About 30 percent of students in 4th grade classrooms never, or hardly ever, use computers to access such reading material in school.

Teachers may assume that young people actually spend too much time on computers and other devices and that they know how to navigate online sources, but, as Heiten's article shows, students need guidance and instruction in how to use digital resources and read online texts independently.

Independent writing occurs as the last stage of writers workshop. Unless students have regular opportunities to write independently, they do not improve. In the National Writing Projects book, *Because Writing Matters: Improving Student Writing in our Schools* (2006) Nagin states, "Schools not only need to have students write more; they must also give students a rich array of writing experiences" (5).

The gradual release of responsibility model of reading and writing provides a framework for biliteracy instruction in dual language classrooms. When teachers include the different components of the model in their instruction, they provide a balanced approach to biliteracy. There are different definitions and models of balanced literacy and biliteracy. Some have claimed it's a balance of whole language and phonics or a balance of a skills-based approach and a meaning construction-based approach. However, we would argue that a balanced literacy program should include a balance of the components of a gradual release of responsibility model.

In effective dual language classes, reading and writing are closely connected. Francisco, a first grade dual language teacher, reads to and with his students each day. He also engages his students in writing every day. Figure 7.2 shows a variation on an "I Am" poem as a "We Are" poem with its repeated phrase, "Somos bilingües y muy trabajadores" (We are bilingual and hard-working). This is a poem Francisco and his students wrote together using language experience. The lines of the poem demonstrate how involved and excited Francisco's students are about reading and writing. By connecting reading and writing during activities in his classroom, Francisco helps his emergent bilingual students become biliterate and builds their academic language in two languages.

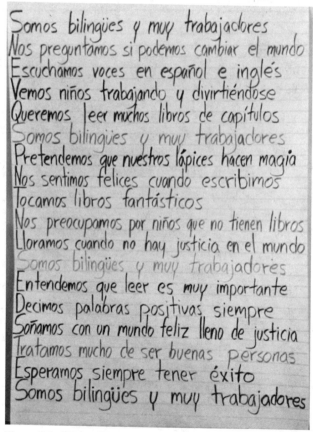

Figure 7.2 "We Are" Poem

Consider the Choice of Language or Languages for Initial Literacy Instruction

The next biliteracy essential focuses on the question of the language or languages for initial literacy instruction. To begin, program developers must decide whether initial literacy instruction should be sequential or simultaneous. Many programs follow a sequential model. Students are taught to read and write in one language, and then literacy in the second language is added. In other programs, language arts is taught in both languages from the start. In programs that incorporate simultaneous biliteracy, language arts is offered in both English and the language other than English.

Sequential Biliteracy ◆ In some dual language programs, literacy is first developed in one language, and then literacy in the second language is taught. This approach is based on the research showing that literacy skills and knowledge transfer from one language to another. As Baker and Wright (2017) report:

> Despite differences in orthography, vocabulary, and grammar, generalizable skills in decoding and reading strategies may transfer from first language literacy to second language literacy (Bialystok 2013; Koda & Zehler, 2008). Concepts and strategies easily transfer from first to second language literacy such as scanning, skimming, contextual guessing of words, skipping unknown words, tolerating ambiguity, reading for meaning, making inferences, monitoring, recognizing the structure of text, using previous learning, using background knowledge about text. (314)

In some sequential biliteracy models, all students are given initial literacy instruction in their home language. The reasoning behind this approach is that students more readily learn to read and write in a language they already understand. For that reason, students whose home language is English are first given literacy instruction in English, and literacy in the second language is added later. Students whose home language is Spanish or Chinese begin literacy instruction in their home language and later add English.

In many dual language programs all students receive literacy instruction in the non-English language. Then, English literacy is added at about second grade. One assumption behind this approach is that parents of English-speaking children can better support their children in learning to read and write than parents of children who speak other languages. They may have more access to books and may be better educated. A second assumption is that because English is a dominant language that is evident in the print environment, English-speaking children will begin to acquire literacy skills more quickly than children who speak other languages, so their initial English literacy can be delayed. An additional reason for offering literacy instruction initially in the non-English language is to counteract the influence of the dominant

Text Analysis to Improve Student Reading and Writing

Omaly IsaacCura engages fourth-grade TWDL students in a series of activities designed to help them learn how to use the elements of a text analysis pyramid during a small-group guided-writing lesson.

Presents Pyramid of Text Analysis

Omaly IsaacCura presents pyramid of text analysis.

language. In this respect, providing literacy instruction in the non-English language helps promote equity. As Howard et al. (2018) point out, "To promote the prestige of the partner language and counteract the dominant status of the mainstream society's language, the partner language must receive more focus in the early stages of a dual language program" (16).

Although these assumptions are not supported by empirical research, many dual language programs provide initial literacy instruction in Spanish, Chinese, or another language. This is especially true of a 90/10 model. In this model, language arts is offered in the non-English language, and during the short time for English instruction (10 percent of the day) the content taught is science or math. One problem with delaying instruction in English language arts until second grade is that high-stakes tests in reading in English are given in third grade, and students may not have developed high enough reading ability in English if they have only been instructed in English language arts for less than one year.

In the study we described in Chapter 1, Valentino and Reardon (2014) reported that by second grade, students' scores in English language arts were significantly higher for students in transitional bilingual and developmental bilingual programs than for students in the dual language program. The dual language program followed

Introduces the Story, Discusses Tone and Theme

Omaly IsaacCura introduces the story and discusses tone and theme.

Reviews the Elements of the Text Analysis Pyramid

Omaly IsaacCura reviews the elements of the text analysis pyramid.

a 90/10 model with only limited English instruction by second grade. It should be pointed out, however, that the test results also showed that the dual language students caught up to the state average in English language arts by fifth grade and surpassed the state average by seventh grade.

Collier and Thomas (2009) found similar results for students in their longitudinal study. By fifth grade dual language students reached national averages, and they continued to accelerate their growth in later grades. Despite this research evidence, there is strong pressure in schools for students to achieve at a high level in state-mandated tests in reading, and so they introduce English reading earlier than second grade. This was true for both Jeff and Vivian in their effective dual language programs.

Sequential biliteracy is often the approach taken in one-way dual language programs. Because most or all of the students in these classes speak a language other than English, initial literacy instruction is given in the non-English language first and English is added later. New understandings of bilingualism, however, suggest that even in one-way programs emergent bilinguals come to school with some proficiency in two languages and may be better served in a simultaneous (or paired) biliteracy program.

Simultaneous Biliteracy ◆ Dual language programs that follow a simultaneous biliteracy model teach language arts in both languages throughout the grades. This approach is most often used in a 50/50 model. Simultaneous biliteracy instruction may be adopted for several reasons.

First, as mentioned earlier, pressure from high-stakes tests may lead dual language program developers to adopt a model that teaches reading and writing in two languages from the start, to ensure that emergent bilinguals have sufficient time to develop English reading proficiency by third grade, when they take high-stakes reading tests in English. A second reason for providing literacy instruction in two languages from the beginning may be the belief that reading and writing knowledge and skills are acquired in a similar way in any language—through exposure to and interactions with comprehensible written texts. The idea is that reading and writing in one language reinforces the ability to read and write in an additional language. Therefore, if language arts is offered in two languages every day, then students are receiving more language arts instruction and will learn to read and write more quickly. In addition, simultaneous biliteracy instruction facilitates immediate transfer of literacy skills and knowledge from one language to another.

Whether literacy instruction is sequential or simultaneous, research by Goldenberg and his colleagues indicates that initial English literacy and Spanish literacy should be taught differently because of differences between the two languages. Their findings may also apply to literacy in other languages.

Goldenberg and his colleagues (2014) conducted research to determine the importance of teaching phonemic awareness to children learning to read in Spanish. The research showed that although phonemic awareness is commonly taught to English speakers learning to read in English, it is not taught in Spanish-speaking countries.

In their research study Goldenberg and his colleagues compared reading performance for three groups of Spanish-speaking first and second graders—children in Mexico receiving reading instruction in Spanish, children in the United States receiving reading instruction in Spanish, and children in the United States receiving reading instruction in English. They reported:

> Children in Mexico begin first grade well behind Spanish-instructed U.S. students in reading achievement and phonemic awareness, but within two years catch up or surpass them in reading—while remaining below both English- and Spanish-instructed children on phonemic awareness. These results call into question whether phonemic awareness instruction actually helps promote, much less is necessary for acquiring, Spanish reading skills. (21)

In traditional approaches to Spanish reading, initial instruction begins with a focus on syllables rather than on phonemes. This approach fits better with the structure of the language. At the same time, many schools in Latin America have adopted a constructivist, meaning-oriented approach to reading. When reading achievement is measured by assessing comprehension, as it was in Goldenberg's study, the results show that the Mexican students scored higher in comprehension than either the English-speaking or Spanish-speaking students being taught Spanish with a focus on phonemic awareness.

This study suggests that teachers should use different methods when teaching reading in Spanish and English and also provides evidence that a meaning construction approach to reading instruction produces higher levels of comprehension than a skills-based approach. In addition, research by Freeman and Freeman (2006, 2007) shows differences in writing development for English speakers writing in English and Spanish speakers writing in Spanish. Both these studies suggest that there should be differences in how language arts is taught in the two languages. However, in many dual language classes language arts in Spanish is taught using methods used for teaching English language arts.

García (2009) has analyzed two models of biliteracy used in dual language bilingual classes. In one model, the separation biliterate model, "children and teachers match the language in which they are communicating around writing to the language of the written text" (343). In other words, if students are writing or reading texts in English, they use English as they communicate, and if the class is reading or writing in Spanish, Spanish is used for discussion. In classes that follow the separation model students are taught literacy in English using English texts and English language arts methods and in Spanish using Spanish texts and methods of teaching language arts used for Spanish speakers. The two languages are kept separate. García and her colleagues (2017) add, "however, we rarely find the sociocultural and discourse norms of Spanish-speaking cultures reflected in bilingual classes" (143). Often, when different methods are used for teaching initial literacy in Spanish and English, Spanish literacy is taught using traditional methods rather than a constructivist approach that emphasizes meaning construction.

A second model, which supports translanguaging, is the flexible multiple model. Here "the two languages are used to interact with texts written in both languages and in other media according to a bilingual flexible norm capable of both integration and separation" (García 2017,143). For example, during English language arts students might read or write texts in either English or Spanish and discuss them in either language (integration). However, there would be times when the reading, writing, and discussion would be primarily in English or primarily in Spanish (separation). This model reflects current research on bilingualism but is not commonly used in the dual language classrooms that we have observed.

Literacy Squared—A Paired Biliteracy Instructional Model ◆ Escamilla and her colleagues (2014) have developed a research-based simultaneous or paired biliteracy model for emergent bilinguals. This model is consistent with García's flexible multiple model and reflects the translanguaging *corriente*. Research (Sparrow and Escamilla 2012) has shown that this model, Literacy Squared, is effective in developing biliteracy. Their research studies in one-way dual language classrooms have involved over 4,000 students and 250 teachers at sites in five different states.

The authors of *Literacy Squared* explain, "The instructional approaches, strategies, and assessment practices in this book are meant to align and address the language resources and strengths of children who enter school with nascent knowledge of linguistic systems and literacy in two languages" (Sparrow and Escamilla 2012, 4). They refer to students in dual language programs as simultaneous emerging bilingual children, and they point out that these children are the "new normal" in dual language programs.

They write that "research over the past four decades has concluded definitively that teaching emerging bilingual students to read in Spanish as well as English promotes both biliteracy and higher levels of reading achievement in English" (5). Literacy Squared has four components: authentic Spanish literacy instruction, literacy-based English language development (ELD) instruction, oracy, and cross-language connections. The authors have also developed a system for assessment that includes trajectories for monitoring literacy in reading and writing.

Spanish literacy instruction is based on methods that have been found to be effective in Mexico, such as focusing on syllables rather than phonemes in reading and using methods such as a dictation (*dictado*) for writing. Literacy instruction follows a gradual release of responsibility model that includes interactive read-alouds, shared reading, and collaborative reading. Independent practice occurs during teacher-led small groups. Independent reading time is provided, but more time in is spent on whole-class and teacher-led small-group instruction to provide more explicit and interactive teaching.

Literacy-based ELD lessons include the same components as Spanish literacy instruction. In other models of dual language ELD is taught through one of the content areas rather than through language arts. In addition, in Literacy Squared, rather than placing students in English literacy based on their English literacy proficiency, they are placed based on their Spanish literacy levels.

In Literacy Squared the difference between the Spanish literacy and the literacy-based ELD is that in literacy-based ELD, there is a greater emphasis on oracy development and on comprehension. Instruction is more sheltered, and students are not expected to perform at the same levels as in Spanish. The focus is on language structures, vocabulary expansion, and dialogue rather than on decoding. Students may use Spanish or English in discussing texts read in English. Each lesson includes cross-linguistic connections.

In Literacy Squared emergent bilinguals in kindergarten receive two hours of Spanish literacy and forty-five minutes of literacy-based ELD. Each year the time for ELD increases and the time for Spanish decreases. By third grade there are sixty minutes of Spanish and ninety minutes of English, and by fifth grade, forty-five minutes of Spanish and two hours of English. In this way, students can fully develop biliteracy in Spanish and English.

Writing instruction includes modeled writing, shared writing, collaborative writing, and the *dictado*. Here again, the emphasis is on whole-group instruction and teacher-led small-group instruction that is explicit. Each lesson includes attention to oracy development. In addition, there is carefully planned cross-language instruction to develop metalanguage.

Literacy Squared provides a balance of oracy, reading, writing, and metalanguage in each lesson. Spanish literacy instruction is authentic. It is based on methods used in Spanish-speaking countries and it differs from English instruction in initial literacy that focuses more on phonemic awareness and phonics. Instruction follows a gradual release of responsibility model. At the same time, there is more time given to large-group and teacher-directed instruction, collaborative small-group instruction, and practice with explicit instruction than to independent reading and writing, although there is time for independent work. Students' progress is carefully tracked to ensure that they are meeting expectations established in the assessment trajectories that have been developed.

Use Translanguaging Strategies to Promote Literacy Transfer and Biliteracy Development

Based on his extensive research, Cummins (2007) argues for a shift away from monolingual instructional strategies. He argues for a use of both languages during instruction. He points out that both languages should be used because of "the interdependence of literacy-based skills and knowledge across languages and the fact that cross-lingual transfer is occurring as a normal process of bilingual development" (231). However, Cummins adds a caution, "Rather than leaving the process to unfold in a potentially sporadic and haphazard manner, it seems reasonable to teach for two-way cross-lingual transfer" (231). Two of the ways he suggests for promoting transfer are using cognates to expand vocabulary and creating bilingual books.

Lindholm-Leary and Genesee (2010) reported on research contrasting more and less successful English learners in dual language programs. They found the following:

> Successful English learner readers/writers employ effective strategies (such as drawing inferences, the use of context and prior knowledge, and monitoring comprehension) to comprehend text in English, and that they use these strategies during both first- and second-language literacy tasks . . . In contrast, less successful English learners view reading in their first and second languages as separate abilities and, in fact, see the first language as a source of confusion. (231)

This research also points to the importance of using strategies to promote cross-language transfer.

In Chapter 2 we explained that translanguaging is the strategic use of students' full linguistic repertoires. Both languages of a bilingual are constantly active, and by using translanguaging strategies teachers can tap into the translanguaging *corriente* that runs through bilingual classrooms. In Chapter 6, we discussed some examples of a translanguaging pedagogy. In this chapter we provide additional examples that focus specifically on translanguaging to support biliteracy development.

The English term *translanguaging* comes from the Welsh word *trawsiethu*. It was coined by the Welsh educator, Cen Williams. He used translanguaging specifically for literacy development in Welsh/English bilingual classes. According to Baker and Wright (2017), "In Cen Williams (1994, 1996) pedagogical use of 'translanguaging', the input (reading and/or listening) tends to be in one language, and the output (speaking and/or writing) in the other language, and this is systematically varied" (280). For example, students might read a text in English and then write a summary in Welsh one day. The next day they might listen to a short lecture in Welsh and then discuss it in English. They could also use both Welsh and English during the discussion. García (2009) and García and Wei (2014) have expanded the use of translanguaging as a pedagogical practice, as discussed in Chapters 2 and 6.

Successful dual language biliteracy programs make extensive use of translanguaging strategies to promote transfer and to build literacy in two languages. Programs such as Literacy Squared build translanguaging into every lesson. In the following sections we discuss several ways that teachers can tap into the translanguaging *corriente* as they teach for biliteracy.

The Bridge ● In their book, *Teaching for Biliteracy: Strengthening Bridges Between Languages*, Beeman and Urow (2013) develop the concept of using translanguaging as a "bridge" to connect languages and help students develop biliteracy. As they explain:

> The Bridge is a powerful concept: with strategic planning, the Bridge allows students who are learning in two languages to strengthen their knowledge of both languages. The Bridge is a tool for developing metalinguistic awareness, the understanding of how language works and how it changes and adapts in different circumstances. An important aspect of the Bridge is that it is two-way. It goes from Spanish to English and English to Spanish. (4)

Adding the Bridge to lessons allows for building metalinguistic knowledge in a structured way. English and Spanish are contrasted during the Bridge. The authors provide specific examples that focus on phonology, morphology, syntax and grammar, and pragmatics.

During Bridge lessons, students learn how to comprehend and express academic content they have learned in one language in the second language. For example, in a 50/50 dual language program that is structured so that the various content areas are taught in different languages, math might be taught in English and science in Spanish. In that case, a Bridge lesson would follow the English math lesson to provide students with the vocabulary and language structures needed to read, write, and discuss math in Spanish. The science lesson in Spanish would be followed by a Bridge to provide vocabulary and structures for science in English.

Beeman and Urow outline a curriculum based on an integrated, thematic approach. As they write, "A comprehensive approach to literacy instruction integrates content, literacy, and language instruction and connects reading with oral language and writing" (2013, 2). Biliteracy is developed by teaching literacy within the context of math, science, and social studies as well as during language arts. The authors give examples of units and explain how teachers can use the Bridge to link the two languages.

Although translanguaging is used during the Bridge to build vocabulary and to increase metalinguistic knowledge by comparing and contrasting the languages, the authors do not suggest translanguaging strategies for use during the lessons in each content area that introduce the concepts. So, for example, a math lesson taught in English would not make use of Spanish. In Chapter 3 we explained the concept of macro- and micro-language alternation. There should be a dedicated time for each language during the day, but there should also be translanguaging spaces within the dedicated Spanish or English time during which the teacher can tap into the translanguaging *corriente* strategically to draw on students' full linguistic repertoires.

Cognates ◆ There are several ways teachers can use translanguaging to build biliteracy. As we have pointed out earlier, the most common strategy is to teach students to find cognates. Although this strategy is not useful in programs where the second language is Mandarin, Korean, or Japanese, it is useful in languages related to English, such as Spanish, French, and Portuguese. Many teachers in dual language programs with these languages have cognate walls. It is important to take cognates from the content areas that students are currently studying to integrate language and content teaching and to give students a purpose for using their knowledge of cognates as they read and write in two languages. For a useful list of Spanish-English cognates, visit the website www.colorincolorado.org.

Teachers can support students by teaching them how to recognize cognates. A lesson might start by having the teacher explain that cognates are words that come from the same root. They often look and sound the same in two languages although there may be some variations in spelling or pronunciation. After the teacher gives examples of some cognates, she can project the page of a book up so that all the students can see it and ask them to find cognates. Students can also work in pairs to identify cognates in a text the class is reading. Each pair might work with a different page, and then the class could work together to create a cognate wall. Students could also add words to a cognate dictionary (Williams 2001).

Ann, a researcher working on the City University of New York–New York State Initiative on Emergent Bilinguals team studying translanguaging in New York schools, observed how a teacher built biliteracy during a math lesson. She gave her students a short reading on measurement in English and also put a Spanish translation next to it. The students first read the text in English and then in Spanish. They highlighted words that looked similar in the two languages. They added these words to their list of math-related English/Spanish cognates. The teacher then added words that students had found, such as *liter* and *litro*, to a whole-class math cognate chart.

Bilingual Books ◆ In addition, teachers can use bilingual books (Freeman and Freeman 2011) to help students build metalinguistic awareness. Bilingual books in Spanish and English are increasingly available. Teachers can use bilingual books in several ways to build biliteracy. For example, students could read the book in one language and use the book in the other language as a resource when they are having difficulty understanding a passage. They could read the book in one language and later read it in the other language to reinforce their understanding. If the first reading is in the student's dominant language, then that reading would build background for later reading the book in the other language.

Teaching Syllables in Spanish

Sandra Cordúa teaches her kindergarten TWDL students about syllables by showing vowels with the letter J.

The most common use of bilingual books is to provide opportunities to compare and contrast the two languages. For example, Carmen Lomas Garza's bilingual book, *In My Family/En mi familia* (Garza 2013), has short readings in English and Spanish on each page accompanied by a picture. One page shows all the family engaged in making empanadas. In addition to finding cognates, such as *dozens* and *docenas*, the student could examine differences between the languages. For example, in Aunt Paz and Uncle Beto, *Aunt* and *Uncle* are capitalized, but in Spanish, *tía* and *tío* are not capitalized. Although *tía* and *tío* are related words with a change in the ending to signify gender, *aunt* and *uncle* are not related. In addition, Spanish uses accent marks to signal which syllable to stress but English does not.

In English, the pronoun *they* is used to start a sentence, but in Spanish the pronoun is optional, and person and number are indicated by the suffix (an) of the verb *invitaban*. Another difference is that in English adjectives usually precede nouns, so Aunt Paz has a *yellow dress* but in Spanish, the adjective usually follows the noun, *vestido amarillo*. By contrasting the two languages, students could note differences in language structures as well as differences in punctuation and capitalization. Through these comparisons, students build metalinguistic awareness.

There are several other translanguaging strategies teachers can use with bilingual books to build students' metalinguistic awareness and help them develop biliteracy. For example, after reading the Spanish version of a bilingual book, such as Xavier Garza's (2005) *Lucha Libre: The Man in the Silver Mask*, the teacher could have students summarize the book in English. They could read the book in English and discuss it in their home language. They could transform the book into a play for a particular audience—Spanish, English, or bilingual. They could write dialogue for bilingual characters or write a speech for a bilingual audience. They could create bilingual poems in two voices.

Bilingual Texts ◆ In some books, both bilingual books and books written primarily in one language, the author includes words from two languages in the text. A good example is Alma Flor Ada's *I Love Saturdays y domingos* (Ada 2002) and *Me encantan los Saturdays y los domingos* (Ada 2004). The narrator, a little girl, visits her English-speaking grandparents on Saturdays and her Spanish-speaking grandparents on *los domingos* (Sundays). In the English version, she refers to her Spanish-speaking grandparents as *Abuelito* and *Abuelita*. She reports her conversation with them in Spanish—*¡Hola, Abuelito! ¡Hola Abuelita!*—and they say—*¡Hola, hijita! ¿Cómo estás? ¡Hola me corazon!* In the Spanish version of the book, the conversation with the English-speaking grandparents is in English.

Teachers can then discuss with students why the author switched languages in writing these books. Students could try writing books with words or phrases from two languages themselves. Ann, the researcher studying translanguaging, reports on one eighth-grade teacher, Chaarene Chapman-Santiago, whose multilingual classroom included students who spoke Arabic, Bengali, French, Fulani, Haitian Creole, and Spanish (Ebe 2016).

The students read a section from *Inside Out and Back Again*, an award-winning book written in verse by Tanhha Lai (2011). In the book, the author translanguages in Vietnamese and English. The students read the chapter on the New Year's Eve celebration that contained many Vietnamese words. The teacher grouped the students into home language groups and gave them questions in English also translated into the students' home languages. She wrote, "The author uses a lot of words in Vietnamese in this book. Explain your thoughts as to why she didn't use all English words? How did you infer the meanings of the Vietnamese words?" The students discussed these questions using their home language and English and wrote responses to the questions in their journals in English. The teacher then led a whole class discussion on the use of two languages in a book. After this, the students each wrote about their own New Year's traditional poems from their own countries, using some home language words and English. The poems were edited at home by parents who added cultural information and checked the home language. The individual papers were made into a whole-class book.

Several well-known authors have used words from other languages as a literary device. This activity helped Mrs. Santiago-Chapman's students better understand how two languages could be used in literary writing. Producing the class book with words from all the students' home languages also tapped into the translanguaging *corriente* in the class and affirmed the students' bilingual identities.

Mary, a teacher educator in California, modeled a bilingual "I am from" poem for her students. In her own "I am from" poem, student Adriana Ruiz recalls events from her life. Adriana writes in Spanish about famous books and authors, her cultural ancestors who give her identity. She writes in English about childhood games, Mc-Donald's, and Care Bear. Bilingual students can write their memories in either their home language or in English. They use the language they most fully associate with the event or practice they are describing. An example of the first page of the bilingual "I am from" poem that Adriana wrote is shown below.

I am from poem

Soy del Laberinto de La Soledad
Paso por paso recojo mi identidad,
Soy de Sor Juana Inés de La Cruz y de Jesusa Palancares
Las revolucionarias silenciadas.
Soy de los teocallis
de la Luna y del Sol
Que sigue derramando mi sangre.

I am from the midnight hide and go seeks,
De la segunda and the .99 bags full of McDonald's toys,
From the Care Bear purse that turned to rags,
To the tight lemon ponytails that gave me cat eyes,
The long cries wishing to get out of my itchy Sunday best.

A reading strategy teachers often used is to have the students write down the gist, or main idea, of a text passage as they read. In one teacher's dual language classroom the students read in both English and in their home language. As they were reading, they added sticky notes to the text on which they wrote the gist of the passage. The teacher encouraged them to write their gist notes in either language. When students read a text in Spanish, they could post their notes either in Spanish or English. Then they used the notes when they reviewed the text.

Daily News ◆ Another translanguaging strategy used regularly in many dual language classes to build biliteracy is daily news (or morning message). Figure 7.3 shows two days of daily news from one class. Daily news is a gathering time and a time for students to share and at the same time develop reading and writing skills.

At a one-way dual language bilingual school in south Texas where we worked, prekindergarten, kindergarten, and first-grade teachers used techniques to both assess student progress and support young writers as they developed reading and writing in two languages. One teacher had students gather at the rug. At the large writing chart, she worked with the students to create the daily news. They first constructed a written greeting that included a salutation, the day, and the date. The class discussed

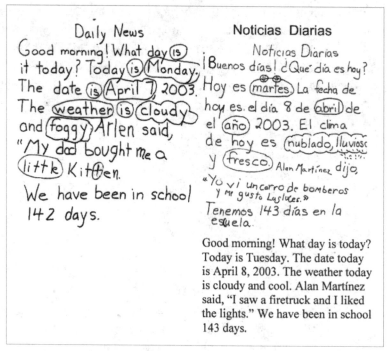

Figure 7.3 Daily News

the weather and then the students and teacher composed a sentence to describe the weather. Next, a designated student shared some personal or class news, and the teacher helped the student add the information. The last part of the daily news was a sentence about how many days students have been in school.

Teachers can use two days' entries to have students find cognates and compare and contrast Spanish and English sentence structures, capitalization, and punctuation. Using the two entries of daily news shown in Figure 7.3, the teacher could point out that *daily* and *diarias* are cognates. This follows a pattern—*ia* in Spanish becomes *y* in English. Other cognates include *April* and *abril* and *school* and *escuela*. Teachers can also point out differences in capitalization. Days of the week and months of the year are capitalized in Spanish but not in English. There are also differences in punctuation. English uses an exclamation point at the end of an exclamation and a question mark at the end of a question. Spanish adds an inverted exclamation point and an inverted question mark at the beginning. Teachers also work on spelling. In the English version one student identifies that *kitten* has two *t*'s.

Morning Message

Dora Baxter begins morning message by having her preK TWDL students connect sounds and letters, recognize punctuation effects, and identify the date. Then the students reread the morning message and identify words. She uses red and blue colored pens to indicate whether a student's home language is Spanish or English.

The daily news at the south Texas dual language school was conducted one day in Spanish and the next in English. During daily news time, teachers wanted to be sure they were aware of which students were contributing in each language. They also wanted all students to eventually contribute in both languages. The teacher wrote the daily news with a blue pen for English and a red pen for Spanish. Then students wrote or corrected with a black pen. The teacher circled the oral and written contributions of students with a red or blue marker, depending on the dominant language of the student. So, for example, when Felipe, a Spanish dominant student, identified *Monday* in the English text and wrote a capital *M* on *Monday* using a black pen, the teacher circled the word in red to show this was done by a Spanish-dominant student.

When Andrea, an English-dominant girl, identified the word *weather* in the English daily news, the teacher circled the word in blue. Using the red and blue markers provided the teachers with a record of how many Spanish- and English-dominant children were contributing in each language during daily news. This helped teachers see if they were only calling on Spanish speakers on Spanish day and English speakers on English day or if they were including speakers of both languages each day. The daily news entries were kept in a center, and children often came there to reread the news. The structure of each daily news stayed the same, so students became accustomed to this daily routine. Daily news, bilingual texts, bilingual books, and cognates all provided opportunities for teachers to use translanguaging strategies to build biliteracy for bilingual students.

Chapter Overview

In this chapter, we discussed three essentials for biliteracy. The first essential, base methods on a theory that views reading and writing as meaning construction, is important because in some dual language schools we have observed, students can decode texts in Spanish and English. These students can name words rapidly, but they do not comprehend what they read. Unless instruction maintains a focus on comprehension, students will not build the competence they need to succeed academically. Similarly, if writing instruction centers on correctness rather than on conveying a meaningful message, students may have good handwriting and may learn to spell words correctly and write complete sentences. Yet, they may not come to view writing as a way to express their ideas.

We contrasted skills-based approaches to meaning construction programs designed to build students' ability to comprehend and compose texts. We described a transactional sociopsycholinguistic theory of reading that is supported by research in miscue analysis and by eye movement studies.

The second essential is to ensure a good match between the theory and the teaching methods. We described an approach to biliteracy instruction that follows a gradual release of responsibility. In this model, the teacher does most of the work in reading and writing in the beginning and then gradually releases the responsibility to the students. Some stages for reading in the gradual release model are read-alouds or storytelling, shared reading, interactive reading, guided reading, and independent reading. A similar set of activities are used in writing instruction—modeled writing, shared writing, interactive writing, and independent writing. The gradual release model is based on Vygotsky's theory of a ZPD. It provides carefully scaffolded instruction to help students become biliterate.

Next we discussed the third essential, consider the choice of language or languages for initial literacy instruction. We described two models, sequential biliteracy where students receive literacy instruction, usually in the language other than English, and then literacy instruction in English is added. We contrasted the sequential model with the simultaneous model where reading and writing instruction in two languages is offered for initial literacy.

We also described two models of biliteracy that García and her colleagues have identified—a separation biliterate model and a flexible multiple model that is used in translanguaging classrooms. García and her colleagues point out that many programs use the same methods for teaching reading in Spanish and English and argue that Spanish and English initial literacy instruction should be different.

Goldenberg and his colleagues (2014) found that phonemic awareness instruction, a cornerstone of initial literacy instruction in English, is not used in Mexico. Despite this, Spanish-speaking children from Mexico have higher reading achievement after two years than either English- or Spanish-speaking students in a dual language program where they received literacy instruction including phonemic awareness instruction in both Spanish and English. This study suggests initial literacy instruction in Spanish should be different from initial literacy instruction in English.

Next, we described an effective paired or simultaneous biliteracy instructional model, Literacy Squared, developed by Escamilla and her colleagues (2014). This research-based model uses authentic Spanish literacy, literacy-based ELD instruction, oracy development, and metalanguage instruction. The authors have also developed an assessment system that measures how well students are meeting learning trajectories.

The fourth essential is that teachers in dual language programs should use translanguaging strategies to promote literacy transfer and biliteracy. The Bridge, developed by Beeman and Urow (2013), provides a way for teachers to follow a lesson in one language with a time to teach the vocabulary and language structures needed to read, write, and discuss the content of the first language in a second language. During the Bridge, students compare and contrast languages to develop metalinguistic awareness. The Bridge is designed to promote language transfer. We then described several translanguaging strategies that can promote biliteracy development. These include identifying cognates to increase vocabulary, using bilingual books to compare and contrast languages, reading and writing bilingual texts, and using daily news during initial literacy instruction. All of these strategies tap into the translanguaging *corriente* that runs through bilingual classrooms.

Reflect and Apply

1. We contrasted skills-based theories of literacy with meaning construction-based theories. Consider a dual language program you work in or that you have observed. Which type of theory guides literacy instruction in this program?

2. We described an approach to literacy that is based on a gradual release of responsibility model. In the program you have observed or where you teach, is the gradual release model being used? If not, list some steps you could suggest for adapting or revising the model and implementing a gradual release model.

3. Which model of initial reading instruction is used in the dual language program you have observed or that you work in—sequential or simultaneous? List some pros and cons of these two approaches. Which one do you think is more effective?

4. We described several translanguaging strategies to promote literacy transfer and biliteracy development. Which of these strategies have you observed or used? Which ones would you like to try out?

5. In this book we have listed whole-school, administrator, teacher, curriculum, and biliteracy essentials. Make a composite list of the dual language essentials. Which of these are being used in the program you have observed or that you teach in? Which are missing? Based on your results, list some changes you would recommend to improve your program.

References

Ada, Alma Flor. 2002. *I Love Saturdays y Domingos*. New York: Atheneum Books.

———. 2004. *Me encantan los Saturdays y los domingos*. Miami, FL: Santillana.

Amistad Dual Language Schools. n.d. www.amistadschool.org/about-our-school.html.

Amistad Dual Language Schools n.d. www.amistadschool.org/mission-vision.html and https://translate.google.com/translate?sl=en&tl=es&u=amistadschool.org.

Anberg-Espinosa, Michele. 2008. "Experiences and perspectives of African American students and their parents in a Two-Way Spanish Immersion Program." PhD diss., University of San Francisco. http://repository.usfca.edu/diss/155.

Armbruster, Bonnie, and Jean Osborn. 2001. *Put Reading First: The Building Blocks for Teaching Children to Read*. Washington, DC: U.S. Department of Education.

August, Diane, Peggy McCardle, and Timothy Shanahan. 2014. "Developing Literacy in English Language Learners: Findings from a Review of the Experimental Research." *School Psychology Review* 43 (4): 490–498.

Austin Independent School District. n.d. www.austinisd.org/multilingual/dual-language.

Baker, Colin. 2011. *Foundations of Bilingual Education and Bilingualism*. Bristol, UK: Multilingual Matters.

Baker, Colin, and Wayne Wright. 2017. *Foundations of Bilingual Education and Bilingualism*. 6th ed. Blue Ridge Summit, PA: Multilingual Matters.

Bartalova, Jeanne, and Jie Zong. 2016. *Language Diversity and English Proficiency in the United States*. Washington, D.C.: Migration Policy Institute.

Beeman, Karen, and Cheryl Urow. 2013. *Teaching for Biliteracy: Strengthening Bridges Between Languages*. Philadelphia: Caslon.

Bialystok, Ellen. 2011. "Reshaping the Mind: The Benefits of Bilingualism." *Canadian Journal of Experimental Psychology* 65 (4): 229–35.

Bransford, John, Ann Brown, and Rodney Cocking. 2000. *How People Learn: Brain, Mind, Experience, and School*. Washington, D.C.: National Academy Press.

Brisk, María. 2015. *Engaging Students in Academic Literacies: Genre-Based Pedagogy for K–5 Classrooms*. New York: Routledge.

Bruner, Jerome. 1985. "Models of the Learner." *Educational Researcher* 14 (6): 5–8.

Bunch, George, Amanda Kibler, and Susan Pimentel. 2013. "Realizing Opportunities for English Learners in the Common Core English Language Arts and Disciplinary Literacy Standards." In *AERA*. San Francisco, CA: AERA.

Cabezón, Mary, Elena Nicoladis, and Wallace E. Lambert. 1998. Becoming Bilingual in the Amigos Two-Way Immersion Program. Washington, DC: CREDE.

California English Language Arts Anchor Standards. n.d. Retrieved on May 20, 2017 from www.corestandards.org/ELA-Literacy/CCRA/SL/#.ELA-Literacy.CCRASL.1.

Callahan, Rebecca, and Patricia Gándara. 2014. *The Bilingual Advantage: Language, Literacy, and the US Labor Market.* Bristol, UK: Multilingual Matters.

Celic, Christina, and Kate Seltzer. 2011. *El translenguar: Una guía de CUNY-NYSIEB para educadores (Versión abreviada en español).* New York: CUNY-NYSIEB.

———. 2011, 2013. *Translanguaging: A CUNY-NYSIEB Guide for Educators.* New York: Graduate Center: The City University of New York.

Clark, Kevin. 2009. "The Case for Structured English Immersion." *Educational Leadership* (April): 42–46.

Coles, Gerald. 2000. *Misreading Reading: The Bad Science That Hurts Children.* Portsmouth, NH: Heinemann.

Collier, Virginia. 1989. "How Long? A Synthesis of Research on Academic Achievement in a Second Language." *TESOL Quarterly* 23 (3): 509–32.

Collier, Virginia, and Wayne Thomas. 2009. *Educating English Learners for a Transformed World.* Albuquerque, NM: Dual Language Education of New Mexico Fuente Press.

Common Core State Standards Initiative. 2017. "Comprehension and Collaboration: CCRA .SL.1." www.corestandards.org/ELA-Literacy/CCRA/SL/#CCSS.ELA-Literacy.CCRA .SL.1.

Crawford, James. 1999. *Bilingual Education: History, Politics, Theory and Practice.* 4th ed. Los Angeles: Bilingual Educational Services.

———. 2004. *Educating English Learners.* Los Angeles: Bilingual Education Services.

Cullinan, Bernice. 2000. "Independent Reading and School Achievement." *School Library Media Research* 3: 1–24.

Cummins, Jim. 1979. "Linguistic Interdependence and the Educational Development of Bilingual Children." *Review of Educational Research* 49 (2): 222–51.

———. 1989. *Empowering Minority Students.* Sacramento: CABE.

———. 1996. *Negotiating Identities: Education for Empowerment in a Diverse Society.* Ontario, CA: California Association of Bilingual Education.

———. 2000. *Language, Power and Pedagogy: Bilingual Children in the Crossfire.* Tonawanda, NY: Multilingual Matters.

———. 2007. "Rethinking Monolingual Instructional Strategies in Multilingual Classrooms." *Canadian Journal of Applied Linguistics* 10 (2): 221–40.

de Jong, Ester. 2002. "Effective Bilingual Education: From Theory to Academic Achievement in a Two-Way Bilingual Program." *Bilingual Research Journal* 26 (1): 1–15.

Dual Language Schools website. n.d. https://duallanguageschools.org.

Duffy, Erin. 2016. "OPS Dual-Language Program Caters to Students New to English or Spanish." *Omaha World-Herald*, September 15.

Ebe, Ann. 2016. "Student Voices Shining Through: Exploring Translanguaging as a Literary Device." In *Translanguaging with Multilingual Students: Learning from Classroom Moments*, edited by Ofelia García and Tatayana Kleyn, 57–82. New York: Routledge.

Escamilla, Kathy, Susan Hopewell, Sandra Butvilosky, Wendy Sparrow, Lucinda Soltero-González, Olivia Ruz-Figueroa, and Manuel Escamilla. 2014. *Biliteracy from the Start: Literacy Squared in Action*. Philadelphia: Caslon.

Espinosa, Linda M. 2013. "PreK–3rd: Challenging Common Myths About Dual Language Learners." In PreK–3rd Policy to Action Brief. New York: Foundation for Child Development.

Fang, Zhihui. 2004. "Scientific Literacy: A Systemic Functional Linguistics Perspective." *Wiley InterScience* 89 (2): 335–47.

Feinberg, Rosa Castro. 1999. "Administration of Two-Way Bilingual Elementary Schools: Building on Strength." *Bilingual Research Journal* 23 (1): 47–68.

Ferrón, Mario. 2012. *Educational Effects of Implementing a K–12 Dual Language Instruction Program in a Community with a High Percentage of Hispanics and Hispanic English Language Learners*. Brownsville, TX: The University of Texas at Brownsville.

Freeman, Ann. "The Eyes Have It: Oral Miscue and Eye Movement Analyses of the Reading of Fourth Grade Spanish/English Bilinguals." PhD diss., University of Arizona, 2001. www.arizona.openrepository.com/arizona/handle/10150/289704.

Freeman, David, and Yvonne Freeman. 2011. *Between Worlds: Access to Second Language Acquisition*. Portsmouth, NH: Heinemann.

Freeman, Rebecca D. 1995. "Equal Educational Opportunity for Language Minority Students: From Policy to Practice at Oyster Bilingual School." *Issues in Applied Linguistics* 6 (1): 39–63.

Freeman, Rebecca. 1996. "Dual Language Planning at Oyster Bilingual School: 'It's Much More Than Language.'" *TESOL Quarterly* 30 (3): 557–82.

Freeman, Yvonne, and David Freeman. 2006. *Teaching Reading and Writing in Spanish and English in Bilingual and Dual Language Classrooms*. Portsmouth, NH: Heinemann.

———. 2007. *La enseñanza de la lectura y la escritura en español e inglés en salones de clases bilingües y de doble inmersión*. Portsmouth, NH: Heinemann.

Freeman, Yvonne, David Freeman, and Ann Ebe. 2011. "Bilingual Books, Bridges to Literacy for Emergent Bilinguals " In *Reclaiming Reading: Teachers, Students and Researchers Regaining Spaces for Thinking and Action*, edited by Richard Meyer and Kathryn Whitmore, 224–235. New York: Taylor and Francis/Routledge.

Freeman, Yvonne, David Freeman, Mary Soto, and Ann Ebe. 2016. *ESL Teaching: Principles for Success*. Portsmouth, NH: Heinemann.

Garan, Elaine. 2002. *Resisting Reading Mandates*. Portsmouth, NH: Heinemann.

García, Amaya. 2015. "What the Rising Popularity in Dual Language Programs Could Mean for Dual Language Learners." In *New America: Education Policy*, Jan. 16. Washington, DC: New America.

García, Ofelia. 2009. *Bilingual Education in the 21st Century: A Global Perspective*. Malden, MA: Wiley-Blackwell.

———. 2010. "Misconstructions of Bilingualism in U.S. Education." *NYSABE News* 1 (1): 2–7.

———. 2014. "Countering the Dual: Transglossia, Dynamic Bilingualism and Translanguaging in Education." In *The Global-Local Interface, Language Choice and Hybridity*, edited by R. Rubdy and L. Alsagoff, 110–18. Bristol, UK: Multilingual Matters.

García, Ofelia, Susana Ibarra Johnson, and Kate Seltzer. 2017. *The Translanguaging Classroom: Leveraging Student Bilingualism for Learning*. Philadelphia, PA: Caslon.

García, Ofelia, and Jo Anne Kleifgen. 2010. *Educating Emergent Bilinguals: Policies, Programs, and Practices for English Language Learners*. New York: Teachers College Press.

García, Ofelia, and Tatyana Kleyn. 2016a. *Translanguaging with Multilingual Students: Learning from Classroom Moments*. New York: Routledge.

———. 2016b. "Translanguaging Theory in Education." In *Translanguaging with Multilingual Students: Learning from Classroom Moments*, edited by Ofelia García and Tatyana Kleyn, 9–33. New York: Routledge.

———. 2016c. "A Translanguaging Educational Project." In *Translanguaging with Multilingual Students: Learning from Classroom Moments*, edited by Ofelia García and Tatyana Kleyn, 34–54. New York: Routledge.

García, Ofelia, and Li Wei. 2014. *Translanguaging: Language, Bilingualism, and Education*. New York: Palgrave Macmillan.

Garza, Carmen Lomas. 2013. *In My Family/En mi familia*. San Francisco: Children's Book Press.

Garza, Xavier. 2005. *Lucha Libre: The Man in the Silver Mask*. El Paso, TX: Cinco Puntos Press.

Genesee, Fred, and Patricia Gándara. 1999. "Bilingual Education Programs: A Cross National Perspective." *Journal of Social Issues* 55: 665–85.

Gibbons, Pauline. 2014. *Scaffolding Language: Scaffolding Learning.* 2nd ed. Portsmouth, NH: Heinemann.

Goldenberg, Claude, Tammy Tolar, Leslie Reese, David Francis, Antonio Bazán, and Rebeca Mejía-Arauz. 2014. "How Important Is Teaching Phonemic Awareness to Children Learning to Read in Spanish?" *American Educational Research Journal* 51 (3): 604–633.

Gómez, Leo, and Richard Gómez Jr. 2015. "Gómez and Gómez Dual Language Enrichment Model." Dual Language Training Institute. http://dlti.us/doc/DLE_MODEL -2015.pdf.

Goodman, Kenneth. 1984. "Unity in Reading." In *Becoming Readers in a Complex Society: Eighty-Third Yearbook of the National Society for the Study of Education*, edited by A. Purves and O. Niles, 79–114. Chicago, IL: University of Chicago Press.

———. 1996. *On Reading.* Portsmouth, NH: Heinemann.

Greene, Jay. 1998. *A Meta-Analysis of the Effectiveness of Bilingual Education.* Claremont, CA: Tomas Rivera Policy Institute.

Grosjean, Francois. 2010. *Bilingual: Life and Reality.* Cambridge, MA: Harvard University Press.

———. 2016. "Bilinguals in the United States." www.psychologytoday.com/blog/life -bilingual/201205/bilinguals-in-the-united-states.

Halliday, M. A. K. 1975. *Learning How to Mean.* London: Edward Arnold.

Hamayan, Else, Fred Genesee, and Nancy Cloud. 2013. *Dual Language Instruction from A to Z: Practical Guidance for Teachers and Administrators.* Portsmouth, NH: Heinemann.

Hayward Unified School District. 2017–2018. "Stonebrae's Mandarin Dual Language Immersion Program." www.husd.k12.ca.us/SDLI.

Heitin, Liana. 2016. "How Should Reading be Taught in a Digital Era?" *Education Week.* www.edweek.org/ew/articles/2016/11/09/how-should-reading-be-taught-in-digital -era.html?_ga=2.245506374.358978076.1495295834-874091391.1484074790.

Hernandez, Sera. 2017. "Are They All Language Learners? Educational Labeling and Raciolinguistic Identifying in a California Middle School Dual Language Program." CATESOL Journal 29 (1): 133-154.

Hesson, Sarah, Kate Seltzer, and Heather Woodley. 2014. *Translanguaging in Curriculum and Instruction: A CUNY-NYSIEB Guide for Educators.* New York: CUNY-NYSIEB, The Graduate Center, The City University of New York.

Houston Independent School District. www.houstonisd.org/Page/32054.

Howard, Elizabeth R., and Donna Christian. 2002. *Two-Way Immersion 101: Designing and Implementing a Two-Way Immersion Education Program at the Elementary Level.* Santa Cruz: Center for Research on Education, Diversity & Excellence, University of California, Santa Cruz.

Howard, Elizabeth, Kathryn Lindholm-Leary, David Rogers, Natalie Olague, José Medina, Barbara Kennedy, and Julie Sugarman. 2018. *Guiding Principles for Dual Language Education.* 3rd ed. Washington, D.C.: Center for Applied Linguistics.

Howard, Elizabeth R., Julie Sugarman, and Donna Christian. 2003. *Trends in Two Way Immersion Education: A Review of the Research.* Baltimore, MD: Center for Research on the Education of Students Placed at Risk.

Howard, Elizabeth R., Julie Sugarman, Donna Christian, Kathryn J. Lindholm-Leary, and David Rogers. 2007. *Guiding Principles for Dual Language Education.* Washington, DC: Center for Applied Linguistics.

Institute of Educational Sciences. 2008. *Reading First Impact Study: Final Report.* Washington, DC: U.S. Department of Education.

Jiménez, Francisco. 2000a. *La mariposa (Spanish edition).* Boston: Houghton Mifflin.

———. 2000b. *La Mariposa (English edition).* Boston: Houghton Mifflin.

Kirst, Michael, Ilene Straus, Sue Burr, Carl Cohn, Bruce Holaday, Josephine Kao, Aida Molina, Patricia Ann Rucker, Nicolasa Sandoval, and Trish Boyd Williams. 2013. *California Common Core Standards: English Language Arts and Literacy in History/Social Studies, Science and Technical Subjects.* Sacramento, CA: California Department of Education.

Koulentes, Tom, Jesse Villanueva, and Scott Russell. "How to Create a High School Dual Language Program." Paper read at Illinois State Conference for Teachers Serving Linguistically and Culturally Diverse Students Celebrating 40 Years, Chicago, Dec. 8, 2016.

Krashen, Stephen. 2001. "What really happened in Calfornia: Dropping bilingual education did not increase test scores." *The Oregonian.*

Krashen, Stephen. 2003. *Explorations in Language Acquisition and Use.* Portsmouth, NH: Heinemann.

Krashen, Stephen. 2004. "Skyrocketing scores: An urban legend." *Educational Leadership* 62 (4): 37–39.

Kucer, Stephen B., Cecilia Silva, and Esther L. Delgado-Larocco. 1995. *Curricular Conversations: Themes in Multilingual and Monolingual Classrooms.* York, ME: Stenhouse.

Kucer, Stephen, and Jenny Tuten. 2003. "Revisiting and Rethinking the Reading Process." *Language Arts* 80 (4): 284–90.

Lai, Tanhha. 2011. *Inside Out and Back Again*. New York: Harper Collins.

Lambert, Wallace. 1974. "Culture and Language as Factors in Learning and Education." In *Cultural Factors in Learning and Education*, edited by F. E. Aboud and R. D. Meade, 91–122. Bellingham, WA: Western Washington State College.

Lambert, Wallace E., and Richard Tucker. 1972. *Bilingual Education of Children: The St. Lambert Experiment*. Rowley, MA: Newbury House.

Lessow-Hurley, Judith. 1996. *The Foundations of Dual Language Instruction*. White Plains, NY: Longman Publishers USA.

Lindholm-Leary, Kathryn J. 2001. *Dual Language Education*. Clevedon, UK: Multilingual Matters.

———. 2013. "Education: Dual Language Instruction in the United States." *Americas Quarterly* (Fall). www.americasquarterly.org/content/education-dual-language-instruction-united-states.

Lindholm-Leary, K., and Fred Genesee. 2010. "Alternative Educational Programs for English Language Learners." In *Improving Education for English Language Learners: Research-Based Approaches*, edited by California Department of Education, 323–382. Sacramento, CA: California Department of Education Press.

Lindholm-Leary, K., and A. Hernandez. 2011. "Achievement and Language Proficiency of Latino Students in Dual Language Programmes: Native English Speakers, Fluent English/Previous ELLs, and Current ELLs." *Journal of Multilingual and Multicultural Development* no. 32 (6): 531–545.

Lindholm-Leary, Kathryn, and Elizabeth R. Howard. 2008. "Language Development and Academic Achievement in Two-Way Immersion Programs." In *Pathways to Multilingualism: Evolving Perspectives on Immersion Education*, edited by T.W. Fortune and D. J. Tedick, 177–200. Clevedon, UK: Multilingual Matters.

Loewus, Liana. 2017. "Study: Teachers Value Independent Reading But Lack Class Time for It." In *Curriculum Matters*. Bethesda, MD: Education Week. http://blogs.edweek.org/edweek/curriculum/2017/04/study_teachers_value_independent_reading_but_lack_time.html.

López, Mary Jean Habermann. 2003. *History and Importance of Bilingualism and Bilingual Education in New Mexico*. Albuquerque, NM: New Mexico State Dept. of Education and The University of New Mexico.

Los Angeles Unified School District website. n.d. https://lausd.net.

Mansilla, Veronica, and Anthony Jackson. 2011. *Educating for Global Competence; Preparing our Youth to Engage the World*. New York: Asia Society.

Mercuri, Sandra. 2015. "Teachers' Understanding of Practice: Planning and Implementing Preview/View/Review in the Dual Language Classroom." In *Research on Preparing Inservice Teachers to Work Effectively with Emergent Bilinguals*, edited by Yvonne Freeman and David Freeman, 81–106. Bingley, UK: Emerald Books LTD.

Miles, Heidi. 2014. *Teaching Content and Literacy Across the Curriculum*. Portsmouth, NH: Heinemann.

Mlawer, Teresa. 2016. *The Tortoise and the Hare/La liebre y la tortuga*. Canandaigua, NY: Adirondack Books.

Monthey, Wanda, Heather Singmaster, Jennifer Manise, and Kate Blosberen Kreamer. 2016. *Preparing a Globally Competent Workforce Through High-Quality Career and Technical Education*. Washington, DC: Asia Society and the Longview Foundation.

National Center for Education Statistics. n.d. "Digest of Education Statistics. Table 204.27. English Language Learner (ELL) Students Enrolled in Public Elementary and Secondary Schools, by Grade and Home Language: Selected Years, 2008–09 Through 2013–14." http://nces.ed.gov/programs/digest/d15/tables/dt15_204.27.asp.

National Institute of Child Health and Human Development, National. 2000. Report of the National Reading Panel. *Teaching Children to Read: An Evidence-Based Assessment of the Scientific Research Literature on Reading and Its Implications for Instruction*. Washington, DC: U.S. Government Printing Office.

National Writing Project, and Carl Nagin. 2006. *Because Writing Matters: Improving Student Writing in our Schools*. San Francisco: Jossey-Bass.

No Child Left Behind (NCLB) Act of 2001, Pub. L. No. 107–110, § 115, Stat. 1425 (2002).

Olsen, Laurie. 2010. *Reparable Harm: Fulfilling the Unkept Promise of Educational Opportunity for Long-Term English Learners*. Long Beach, CA: Californians Together.

———. 2014. *Meeting the Unique Needs of Long Term English Language Learners: A Guide for Educators*. Washington, DC: National Education Association.

Ovando, Carlos, and Virginia Collier. 1998. *Bilingual and ESL Classrooms: Teaching in Multicultural Contexts*. 2nd ed. New York: McGraw Hill.

P21 Partnership for 21st Century Learning. 2007. Framework for 21st Century Learning. PDF retrieved Nov. 7, 2017 from www.p21/org/Framework.

———. 2015. P21 Framework Definitions Document. PDF retrieved Nov. 7, 2017 from www.p21/org.

Paulson, Eric, and Ann Freeman. 2003. *Insight from the Eyes: The Science of Effective Reading Instruction*. Portsmouth, NH: Heinemann.

Pearson, P. D., and M. C. Gallagher. 1983. "The Instruction of Reading Comprehension." *Contemporary Educational Psychology* 8 (3): 317–44.

Pérez, Bertha. 2004. *Becoming Biliterate: A Study of Two-Way Bilingual Immersion Education*. Mahwah, N.J.: Lawrence Earlbaum Associates.

Riley, Richard W. 2000. "Excelencia para todos-excellence for all: The Progress of Hispanic Education and the Challenges of a New Century." March 15, 2000. https://eric.ed.gov/?q=Excelencia+para+todos&id=ED440542.

Rolstad, Kellie, Kate Mahoney, and Gene Glass. 2005. "A Meta-Analysis of Program Effectiveness Research on English Language Learners." *Educational Policy* 19 (4): 572–94.

Rosenblatt, L. 1978. *The Reader, the Text, the Poem: The Transactional Theory of the Literary Work*. Carbondale, IL: Southern Illinois University Press.

Ruíz, Richard. 1984. "Orientations in Language Planning." *Journal of the National Association of Bilingual Education* 8: 15–34.

San José Elementary School. 2017. "Dual Language Program." www.duvalschools.org/Page/9102.

SBISD. 2017. "SBISD Principals of the Year Named." *The School Zone, Spring Branch ISD's Online News Room*. www.sbisdsnapshots.blogspot.com/2017/02/sbisd-principals-of-year-named.html.

Schleppegrell, Mary J. 2004. *The Language of Schooling: A Functional Linguistics Perspective*. Mahwah, NJ: Lawrence Erlbaum.

Singleton, Glenn. 2015. *Courageous Conversations About Race: A Field Guide for Achieving Equity in Schools*. Thousand Oaks, CA: Corwin.

Slavin, Robert, and A. Cheung. 2004. "Effective Reading Programs for English Language Learners: A Best-Evidence Synthesis." www.bestevidence.org/word/ell_read_2005_BRJ.pdf.

Soltero, Sonia. 2016. *Dual Language Education: Program Design and Implementation*. Portsmouth, NH: Heinemann.

Sparrow, Wendy, and Kathy Escamilla. 2012. *Literacy Squared Phase II: Oregon Replication Study Technical Report, 2009–2012*. BUENO Center for Multicultural Education, University of Colorado, Boulder.

Steel, J. L., R.O. Slater, G. Zmarro, T. Miller, J. Li, S. Burkhauser, and M. Bacon. 2017. "Effects of Dual-Language Immersion Programs on Student Achievement: Evidence for Lottery Data." *American Educational Research Journal* 54 (1s): 282s–306s.

Sugarman, Julie Sarice. 2012. *Equity in Spanish/English Dual Language Education: Practitioners' Perspectives*. College Park, MD: Graduate School, University of Maryland.

TEA. 2015. *Texas Essential Knowledge and Skills for Grade 4*. Austin, TX: Texas Education Agency.

Thomas, Wayne P., and Virginia P. Collier. 2002. "A National Study of School Effectiveness for Language Minority Students' Long-Term Academic Achievement." http://files.eric.ed.gov/fulltext/ED475048.pdf.

Thomas, Wayne, and Virginia Collier. 2012. *Dual Language Education for a Transformed World*. Albuquerque, NM: Dual Language Education of New Mexico-Fuente Press.

Torres-Guzman, María E. 2002. *Dual Language Programs: Key Features and Results*. Washington, D.C.: National Clearinghouse for English Language Acquisition and Language Instruction Educational Programs.

Umansky, Ilana, and Sean Reardon. 2014. "Reclassification Patterns Among Latino English Learner Students in Bilingual, Dual Immersion, and English Immersion Classrooms." American Educational Research Journal 51 (5): 879-912.

U.S. Commission on Civil Rights. 1972. "Language Rights and New Mexico Statehood." www.languagepolicy.net/archives/nm-con.htm.

U.S. Department of Education, Office of English Language Acquisition. 2015. *Dual Language Education: Current State Policies and Practices*. Washington, D.C. https://ncela.ed.gov/files/rcd/TO20_DualLanguageRpt_508.pdf.

Utah Dual Language Immersion. www.utahdli.org/whyimmersion.html.

Valdés, Guadalupe. 1997. "Dual-Language Immersion Programs: A Cautionary Note Concerning the Education of Language-Minority Students." *Harvard Educational Review* 67 (3): 391–429.

———. 2017. "Foreword." In *The Translanguaging Classroom: Leveraging Student Bilingualism for Learning*, edited by Ofelia García, Susan Ibarra Johnson and Kate Seltzer. Philadelphia, PA: Caslon.

Valdez, Verónica, Juan Freire, and Garrett Delavan. 2016. "The Gentrification of Dual Language Education." *Urban Review* 48 (4): 601–27.

Valentino, Rachel, and Sean Reardon. 2014. "Effectiveness of Four Instructional Programs Designed to Serve English Language Learners: Variation by Ethnicity and Initial English Proficiency." Stanford University Graduate School of Education. http://cepa.stanford.edu/sites/default/files/Valentino_Reardon_EL Programs_14_0326_2.pdf.

van Lier, Leo. 2007. "Action-based Teaching, Autonomy and Identity." *Innovation in Language Learning and Teaching* 11: 46–65.

van Lier, Leo, and Aida Walqui. "Understanding Language: Language, Literacy, and Learning in the Content Areas." Paper read at Understanding Language Conference, Palo Alto, CA, January 13–14, 2012.

Villaseñor, Victor. 1991. *Rain of Gold*. New York: Dell.

Vygotsky, L. 1962. *Thought and Language*. Translated by Eugenia Hanfmann and Gertrude Vakar. Cambridge, MA: MIT Press.

Wagner, Tony, and Ted Dintersmith. 2015. *Most Likely to Succeed: Preparing our Kids for the Innovation Era*. New York: Scribner.

Whiteley, Greg. 2015. *Most Likely to Succeed* (documentary). Washington, DC: 21st Century Skills.

Wiggins, Grant, and Jay McTighe. 2005. *Understanding by Design*. Alexandria, VA: ASCD.

———. 2011. *The Understanding by Design Guide to Creating High-Quality Units*. Alexandria, VA: ASCD.

———. 2012. *The Understanding by Design Guide to Advanced Concepts in Creating and Reviewing Units*. Alexandria, VA: ASCD.

Williams, Joan. 2001. "Classroom Conversations: Opportunities to Learn for ESL Students in Mainstream Classrooms." *The Reading Teacher* 54 (8): 750–57.

Wilson, David McKay. 2011. "Dual Language Programs on the Rise." *Harvard Education Letter* 27 (2). http://hepg.org/hel-home/issues/27_2/helarticle/dual-language-programs-on-the-rise.

Wong, Kevin. "Five Fundamental Strategies for Bilingual Learners." *The Blog*, Huffington Post, Dec. 23, 2015. www.huffingtonpost.com/kevin-wong2/five-fundamental-strategi_b_8870038.html.

Woodley, Heather. 2015. "Empowering Language and Learning with Muslim Immigrant Youth." In *Research on Preparing Inservice Teachers to Work Effectively with Emergent Bilinguals*, edited by Yvonne Freeman and David Freeman, 233–63. Bingley, UK: Emerald Group Publishing.

Zwiers, Jeff. 2011. *Academic Conversations: Classroom Talk That Fosters Critical Thinking and Content Understanding*. Portland, ME: Stenhouse.

———. 2014. *Building Academic Language: Meeting Common Core Standards Across the Disciplines, Grades 5–12*. 2nd ed. San Francisco, CA: Jossey Bass.

Index